MADE YOU LAUGH!

MADE YOU LAUGH!

THE FUNNIEST MOMENTS IN RADIO, TELEVISION, STAND-UP, AND MOVIE COMEDY

JOE GARNER

Andrews McMeel
Publishing

Kansas City

Made You Laugh! © 2004 by Garner Creative Concepts, Inc. All rights reserved. Printed in the United States of America. No part of this book may be used or reproduced in any manner whatsoever without written permission except in the case of reprints in the context of reviews. For information, write Andrews McMeel Publishing, an Andrews McMeel Universal company, 4520 Main Street, Kansas City, Missouri 64111.

04 05 06 07 08 RR3 10 9 8 7 6 5 4 3 2 1

Library of Congress Cataloging-in-Publication Data
Garner, Joe.
    Made you laugh! : the funniest moments in comedy / Joe Garner.
        p. cm.
    ISBN 0-7407-4695-2
        1. Comedy programs—United States—History and criticism. 2. Stand-up comedy—United States—History—20th century.
    3. Comedy films—United States—History and criticism. I. Title.

PN1991.8.C65G37 2004
791.44'617—dc22

2004053712

Book design by Holly Camerlinck

Attention: Schools and Businesses:
Andrews McMeel books are available at quantity discounts with bulk purchase for educational, business, or sales promotional use. For information, please write to: Special Sales Department, Andrews McMeel Publishing, 4520 Main Street, Kansas City, Missouri 64111.

IN GRATITUDE TO THOSE WHO HAVE MADE
THEIR LIFE'S WORK MAKING US LAUGH . . .
AND TO COLLEEN, J.B., AND JILLIAN
FOR THE LAUGHTER THEY BRING TO MY LIFE

CONTENTS

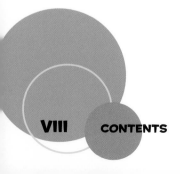

FOREWORD
BY RICHARD PRYOR

A book about comedy is a scary thing to pull off. So the guy that did this one you're holding, Joe Garner, is either too brave or too dumb to be scared. Because taking comedy apart and analyzing "funny" is like taking apart a frog—yeah, you learn how the frog is put together, but ya end up with one dead Kermit.

Too brave or too dumb?

People always feel they gotta know where comedy "comes from." No, you don't. David Copperfield doesn't tell you how he yanks the bunnies out of his ass. And once you start analyzing it, some white man with a pipe comes by, saying things (imagine my uptight white guy voice here) like "True comedy comes from pain." And he says it like he's the first guy who ever thought that up. Yeah, it's true, but don't be saying it like you discovered radium. We *know* comedy comes from pain—that's why there's hardly anybody *in* this book who isn't black or a Jew. (We don't count Carlin, because he had nuns, and if you get enough nuns early in your life beating on your ass, you end up basically a black Jew.)

And that's basically the story of everybody in this book. The great comics all have a hole in their chest where their heart should be. Somebody yanked their heart out when they were just kids, and they've been spending their whole lives trying to fill that hole. Or kill the pain. Hell, I know I did. And I tried *everything*: drugs ("Damn right! I have prescriptions for all of it, Your Honor), money (I've been rich and poor, and I've been happy and miserable being both), sex (Jenny tells me, "You've had enough to last a lifetime." But I tell her, "There ain't no such thing"), marriage (Eight times! Twice to two women I'd already been married to once! Don't tell *me* I can't commit), fame (I was the Number One Box Office Comic In The World and the Least Happy Human In The World—all at the same time). But the only thing that could numb that hole in my chest—if only for the moment—was the sound of somebody laughing.

And if you're wondering why this book is a little light on the newest comics working today, I'll tell ya why: If "comedy comes from pain," seems like very few comics today are in any pain at all. 'Cause there ain't but four and a half who actually make me laugh, and you *know* who they are. No, I'm not going to name them and have the rest of those vindictive bruthas coming to *my* house to burn *my* albums on *my* front lawn. Let them think they're one of the four and a half.

Brave or dumb . . . dumb or brave . . .

Jennifer (wife number six and number eight, I think) and I went to a comedy club last Monday, and, man, this shit is *over*. Nobody's got nothin' to say 'bout nothin. It's all just "Nigga this." And then these newbies say I was a "big influence" on them. Say what?! Listen to my stuff. If all you hear is a black man saying "nigga" and "mutha-f," there's either something wrong with you or something wrong with me, and I know there's nothing wrong with *me*. (Except for the M.S., which is no big deal unless you want to do something crazy like get up and walk.) Yeah, those words are *in* my stuff, but that's not what the stuff is *about*.

These guys on stage now, being all cool, saying they were influenced by me, show me when I was cool. I never said "Dig me. Look how cool I am and how messed up everybody else is." Hell, I got all the material I *need* just on how messed *up* I am. I mean, how screwed up a brother I gotta be to stand up in front of a million strangers and say "Listen to *me*"? Yes, stop what you're doing and listen to me so I can make you laugh—so the sound of your laughing drowns out the voices in my head.

So it boils down to this. If you want to be a good comic, you gotta have some pain, and you need to know your history. Whoever your people are, learn about them. If you're a Guatemalan, you study the Guatemalans that came before you. Architects study past architects. Doctors, doctors. And comics, comics. The people who came before you—those are your ancestors—the giants. And to be great, you have to find a giant who'll let you stand on his shoulders.

And this book you're holding has got all the comedy giants.

The past is what you build your future on. Comedy deserves no less respect. Comedy is a craft, it's an art, it's a sickness. Ya gotta work *hard* to make it look *easy*. If you don't want to do the kinda work that the people in this book did, then get the hell off the stage!

Comedy is some serious shit.

And Joe Garner is a brave, brave man.

FOREWORD BY RICHARD PRYOR

ACKNOWLEDGMENTS

It would have been impossible to complete this book without the support of these wonderful, dedicated people:

Once again, my heartfelt gratitude to Kathleen Andrews, John McMeel, Tom Thornton, Hugh Andrews, and Jim Andrews. (This is a group that loves to laugh!) I remain grateful for their unwavering support and enthusiasm. A very special thank-you to Chris Schillig and her wonderfully creative staff. I feel fortunate to be in her incredibly capable hands.

I would like to extend my deepest gratitude to Carl and Rob Reiner. Their contributions of their enormous talent, expertise, and integrity are invaluable to this project. It was an honor to work with them both.

I am also extremely grateful to Richard Pryor and Jennifer Lee Pryor for the funny and insightful foreword. Again, I am honored and humbled by such a contribution.

My sincerest gratitude to Jerry Lewis for a wonderfully candid and insightful interview—and one of the most memorable events of my life.

I would also like to thank George Shapiro for bringing Carl and Rob to this project. George truly loves comedy, and I am proud to have had his support and encouragement.

I am also grateful to Aimee Hyatt in George's office, Pam Jones in Rob's office, and Bess Scher in Carl's office for their graciousness and skillful coordination of the scheduling and the endless details inherent in this kind of endeavor.

As always, I am grateful to my agent, Sloan Harris, for his friendship, his willingness to knock around my ideas, and his very savvy counsel.

Abigail Ray deserves her own page of thanks. One minute she's GCC office administrator, then photo editor, then production coordinator—and everything in between. I do know that she does it all with grace, enthusiasm, and a wonderful sense of humor. She makes it happen.

Once again, I am grateful to designers Tim Lynch and Holly Camerlinck, copy chief Michelle Daniel, and administrative assistant JuJu Johnson of Andrews McMeel Publishing for their valued contributions of their talents and enthusiasm for making this book the best it can be.

Thank you to Kristine Campbell and her dedicated and talented group in the public relations department at Andrews McMeel Publishing, and to Tess Woods and everyone at Newman Communications for their tireless efforts to make sure the word gets out. Thank you to Rita Rapp for all of her efforts in making sure I am where I'm supposed be.

A very special thank-you is due Stephan Michaels. He is a man of many talents who willingly contributed them wherever and whenever they were needed "24/7." As talent/clip/music clearance manager his meticulous attention to detail was invaluable, and this book is better for it.

Once again, thank you to Chris Monte for his masterful editing and boundless creativity; Jim Castle for his uncompromising commitment to the quality of his work; and to Kris Wilson for his expertise and warm easygoing demeanor that kept us on track in the studio.

My gratitude to Kali Londono at C. R. Enterprises for facilitating the inclusion of an excerpt of Chris Rock's performance. And thank you to Mr. Rock for permitting its inclusion.

Thank you to Shiela Griffiths at *Real Time with Bill Maher* for introducing this project to Mr. Maher, and to Mr. Maher for his interview and for his permission to include excerpts of his performance. Thanks also to Avrielle Gallagher for coordinating the interview.

Thank you to Larry Brezner, David Steinberg, Stephen Tenenbaum, and everyone at MBST Entertainment for facilitating the inclusion of performances of their clients Billy Crystal and Robin Williams.

I am grateful to Rory Rosegarten and Bryan Friedman at the Conversation Company for arranging our interview with Robert Klein, and for facilitating the permission to include excerpts of Ray Romano's performance in *Everybody Loves Raymond*.

Thank you to April Mosel for her assistance in coordinating our interview with David Brenner.

A special thank-you to Wendy Blair at Knave Productions for all of her help in coordinating the interview with the Smothers Brothers and for her assistance in locating just the right clips and stills to illustrate their portion of the chapter.

Thank you to Rick Nasch and Mark Biase at the Production Group in Hollywood for their wonderful facilities and hospitality.

Thank you to Anthony Lewis and Matthew Braun at Airborne Productions, and Rich Pina and Aaron Johnson at Sterling Productions, for the magnificent way they shot the numerous interviews, sometimes under less-than-ideal conditions.

Thank you to makeup artist Gail Katz for making our interview guests look their best.

I am grateful to Jeff Abraham, a comedy historian with a true love of the art, for willingly fielding numerous questions, opening his amazing library and archive, and for facilitating the interview with David Brenner.

My heartfelt thanks to Janel Syverud for her friendship, encouragement, and adaptability, and for making sure that things run smoothly at GCC, and to Scott Sturgis for all of his support and keeping the information flowing.

Once again, thank you to my friend Wendy Heller-Stein for her friendship and willingness to share her expertise.

I am particularly grateful to Lorra-Lea Bartlett at CBS Entertainment, Lee Ann Platner at NBC Entertainment, Larry McCallister at Paramount Pictures, Julie Heath at Warner Bros., Laura Sharp at Warner Bros. Television, Andy Bandit at Twentieth Century Fox, Deidre Baxter at Whacko Inc., Kali Londono and Chris Rock at C. R. Enterprises, Ward Grant and Jim Hardy at Bob Hope Enterprises, Cecily Schaefer at Castle Rock Entertainment, Ed Zimmerman at Sony Pictures TV, Margarita Harder at Columbia TriStar Motion Picture Group, Joshua Baur at MGM, Jeremy Laws and Roni Lubliner at Universal Studios, Robin Zlatin at New Line, Ruth Englehardt at Clavada Productions, Steve Sellers at StudioCanal Roger Saunders—Python (Monty) Pictures Inc., Steve Rogers at Peter Rogers Organization, Larry O'Daly at the Television Distribution Company, Garry Shandling, Jerry Hamza at Carlin Productions, Sandy and Lisa Hackett at Hackett Entertainment, Michael Wright, and Faye Tucker at HBO for permitting me to include these landmark television and motion picture moments.

Thank you to the following people for their determination in providing us with the very best images: Deidre Thieman at Universal Studios, Cynthia Litman at New Line Cinema, Gilbert Emralino at Columbia TriStar, May Beth Whelan at Globe Photos, Jeni Rosenthal at AP Wide World, Jay Williams at Shooting Star, Chad Witt at Getty, Howard and Ron Mandelbaum and Robert Milite at Photofest, Geoff Murillo and Jeff Briggs at Warner Bros., Kristoph Yniquez at Twentieth Century Fox, Amber Noland/Edie Baskin (SNL), Dominic LaCarrubba—Lanndov LLC, and Jonathan Hyams at Michael Ochs Archive.

I am always grateful to Bill Kurtis and Bob Costas for being there in the beginning.

And, finally, none of this is possible without the sacrifice and unwavering devotion from my wife, Colleen; my son, James (J.B.), and my daughter, Jillian; and my parents, Jim and Betty Garner, for their boundless love and encouragement, and all the laughter in our house. And my heartfelt thanks to Jerry and Sandi Barnes for their constant love and support.

INTRODUCTION

There was a seminal moment in my early childhood that would seal my love and appreciation for comics, and their importance in our world, for the rest of my life. My dad was a life insurance agent for Northwestern Mutual Life. Every summer we would make the pilgrimage to his company's annual convention in Milwaukee. It was exciting for a starry-eyed kid from the rural Midwest, because they always hired big-name talent to entertain the attendees and their families. And in 1969, the featured entertainer was none other than comedian Bob Hope. Although I was only nine, I was already a big fan, having watched Hope's movies and specials on television. For reasons that must have seemed logical for a nine-year-old, I wrote an impassioned letter to the president of the company asking if he would permit me to meet the man I knew to be a living comedy legend. To my parents jaw-dropping astonishment the president replied by saying that he would gladly try to arrange the meeting. As you can see by the picture, he was successful.

It was just minutes before Hope was to perform to a sold-out crowd at Milwaukee Stadium on July 27, 1969. I'm the kid in the snazzy plaid sport coat; my dad is standing next to me. After signing autographs, cracking jokes, and imparting a few encouraging words, Mr. Hope shook my hand and I watched in awe as he took the stage and—as they say in the comic vernacular—*killed* 'em.

Watching Hope from the wings taught me the power of being able to make people laugh. The ability to take the "truths" of everyday life and hold them up in front of people—twisting them slightly in one direction or another to expose the humor—is a rare gift. It's a moment I'll carry with me my whole life. Thanks for the memory, Mr. Hope.

What makes us laugh is often a mystery. But why we laugh is obvious. Funny is funny. We know it when we hear it or see it. And while much of comedy has a short shelf life, there are certain comics and comedic moments that have stood the test of time. They're embedded in our pop culture and locked in our memories, and they make us laugh every time we think of them.

Like Groucho and Chico Marx debating a "sanity clause." Or an exasperated Lou Costello grappling with "who's on first." Lucy and Ethel's fiasco in the candy factory. Tommy Smother's shouting his senseless comeback, "Mom liked you best!" The campfire scene in *Blazing Saddles*. The Church Lady proclaiming, "Well, isn't that special." Or George Costanza's embarrassing "shrinkage." These hysterical moments and many more like them can be found in this book and on the accompanying DVD.

Comedy's history is rich, complex, and diverse. It comes in all shapes and sizes, from slapstick to sophisticated; from ethnic to surrealistic; from highbrow and wholesome to, well, down and dirty. But seriously, folks, the great comedians have taken an ephemeral entertainment and transformed it into timeless art.

The most difficult task in putting together this collection was deciding which moments and comics to include and which to leave out. I knew that I couldn't cover the absolute, definitive history of comedy; the subject is just too large, dating back centuries. (I'm sure there's a painting in a cave somewhere of a caveman slipping on dinosaur dung.) Instead, my goal was to compile some of comedy's extraordinary highlights since the dawn of the electronic age, a collection of some of the funniest and most memorable moments and performances spanning nearly a century.

The resulting book and DVD—divided into three primary sections of Radio and Television, Motion Picture, and Stand-up—explores the continuum of comedy. Physical comedy or "slapstick" spans the eras from Laurel and Hardy to Peter Sellers to Jim Carrey. Observational stand-up comedians range from Jonathan Winters to Garry Shandling to Chris Rock. Screwball comedies run the spectrum from *His Girl Friday* to *Some Like It Hot* to *Tootsie*. The section on spoofs leaps from Mel Brooks' *Young Frankenstein* to the mockumentary *This Is Spinal Tap* to the very groovy *Austin Powers*.

In researching this enormous subject, I met, interviewed, and worked with some of comedy's most skilled artists. The first interview I conducted was with Jerry Lewis. What was to be a thirty-minute interview turned into an extraordinary, and at times emotional, two-hour tutorial on the last sixty years of comedy. Jerry reminisced about his relationships with Charlie Chaplin, Stan Laurel, and his partner of ten years, Dean Martin. In a startlingly candid moment, tears welling in his eyes, Jerry sat forward in his chair proclaiming, "Dean Martin was funnier than Jerry Lewis could have ever hoped to be, ever."

He spoke with great admiration about the influence of fellow comics from Milton Berle and Jackie Gleason to Robin Williams and Jim Carrey. I knew the task of doing this book and DVD was going to be challenging but after spending time with Jerry, the project took on even greater dimensions than I originally envisioned.

Budd Friedman, founder of the legendary Improv comedy clubs—where thousands of comics launched their careers—generously shared his recollections of the early careers of the likes of Richard Pryor, Rodney Dangerfield, Andy Kaufman, Ellen DeGeneres, and Chris Rock.

Phyllis Diller and Joan Rivers provide a revealing look at what it was like for female comics in the male-dominated comedy world of the 1950s and '60s.

TV writers Bob Schiller (*I Love Lucy, All in the Family, Maude*), Carol Leifer (*Saturday Night Live, Seinfeld, Ellen*), Phil Rosenthal (co-creator of *Everybody Loves Raymond*), and David Crane (co-creator of *Friends*) discuss their influences and the mark they hope to have left on the enduring genre of situation comedy.

Equally as important as determining which moments to include on the DVD was finding the best guides to take us through comedy's storied past. I was lucky enough to land two of comedy's most gifted and time-honored artists, Carl and Rob Reiner. (I was surprised to find out that this would mark the first time that father and son have appeared together.) Working with them was not only a pleasure, it was an education. Their personal experience in comedy would fill volumes, and their encyclopedic knowledge and expertise on the subject emerged in many impromptu and insightful observations during the taping of the narration. They are indeed gracious and genuinely charming people.

In addition to the invaluable contributions made by the Reiners, I can't imagine a more appropriate way to begin this kind of collection than to give the first word to the greatest stand-up comic of all time, Richard Pryor. Richard's brilliance on stage was in expressing his observations on the human condition with brutal, honest street-wise eloquence. He brought that same incisive candor to the foreword. I am honored and humbled by his profound contribution.

While I was interviewing noted entertainment journalist and critic Joel Siegel, he mused, "What is it about these moments? They change the way you look at the world for the better because when you recall them you smile and you laugh. Isn't that the greatest legacy anyone can leave us? I mean, we're all living a joke. And the punch line ain't so funny. It's inevitable, and what's better than a laugh to help us get through?"

Made You Laugh! is a tribute and celebration of these special people who have dedicated their lives to *making us laugh*. I hope this collection brings you much laughter for years to come.

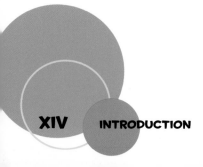

PART 1

COMEDY FROM RADIO AND TELEVISION

THE GILDED COMICS
OF RADIO'S "GOLDEN AGE"

As the nation slipped into the depths of the Depression, comedy was the tonic that kept spirits high. The burgeoning medium of radio delivered the greatest comic talent of the day directly into the nation's living rooms—the best jokes, the funniest wisecracks, and the cleverest routines vaudeville had to offer played out in a grand new venue, the theater of the mind.

One series so captured the nation's imagination that it had a detrimental effect on the movie business. Theater owners surrendered, halting the film during the broadcast, which they played over the theater's sound system. Once the episode was over, the film continued.

That showstopper was *Amos 'n' Andy*, one of the most popular and longest-running radio series of all time. First broadcast by Chicago's WMAQ in 1928, it ran for an astounding thirty-two years, its final broadcast being November 25, 1960. By comparison, the television series it spawned lasted just three seasons, from 1951 to 1953. It's estimated that during *Amos 'n' Andy*'s glory days, forty million people listened to the show religiously—nearly one-third of America's total population at the time, a number that included self-professed fan President Calvin Coolidge.

Amos 'n' Andy was the invention of actor-writers Freeman Gosden and Charles Correll. The pair had teamed up in 1921 to do radio, sketch comedy, and variety shows and were involved with several successful radio shows before they hit big with *Amos 'n' Andy*. Gosden and Correll were two white men who played the title characters: two impoverished black men, Amos Jones and Andy Brown, who owned the Fresh Air Taxi Company, so-named because their only cab had no windshield. The most common of men, they symbolized the poor guy with no "dough," no real job, and no prospects. *Amos 'n' Andy* was the perfect distraction for America during the Depression and war years, and the country responded by tuning in en masse. From 7:00 P.M. to 7:15 P.M., six nights a week, the nation belonged to them.

Gosden and Correll were true innovators—it's hard to overestimate how revolutionary their show was. And it wasn't just because of their use of black characters. This was the first successful serial to combine sympathetic characters, comedy, and suspense. Because it was broadcast in real time, the show could incorporate news of the day, even news of the hour. The humor was gentle, not forced, and it moved beyond vaudeville, coming from character, not jokes. A lot of its comedy came from malaprops and mispronunciations, like "'Splain that to me" and "Holy mack'el dere, Andy!" and "The Fresh Air Taxi Company *Incorpulated*"—words and phrases that made it into the common lexicon.

These were characters whom listeners could identify with, root for. Listeners laughed *with* the characters, not *at* them. Amos, Andy, Kingfish, Ruby, Sapphire, and Calhoun became beloved, as did the nearly 150 other characters Gosden and Correll voiced sitting at a table with a single microphone between them. It wasn't until the show's seventh year that they hired other actors, and their ninth year before they hired their first actress to play Amos's wife, Ruby.

Gosden and Correll were also brilliant at creating dramatic cliff-hangers; like soap operas, you simply had to tune in the next day to find out what happened. When Ruby nearly died, the country was on edge. Listeners were so upset that eighteen thousand of them deluged the sponsor, Pepsodent toothpaste, with letters, threatening to switch to Colgate if she passed away. Needless to say, Ruby quickly recovered.

In 1943, after more than four thousand episodes, *Amos 'n' Andy* went from fifteen minutes six days a week to a weekly half-hour format. The new version was a full-fledged sitcom. For the first time in the show's history, there was a studio audience and an orchestra. More outside actors, including many black comedy pros, were brought in to fill out the cast. Many of the half-hour programs were written by Joe Connelly and Bob Mosher, the writing team who'd later bring *Leave It to Beaver* and *The Munsters* to television.

Although not quite as popular as *Amos 'n' Andy, The Fred Allen Show* was every bit as influential. A former vaudevillian who was billed as "The World's Worst Juggler," Allen worked alongside comedy legends Al Jolson, Ed Wynn, and George Jessel before making his radio debut in 1932. Unlike a lot of stage comedians whose visual talents didn't translate

to the sightless medium, he was perfect for radio, self-taught and exceptionally well read. Allen claimed to read nine newspapers each day, from which he gleaned material. He simply stopped juggling balls and started juggling words, becoming the master of the ad-lib. That was a skill radio rival Jack Benny paid tribute to in responding to a mock insult, "You wouldn't say that if my writers were here." Allen was called "literate, urbane, intelligent, and contemporary" and "the best writer on radio."

Though some famous writers would get tutelage under Fred Allen (notably, novelist Herman Wouk and successful television producer-writer Nat Hiken, creator of *The Phil Silvers Show* and *Car 54, Where Are You?*), Allen did most of his radio scripts on his own, spending an average of a dozen hours a day honing the material for his weekly show.

Depending on which household product was sponsoring him, Fred Allen's radio shows were known by various names—like *The Linit Bath Club Revue* (Linit Bath Oil), *The Salad Bowl Revue* (Hellmann's Mayonnaise), and *Hour of Smiles* (Ipana Toothpaste). But the most famous and most loved version was *Allen's Alley*, in which Allen visited the imaginary street's eccentric (and, some say, overly stereotyped) inhabitants.

From *Allen's Alley* came imaginative and colorful characters like Senator Beauregard Claghorn (Kenny Delmar), a drawling, double-talking caricature of a politician who'd had the "Southern fried chicken pox" and defiantly pro-

claimed that he'd "never go to Yankee Stadium unless a southpaw's pitchin'." Claghorn was later appropriated by Warner Brothers and transformed into their blustery cartoon rooster, Foghorn Leghorn. There were also equally unforgettable folks like the stoic New England farmer Titus Moody (Parker Fennelly) and malaprop-prone Brooklyn housewife Pansy Nussbaum (Minerva Pious), a fan of "Hoagy Carbuncle" who referred to her husband as the "lone stranger."

Allen once said, "An actor's popularity is fleeting. His success has the life expectancy of a small boy who is about to look into a gas tank with a lighted match." Clearly, he underestimated his own importance, because he greatly influenced the generations of entertainers who followed. Allen's influence is present in the routines of personalities like Steve Allen's "Man in the Street" interviews, Johnny Carson's "Mighty Carson Art Players" (Allen had the "Mighty Allen Art Players"), and David Letterman's "People You Didn't Expect to Meet."

Another classic radio series that established a prototype that still exists today is *Fibber McGee and Molly*. The McGees may have been a couple of steps up the financial ladder from Amos and Ruby Jones, but the husband-wife dynamic was just as rich; Fibber was a blowhard buffoon given to exaggeration and dopey get-rich-quick schemes, and long-suffering Molly, who loved him just the same, was smarter and usually two steps ahead:

> *"My wife and I had words, but I never got to use mine."*
>
> —Fibber
>
> *"When a man brings his wife flowers for no reason, there's a reason."*   —Molly

The McGees were played by real-life husband and wife Jim and Marian Jordan, two veterans of vaudeville whose easygoing rapport and obvious love and respect for each other made them believable and beloved. Their show hit a real sweet spot in the comedy spectrum—not as corny and small town as shows like *Lum and Abner* or *Vic and Sade*, yet not as sophisticated and cosmopolitan as shows like Fred Allen's, Jack Benny's, or Bob Hope's. The series was middle-class and middle-of-the-road, starring characters who strove upward without forgetting where they came from. Life at "79 Wistful Vista," was a muted reflection of the Depression years, a bleak time endured best by savoring home and hearth. There was never any money coming in, but the McGees, like a lot of Americans, always managed to squeeze by somehow.

There was hardly any need to venture outside the McGees' living room, because everybody came to visit—classic characters like Horatio K. Boomer and Wallace Wimple (Bill Thompson), Mayor LaTrivia (Gale Gordon), Mrs. Abigail Uppington (Isabel Randolph), and Throckmorton P. Gildersleeve (Hal Peary), who earned radio's first spin-off series, *The Great Gildersleeve*, in 1941. Those characters' main function was to argue with Fibber, trade insults, one-up his outrageous claims, or deflate his overblown ego.

Like most successful shows of the radio era, *Fibber McGee and Molly* spawned familiar phrases like Molly's "'Tain't funny, McGee" and "Heavenly day, dearie" and Fibber's "That's the way I heeerd it." A good portion of the humor was based on verbal gymnastics, and especially Fibber's tendency to alliterate—badly. Here's his description of a former job: "I was the top tin-can designer for the Town Talk Tuna Company. I turned out tuna tins by the ton. I had a type of tin in two tones of tan that was the talk of the tuna trade, but one tan turned tones too tawny, so I had to tone down the tawny tan."

The show also had the most famous running sound gag in radio, and the defining *Fibber McGee and Molly* memory for most folks—their perpetually overloaded front closet. Almost always preceded by Molly's cry of "Don't open that door, McGee!" its imaginary contents would come cascading out. The thunderous effects were produced by sound-effects man Howard Tollefson (who was also Jack Benny's sound-effects man) throwing a variety of objects down a portable staircase in the studio. Sometimes they went on for nearly a minute, with the laughter from the studio audience building and building. Almost always, when the racket finally ended, Fibber would make his now-legendary pronouncement "Gotta clean out that hall closet one of these days."

The closet gag wasn't something the production just happened on. It was planned by the Jordans and writer Don Quinn, who were trying to come up with a running joke as effective as that of a rival show, one that ended each episode with the sound of creaking springs. History has proven they succeeded.

Fibber McGee and Molly ran for an astounding twenty-four years, 1,610 broadcasts, all on NBC and all sponsored by the Johnson Wax Company—a testimony to how devoted not only the audience but also the network and the sponsor could be when a show deserved it.

Six years after *Fibber McGee and Molly* began broadcasting, Bud Abbott and Lou Costello, another pair of shining vaudeville stars, began their own radio show. Bud and Lou had been together since teaming up in a Brooklyn burlesque house in 1936.

Their act was a variation of a classic vaudeville routine known as a "Dutchman act." A Dutchman act consisted of the straight man, and his comic partner, dressed in an oversized jacket, baggy pants, big shoes, and derby playing a fresh-off-the-boat foreigner, someone who barely understands the language and speaks with a "funny" accent, like Dutch, Polish, or Russian. It simultaneously made fun of, and paid tribute to, America's vast influx of immigrants.

Abbott and Costello guested on several radio shows in the late 1930s, eventually replacing Henny Youngman on Kate Smith's top-rated variety program. It was there that America at large was introduced to the pair's classic, stage-honed baseball routine, "Who's on First."

ABBOTT: *You know, they give ballplayers funny names nowadays. On this team, Who's on first, What's on second, I Don't Know is on third.*
COSTELLO: *That's what I want to find out. Who's on first?*
ABBOTT: *Yes.*
COSTELLO: *I mean the fellow's name on first base.*
ABBOTT: *Who.*

"Who's on First" was an instant hit, and the duo was hired to appear on Smith's show once a week and to repeat the baseball routine once a month. In fact, the routine was so beloved that, in 1957, Bud Abbott and Lou Costello became the first non–baseball-playing celebrities to be inducted into the Baseball Hall of Fame in Cooperstown. "Who's on First" plays there continuously.

After scoring big on Kate Smith's radio program, Abbott and Costello joined a Broadway revue called *Streets of Paris* and stole the show. Soon they were offered their own radio program by ABC, and in 1941 *The Abbott and Costello Show* hit the airwaves.

The radio show was essentially a reprise of the act Bud and Lou had polished in their years of burlesque, vaudeville, and Broadway—a half-hour of impeccably timed funny business frequently punctuated by Costello's plaintive cry "Hey-y-y-y-y, Ab-bott!" or his "Oh—I'm a ba-a-a-d boy!"

While Abbott and Costello were performing on radio, they were building a career in the movies. Their first bill-topping roles came in the 1941 Universal Studios film *Buck Privates*, which was phenomenally successful. It brought in more than ten million dollars—then a record for the studio—and was the first of a string of hits that made Abbott and Costello two of the biggest box-office stars of the 1940s.

Comedian Jerry Seinfeld readily acknowledges Abbott and Costello as a primary influence on his long-running television series.

Radio comedy's popularity was immense. For millions of Americans trying to weather the world's woes during the World War II era, they were part of the family—cheergivers who dropped by each week to boost morale during tough times. But the same generation that made them so incredibly popular defected to television in the late 1940s, and with them went the stars, the writers, and the sponsors. Fortunately, a large portion of radio's brilliance has been preserved; this theater-of-the-mind still has the power to enthrall, excite, and tickle the most calcified funny bone.

CHAPTER 2

VAUDIO

With the debut of television in the late 1940s, all those talented vaudevillians who were ineffective on radio—simply because they needed to be seen to be appreciated—suddenly became viable again. It was a gold rush for plate-spinners, animal trainers, pantomimists, and all the physical comedians whose acts didn't translate to the sightless medium. Thus the rise of the man whom famed newspaper columnist Walter Winchell called "the thief of bad gags," Milton Berle.

Born in New York, in 1908, Berle began working in show business almost from birth. His mother, a frustrated actress, firmly nudged him into silent movies at the age of five. In 1914 he appeared in Charlie Chaplin's *Tillie's Punctured Romance* and was tossed from a train in *The Perils of Pauline*. He eventually appeared in fifty films before making his stage debut at the age of twelve and then hitting the vaudeville circuit, where his career in comedy began.

By the time vaudeville collapsed in the late 1930s, Berle had honed his skills as a brash visual comic, earning a living doing predominantly one-night stands, bouncing from nightclubs to B movies to radio, never becoming an A-level star. Television changed all that.

In 1948, Berle was tapped to be one of a set of rotating hosts on a variety show called *The Texaco Star Theater*, but only after big names like Jack Benny and Fred Allen turned it down. The bigger stars didn't see the potential of television, and stuck with radio. When *The Texaco Star Theater* debuted on June 8, 1948, there were approximately five hundred thousand television sets in the United States, concentrated mostly on the East Coast. The program was tantamount to the rebirth of vaudeville, and *Variety* magazine dubbed it "vaudio," praising the new show as the "greatest single hypo" given to the nascent medium.

While Milton Berle's raucous presentation and sight gags had never been right for radio, they were perfect for television. His manic energy, anything-for-a-laugh clowning, dressing in drag, rapid-fire jokes, and pie-throwing, all

interspersed with skits, guest stars, and the best vaudeville-style acts still around, completely captured the public's imagination.

The popularity of the Berle-hosted shows far eclipsed that of other hosts, and by September 1948 the show was given to him alone. At that time, *The Texaco Star Theater* was drawing a mind-boggling 97.4 percent of all sets that were turned on. As in the reigning days of *Amos 'n' Andy*, theaters and restaurants adjusted their hours on Tuesday evenings so their patrons could watch "Uncle Miltie" and still enjoy an evening out. Critics hated his "low comedy," but the masses loved the man of whom Winchell also wrote, "The only ones who like Milton Berle, are his mother—and the public."

Asked to describe what made the manic star so special, comedian Jerry Lewis said, "Speed, a brilliant, brilliant speed. His timing was unlike anyone else's because he knew the hit-and-run. Do not belabor. You're not a dramatic artist, you're a comedian. Get out there and bang, bang, bang, bang. If they don't understand it, give them

something they will. Milton was the originator of the ba da bing bom."

Soon, network executives tried to copy the hit, and before long practically anyone with enough star power to headline a show had one. There were variety programs like *All-Star Revue* with Jimmy Durante, *Toast of the Town* with Ed Sullivan, Ed Wynn's *The Ed Wynn Show*, and *The Admiral Broadway Revue*, which starred Sid Caesar and Imogene Coca.

Just four years after Milton Berle had captured the imagination of America's television-viewing public, his incredible run started losing steam. As the roster of affiliates spread steadily westward, his "New York" humor was less appreciated. As viewers became more sophisticated, Berle's brand of outlandish vaudevillian comedy gave way to the public's desire for dramatic content, and westerns and crime shows began dotting the television landscape. In 1952, Texaco shifted its sponsorship to another night, and from 1954 to 1956 *The Milton Berle Show* alternated with shows hosted by Bob Hope, Martha Raye, and Steve

Allen. Berle was on television intermittently until 1967, but it was his total dominance of the media during television's toddling years that earned him the title "Mr. Television" and a rightful place in the comedy and radio and television halls of fame.

Unlike Milton Berle, Bob Hope had made a smooth transition to radio. By the late 1930s, Hope was already a show-biz veteran, with credits in vaudeville, Broadway shows, and movies. In 1938 he signed to do his own radio program, *The Bob Hope Pepsodent Show*, which went on to become one of the most successful radio shows in broadcast history. During the war years, his Tuesday night show was number one in the country, and his remote broadcasts from military bases around the world helped boost the nation's morale. The program was very much in the tradition of vaudeville, with a variety of musical and comedy acts, skits, and guest stars. The show ran for sixteen years, and by the time it ended in 1954 nearly every great star of stage and screen had visited with Bob.

Television had been trying to recruit Bob Hope since the late 1940s, but Hope refused the call. In 1950, when he was finally persuaded to give the new medium a shot, he was the number-one box-office draw in the nation. But Hope had no interest in the grind of a weekly series. "Back in the old days, you would do one sketch for five years,"

he said, "but if you use that sketch on TV, in one night it's used up." So Hope signed on to do "specials" with NBC. The intense grind of putting on a weekly show, something that had caused Milton Berle and show-runners like him to collapse physically, was averted, and Hope was able to continue to work comfortably with NBC for more than forty years.

Bob Hope had a completely relaxed, wisecracking comedy style; he'd just lay a joke out and wait for the audience to laugh—or not. If one joke didn't work, the next one would.

Comedienne Phyllis Diller, who worked with Hope, says the easygoing guy he portrayed on stage was exactly the way he was in real life. "Working with Bob Hope was the greatest. It's no big deal. You don't have to suffer. And he had such a genuinely funny attitude, from morning to night. And that's heaven to work with someone with that very light touch. Just sweet old Bob, and 'Let's have a ball and make it easy.'"

Hope was not so easy with his writers. Mort Lachman, who in twenty-five years with Hope as a writer, a director, and a producer, says his boss could be very demanding.

"When you worked for Hope, you gave him your life," Lachman says. "Every hour of every day belonged to him, and he called you anytime, day or night."

On the other hand, Hope would also be the first to credit those legions of writers. Jerry Lewis said of Bob, "He worked very hard at his craft. And the one wonderful thing about Hope was that he never made any bones about the fact that the writers had given him the material. He had never had that hang-up with, well, 'I did that.'"

What Bob Hope did do was set the platinum standard for American entertainers—and his many awards prove it. *The Guinness Book of Records* cites Hope as the "Most Honored Entertainer in the World," having received more than two thousand awards, including fifty-four honorary doctorates. In Washington, D.C., Hope has been immortalized in an exhibit at the Library of Congress called "Bob Hope and American Variety." It traces his seventy-year career in comedy, and among the memorabilia featured at the exhibit are eighty-five-thousand pages of jokes.

Like Bob Hope, Jack Benny successfully made the transition from vaudeville to movies to radio to television. And, like Hope, he initially had misgivings about appearing on the new medium. In his memoir, *Sunday Nights at Seven*, Benny wrote, "I saw that the camera was a man-eating monster. It gave a performer close-up exposure that, week

after week, threatened his existence as an interesting entertainer." Nevertheless, Benny took the challenge, signing on with CBS in 1950. But he didn't give up his day job—he continued to do his radio show, which he'd started in 1933 and continued until 1955.

Benny essentially relocated his radio show to television, and with near perfect timing—because as television and its audience grew more sophisticated, they were less interested in vaudeville-style variety shows. They craved something episodic with a group of characters you could follow from week to week. Benny's show fit the bill.

His core cast—wisecracking valet Eddie "Rochester" Anderson, boy singer Dennis Day, and show announcer Don Wilson—came with him. Benny was always portrayed as single, and his real-life wife, Mary Livingstone, was cast as a wisecracking "friend of the family." Jack's persona was that of a vain but endearing penny-pincher who was perpetually thirty-nine years old. (It was an image promulgated in one of his most famous routines. In it Benny is caught in a holdup. The robber says to him, "Your money or your life!" Benny pauses. The agitated robber demands again, "Look, bud, your money or your life!" Benny frustratingly replies, "I'm thinking it over.") Part of the show's brilliance was that Jack played a lightly altered version of his public persona. There was no effort to make an audience believe they were watching a "character"—for all intents and purposes, this was the real Jack Benny. In reality, Benny was actually a competent violinist, and generous with his money.

Class and ethnicity never were an issue on the show; beneath his thin facade of arrogance and braggadocio, Jack was as ordinary as could be, a real Everyman.

Benny once said, "Gags die, humor doesn't." The major innovation of his show was that it didn't rely on gags—it relied on story and character. These were friends you could visit with each week, find out what's new, what's happening. It was a show that proved that human beings, just slightly exaggerated, were infinitely interesting, and in the case of Jack Benny, endlessly entertaining.

The show-biz team of George Burns and Gracie Allen was in vaudeville and radio for three decades before moving their act to television in 1950. The show was an extension of an established public image: George was the model of a straight man, and Gracie was his dizzy and adorable wife—the queen of illogical logic. In vaudeville, their act was called a "Dumb Dora." In *The George Burns and Gracie Allen Show*, the two played a romanticized version of

themselves—a celebrity couple in one of the very first "domestic comedies"—a show Burns described as having "more plot than a variety show but not as much as a wrestling match."

Gracie was the source of the show's humor, which was almost always based on twisted linguistics. Her brilliance was in the way she was able to turn the most mundane events into mind-boggling flights of imagination, creating an entire universe of Gracie-style logic:

"When I misunderstand what you say, I always know what you're talking about."

When asked whether her sister's new baby is a boy or a girl, Gracie replies, "I can't wait to find out if I'm an aunt or an uncle."

"It's harder to work in the movies than on stage," Gracie explains. "Movie stars have to act in black and white."

Allen's essential sweetness and dedication to her family and friends always mitigated all the trouble she caused—she was simply too nice to get mad at. The plots weren't exactly elaborate; if Gracie's cousin was visiting from out of town, or Gracie decided to take Spanish lessons, or if she dented a fender on George's car, that was enough to sustain an episode.

George, for his part, was a real television innovator. Whether it was a holdover from his vaudeville days or a product of his own genius, George Burns was the first person on television to break the "fourth wall" and talk directly to his studio (and television) audience. As each episode began, George would step out in front of the living room set with his ever-present cigar and do a mini-monologue to set up the basic plot of the show to follow. Once the show started, he'd often stop in the middle of a scene—the other actors would "freeze," and Burns would walk out of the scene and out of character, talk to the audience *about* the scene, and then rejoin the other players, who would then unfreeze as if nothing had happened. In his biography of Allen, *Gracie: A Love Story*, Burns facetiously took credit for the concept by explaining, "That was an original idea of mine. I know it was because I originally stole it from Thornton Wilder's play *Our Town*."

George and Gracie ended each of their shows with a short dialogue, a minute or two of their classic routines, and then signed off with one of the best-known closers in show-business history. "Say goodnight, Gracie," George would say, and Gracie would turn to the audience, smile humbly, and say, "Goodnight." (Despite the common misconception, she never did say "Goodnight, Gracie.")

The early 1950s were huge years for the television industry—new stations were rapidly sprouting up across the country, and the number of sets in American homes was increasing exponentially. Nonetheless, radio was still a large influence on television programming as network executives raided radio for its stars and its program ideas. On September 15, 1951, a show born on radio was reborn on television—it was the premiere of a classic program destined to become the most popular television series of all time.

I Love Lucy was the television incarnation of a show that hit radio in 1948 called *My Favorite Husband*. The female lead was a character named Liz Cooper, the scatter-brained wife of a midwestern banker, played by former model and then current movie actress Lucille Ball. Liz

Cooper was a schemer who often got herself, and her husband, into embarrassing messes.

As *My Favorite Husband* gained popularity, Lucy started getting raves, not only for her voice acting but also for acting her radio audience couldn't even see. The *Hollywood Reporter* wrote that it was "too bad that her funny grimaces and gestures aren't visible on the radio." When *Life* magazine did a spread on the show, it had a picture of Lucy and co-star Richard Denning at the microphone with the caption "It could be television—Lucille and Richard look like an awfully cute couple."

It wasn't long before television came knocking. Lucy was ready to make the jump, but there was a major problem—she didn't want Richard Denning jumping with her. Instead, she wanted her husband, Cuban singer and band-leader Desi Arnaz, as her co-star. She thought it'd be a perfect way to corral her nomadic spouse.

Desi was nearly an impossible sell at the network—CBS executives were wary of the "mixed marriage" and Desi's thick Spanish accent and turned them down. So Lucy and Desi decided to put together an act and take it

on the road to prove to the network executives they were wrong. They worked out routines together and booked a tour, hitting the remaining vaudeville houses across the country to let the public decide whether they were acceptable as a team.

That tour was a huge success with audiences and critics alike, and finally, after protracted wrangling, the television show was given the green light.

Like *The George Burns and Gracie Allen Show, I Love Lucy* was ostensibly about a celebrity couple. But Lucy's character was grounded in the everyday travails of married life, even if her husband was a headliner at the fictitious New York supper club, the Tropicana. She represented the urges of 1950s women who thought there was something more for them beyond kitchen and kids. No matter how ditzy her scheme, how outrageous her plots, the audience was always with her.

Lucy writer Bob Schiller says the schemes seemed logical because of the way they were constructed. Each week, the writers would convene in producer Jess Oppenheimer's office and begin at the end. "Getting the story line is the toughest part—once you get a story line, hanging the jokes on it is easy for a comedy writer. It's a process that, on *I Love Lucy*, we did backward. We would think of a funny last scene and work backward to make it logical. If it's not

logical, people are going to say, 'That's silly.' The whole thing falls apart."

It helped that the show was a quality production from top to bottom. William Frawley and Vivian Vance, as Fred and Ethel Mertz, were perfection; Frawley was the quintessential grumpus, and Vance was Lucy's eager co-conspirator. Desi's quick temper and fractured English were an effective counterbalance to Lucy's loopy logic and dizzy machinations.

Of course, none of this would have meant much if Lucy hadn't been one of the greatest physical comediennes who ever lived. She had an amazing arsenal of body language and facial expressions, never baulking at the outlandish stunts the writers would concoct from week to week. Whether they had her wrestling in a vat of grapes, lighting her nose on fire (protected with putty, of course), or covering herself in clay (to appear frozen), "as long as it's funny" was her only stipulation, according to *I Love Lucy* writer Bob Carroll Jr.

In the pantheon of television shows that went before and have come since, there isn't likely to be a show more adored and revered than *I Love Lucy*. It is a testament to its creators and producers, and to the comic genius of its four principal actors.

In the first fifty years of the twentieth century, the ways we experienced entertainment took incredible leaps forward—from live stage shows to broadcast radio to network television. Comedians not only adapted, they were in the forefront of the revolution.

CLASSIC SKETCH COMEDY

By the 1940s, radio had effectively driven a stake into the conjoined hearts of vaudeville and burlesque; the medium was a boon for entertainers whose talents were verbal, and a bust for those who were visual. But in the late 1940s, television brought back to life not only the dancers, the magicians, and the tumbling acts, which had been consigned to entertainment purgatory, but also the entire form of "sketch comedy." As opposed to the half-hour situation comedy format, sketch comedy is fast-moving and hinges on a few characters playing out a warped version of a familiar scenario. Like all successful comedy, sketch comedy has an element of surprise to it, be it unusual characters, an unexpected subject, or simply a fresh look at a common situation.

No one was more responsible for bringing sketch comedy into the television era than early superstar Sid Caesar. A former Juilliard-trained saxophone player, Caesar was assigned to the Coast Guard band during World War II. He was performing in a revue called *Tars and Spars* when he was plucked off the bandstand by entertainment impresario Max Liebman. Liebman had heard Caesar improvising comedy routines with his fellow musicians, using the uncanny ear for dialects he'd developed hanging around the family restaurant in Yonkers, New York. Caesar recalls, "I'd have lunch at my father's restaurant, and then I'd pick up a few dishes at lunchtime to help him out. And every time I went over to a table—like one table was all Italian, the next table was all German, the next table was all French—they would teach me, you know. And I'd listen . . ."

After Liebman heard Sid Caesar cracking up his band-mates, he quickly reassigned him from saxophone to microphone. Then Caesar co-starred in the stage and movie versions of *Tars and Spars*, and after his hitch was up he worked on Broadway and in the Catskill mountains with Liebman as his guide. In 1948, Caesar's notices in the Liebman-produced show *Make Mine Manhattan* led to successful appearances on Milton Berle's *Texaco Star Theater*, which in turn earned him his own show, *The Admiral Broadway Review*.

The Admiral Broadway Review, a variety show produced and directed by Liebman, had a big budget and big talents, chief among them the brilliant comedienne Imogene Coca. Coca, who "readjusted" her age when she was hired, was actually fourteen years older than Caesar; she was a touring professional when he was still a schoolboy. Not classically pretty, she'd given up her dream of becoming a leading actress and earned her living performing ballet parodies and lampooning heavy drama. She proved to be a perfect foil for Caesar.

The Admiral lasted only seventeen weeks, but it set up the series that became one of the hallmarks of early television, *Your Show of Shows*. Using most of the same production crew and writers, Max Liebman added the talents of comic actor Howard Morris and a young Carl Reiner.

It didn't hurt that the show's writers were ultimately the comedic crème de la crème of the last half of the twentieth century. The legendary team included Woody Allen, Mel Brooks, Neil Simon, Larry Gelbart (*M*A*S*H* television series; *Tootsie*), Bill Persky and Sam Denoff (*The Dick Van Dyke Show*), Joe Stein (*Fiddler on the Roof*), and Mike Stewart (*Hello, Dolly!* and *Bye Bye Birdie*).

With everyone trying to get the attention of, and please, Caesar, the writing sessions were famously fractious, with Caesar himself the chief instigator. "Once," Larry Gelbart said, "Sid yanked an offending washbasin out of a wall with his bare hands." The writers would split up into small groups that competed with one another, all fighting for the boss's discriminating ear—all, that is, but a noncombative Neil Simon who reportedly whispered his ideas to Reiner, who would then pitch them to the group. Simon later said that writing for Caesar was like going to "the Harvard of comedy."

There weren't many real college graduates in the writing room, but the comedy could be simultaneously high and low, elite and common, or literate and dopey. The

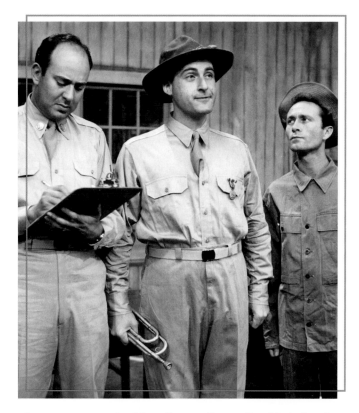

skits in German double-talk usually used Yiddish for the punch lines. Actually, Caesar and Reiner could make *any* language sound Yiddish. One classic skit was set in an Indian restaurant; Sid Caesar plays a customer, Carl Reiner plays the Indian waiter:

> SID: *What have you got to eat?*
> CARL: *Klochmoloppi. We also have lich lop, slop lom, shtocklock, riskkosh, and flocklish.*
> SID: *Yuck!*
> CARL: *We have yuck too. Boiled or broiled?*

One style of comedy the show did best was satire, poking fun at movies, plays, music, politicians—basically whatever needed poking. Satire, Carl Reiner says, requires a large degree of faith in your audience. "It was a kind of comedy that was rather sophisticated," he explains. "Satire was at the root of some of the best things [Sid Caesar] ever did. You have to have great frames of reference. If you're going to do takeoffs of operas and foreign movies, you have to get an audience who have heard operas, have been to operas, have seen foreign movies."

That faith was obviously justified, as Sid Caesar's *Your Show of Shows* and, later, *Caesar's Hour* were a couple of early television's funniest and most popular programs.

Caesar says one of the keys was *who* was made fun of. "When I did comedy, I made fun of myself. If there was a buffoon, I played the buffoon. And people looked at me and said, 'Gee, that's like Uncle David' or 'That's like a friend of mine.' And they related through that. I didn't make fun of them, I made fun of me."

Your Show of Shows drew an estimated sixty million viewers at a time when only forty-four million American households had sets. By comparison, today there are more than one hundred million TV homes, but the most-watched shows get less than half that sixty million.

Another amazing innovator in the art of television sketch comedy was funnyman Ernie Kovacs. In the mellow postwar Eisenhower years, Kovacs was an absolute anomaly, a media anarchist with the comedy skills of a vaudevillian and the curious mind of a mad scientist. What resulted was *The Ernie Kovacs Show*, a totally unique program that took televised entertainment where it had never gone before.

Kovacs wrote and produced the show himself, and a great deal of it was improvised. Unlike almost all other entertainment programs, there was no studio audience and no canned laughter. Kovacs said, "I don't have an audience for my shows. I don't believe in that. An audience with free tickets will laugh at the pause because they've been told, nudgingly, 'You are now to laugh.' And they're trying to be nice—they're fond of the people in the show and they want to show their appreciation and show they're glad to be there, so they'll laugh." Another reason there was no audience was because the show was so heavily invested in "special effects." Kovacs felt that an audience that really couldn't see what was going on was of little use.

To a large degree, those special effects are what made the show so groundbreaking during television's toddling years. Each week, Ernie Kovacs welcomed viewers into his "hallucinatory world"—where, literally, up was down and black was white. His technical innovations are legendary; he utilized camera effects like superimposing images on one another, reversing polarity (which made positive seem negative), and reverse scanning, which flipped images upside down. These were like hallucinations without hallucinogens—with paintings that came to life, books that talked, and candle flames that hovered in mid-air.

A lot of the humor and offbeat innovations were a result of Kovacs's treating his show as kind of an electronic science lab. "This is not primarily a comedy show, this is more or less an experiment that I'm doing. There is a strong element of comedy that runs through it, but it is a unique comedy. My particular affinity for the medium is to make it an electronic one and to use this particular medium for its own intrinsic value and approach. But I don't put it above—nor do I put it below—other forms of comedy. This happens to be mine."

Ernie Kovacs's off-the-wall humor and pioneering production earned him a loyal audience and a place in the ranks of the comedy immortals. As proof, in 1989, on the fiftieth

anniversary of the beginning of television, *People* magazine named him one of television's "Top 25 Stars of All Time."

Another great innovator in sketch comedy spent the first two decades of life as Clerow Wilson before being rechristened "Flip" by Air Force buddies who thought he was "flipped out." After finishing his military service, Flip Wilson began ascending in the ranks of comedians by performing at low-rent clubs across the country, building his reputation and his act. When television came looking for black comics in the 1960s, he was more than ready.

Flip Wilson was an innovator in many small ways and in two big ways: he was the first black host of a TV variety series, and his was the first television show to play "in the round." The audience surrounded the round stage, promoting a real sense of intimacy.

Wilson had built his act on a style of comedy that had seemingly passed and that was embodied by the canceled *Amos 'n' Andy* shows. To many who were racially sensitive, the characters he portrayed were throwbacks to a time when African-Americans were stereotypes. But Wilson proved that these characters, when treated with dignity and respect, were still vital and still very funny.

One of his most famous characters was Reverend Leroy, an unscrupulous pastor whose love of the Lord was surpassed only by his love of money. Wilson based the reverend, head of the "Church of What's Happening Now," on a preacher he'd actually listened to as a child. "I was very impressed with him, and I was always amazed that he wasn't well educated," Wilson said in a 1971 interview, "but in his simple way he was dynamic and exciting."

Flip Wilson is best remembered for his in-drag portrayal of Geraldine Jones, the no-nonsense "sista" with the impeccable coif, chartreuse stockings, and take-no-guff attitude. The wisecracking Geraldine was immensely popular, and a number of her catchphrases—"The devil made me do it," "What you see is what you get," and "When you're hot, you're hot!"—quickly became part of the pop lexicon.

Wilson toed a fine line with Geraldine. If the character hadn't been so well devised, she could easily have been offensive—not only to black women but to women in general. It was something he was quite aware of. "The secret of my success with Geraldine is that she's not a put-down of women," Wilson once said. "She's smart, she's trustful, she's loyal, she's sassy. Most drag impersonations are a

Television sketch comedy continued to thrive into the 1970s, and for eleven seasons, from 1967 to 1978, Carol Burnett and her troupe of regulars—Harvey Korman, Vicki Lawrence, Lyle Waggoner (until 1974), and Tim Conway (a regular from 1975 on)—were an integral part of American life and an unfailing source of creativity and laughs.

Carol Burnett was a popular television personality a decade before she got her own show. After studying in UCLA's theater program and becoming a campus star, she moved to New York City in the mid-1950s and quickly made her mark, scoring her first television gig in 1955 on *The Paul Winchell and Jerry Mahoney Show*—a kids' program where she played second fiddle to ventriloquist Paul Winchell's famous dummies. A raft of guest appearances led to a spot as a regular on the primetime *Garry Moore Show*, where she'd often portray five or six different characters in the hour-long program. Burnett was on the show from 1959 to 1962 and became so popular that she was named America's Favorite Female Performer of 1961–62 by *TV Guide*.

After she co-starred with Julie Andrews on an Emmy-winning 1962 special, *Julie and Carol at Carnegie Hall*, CBS made her an offer no one would refuse—a ten-year exclusive contract. For the first five years, she would do specials and guest appearances on other CBS shows, and for the last five years she'd get her own show. Burnett signed on the dotted line, and five years later, on September 11, 1967, *The Carol Burnett Show* debuted.

The Carol Burnett Show was vaudeville for the Age of Aquarius—an updated version of the entertainment style that had dominated the first half of the century. It was a variety show in the true sense of the word, each week featuring a lineup of great talent—singers, actors, and musical acts—all anchored by a woman who could convincingly portray the essence of class or the trashiest of trailer trollops with a simple change of costume. The ensemble was

drag. But women can like Geraldine, men can like Geraldine, everyone can like Geraldine."

A lot of Wilson's popularity can be attributed to its all-inclusiveness—it was clean comedy everyone could like. *The Flip Wilson Show* ran from 1970 to 1974, during which time it was rated the Most Popular Variety Show and the Second Most Popular Show overall in the United States. The show won two Emmys in 1970, for Outstanding Variety Series—Musical, and Outstanding Writing Achievement in Variety and Music; and a Golden Globe in 1971 for Best Performance by an Actor (TV/Game, Comedy, or Musical). And it drew the biggest names in show business as guest stars.

often aided and abetted by the biggest names in show business, like Lucille Ball, Rock Hudson, Liza Minnelli, and Sammy Davis Jr., and by musical acts like Steve Lawrence, the Jackson Five, the Carpenters, Ray Charles, and The Pointer Sisters. Harvey Korman said of the show, "We did a Broadway musical revue every week."

At the time, television was a veritable variety kingdom. "There were nine variety shows on at the same time," says Burnett. "We had *Flip Wilson* [and] *Laugh-In*. Even Bill Cosby had a variety show for a while. Friday nights at Television City (CBS studios) was like being in a dorm. The Smothers Brothers were down here. Glen Campbell was down there. Sonny and Cher were across the hall. Sometimes when we had a scenery change, I'd run through the ladies' room and get on Sonny and Cher's stage and just kind of watch and see what they were up to."

Sketch comedy was the show's cornerstone, and one of the staples of the sketches was movie parodies—inspired takeoffs on classic films with names like *From Here to Maternity*, *Sunnyset Boulevard*, *Lovely Story*, *Dr. Nose*, and the immortal spoof *Went With the Wind*. Often cited as one of the funniest TV sketches of all time, *Went With the Wind* features Carol as "Starlett O'Hara" reprising the famous scene where Vivian Leigh sweeps down the staircase at Tara in a dress made from the mansion's drapes. When Carol descends the stairs, she's also wearing window drapes—but these drapes still have the curtain rod in them!

Harvey Korman, as "Rat Butler," gasps, "Starlett, I love you. That gown is gorgeous." "Thank you," she replies, "I saw it in the window and I just couldn't resist it." Giving credit where credit is due, Carol Burnett says, "That's one of the greatest sight gags ever. And I have to give Bob Mackie credit. He was our costume designer. He came up with the idea of the curtain rod. The man is a genius."

One of the show's most famous running sketches was "Ed and Eunice" (it was also called "The Family" and inspired the television spin-off *Mama's Family*), in which Burnett and Harvey Korman portrayed Ed and Eunice, a bickering, uptight, lower class couple, and Vicki Lawrence, heavily padded and made up, played Eunice's exceedingly crabby "Momma," a woman about three times Vicki's age. The arguments between the family members ranged from snippy to downright nasty, but they were always "painfully" funny.

Though guest stars were often drafted for "Ed and Eunice," the best-remembered episode is probably the one in which Tim Conway, as Ed's dim-witted assistant, describes a pair of "Siamese elephants" joined at the trunk. When Tim insists the poor beasts can't make noises like the other elephants, just a "fnork," the entire cast falls apart laughing and is barely able to continue.

From his early guest appearances to finally joining the cast in 1975, Tim Conway proved one of the funniest sketch comedians ever. Often Harvey Korman would lose it during their routines—though Tim admits that, most of the time, he was consciously trying to get Korman to break up, as he did in the classic "Dentist" sketch. "We would rehearse what was on the written page. And then when we went to do it, I would do something totally different," Conway confessed. "So, it wasn't until dress rehearsal that I put the Novocain in my hand, in my leg, my head, and the whole thing. Harvey had never seen that. So, he's sitting there hysterical, viewing it as the audience."

One show had a sketch set in a dry-cleaning shop in which Conway was doing his "Old Man" character, a slow-moving turtle of a guy. The Old Man somehow gets hung on the cleaner's rotating clothing rack, and the rack takes

him round and round. It was a funny gag, made hilarious by a problem with the rack's electrical circuitry.

"It actually stuck on," Conway says, "so every time I passed Harvey I would do my line, but they couldn't stop it. Harvey, of course, was wetting his pants because they couldn't stop this thing, and I was hanging from a hanger on it and they were just dragging me around."

Like all good comedy, some of the most popular routines were born out of real life—like the Tudball and Wiggens sketch. "The [Burnett] writers had a room at the end of the hall, and way down at the other end was the secretary who typed our stuff," explained Conway. "So they finally put in an intercom, but one of those really early ones. It just said 'talk' and 'on' and 'off.' So, if you pressed the talk button when you were talking to her, she could no longer hear you. So you go, 'Uh, Charlene, could you—,' and she'd go, 'Hello? Um, Charlene. Could you just— Hello?' And then you'd have to walk down the end of the hall and go, 'Charlene, don't touch the button when I'm talking.' So we had Tudball sitting right next to Miss Wiggens."

Like Tim Conway, the cast members on *The Carol Burnett Show* were consummate professionals who made it obvious that they took great pleasure in their work and respected one another. Audiences loved them right back— especially Carol. Neil Simon says that people were so taken with her because she was "one of them." "She was always a fan," he explains. "People like Sid Caesar hid behind their characters. People like Carol Burnett were part of the audience, identified with them." Carol put her own spin on it: "I'm like your mother, your sister. One lady once came up to me and said, 'I just love you. You're so common.'"

What these remarkably uncommon shows have in common is that they all made important contributions to the renaissance of sketch comedy, a traditional form of humor left for dead by the sightless medium of radio. In the process, they modernized it, repopularized it, and reestablished it, proving that great comedy and great comedians are timeless.

CHAPTER 4

AND NOW FOR SOMETHING COMPLETELY DIFFERENT

In the 1960s, the Beatles, the Rolling Stones, and the Who shook up the world of music with their irreverence, their attitude, and their ability to reflect the changin' times. At the same time, a couple of folksingers, an ensemble of oddball actors, and a British improv troupe were doing the same for comedy. Nothing was sacred—everything was funny. The revolution was televised, and they socked it to us.

The first show to break the mold was an unlikely candidate, a show hosted by a pair of amiable folk musicians, and brothers to boot—one conservative and the other perpetually confused and innocent. But *The Smothers Brothers Comedy Hour* soon proved to be much more. Tom and Dick Smothers had started out performing folk music, but with Tom's between-song patter and the eternal comic appeal of sibling rivalry, the act soon evolved. After appearances on Jack Paar's *Tonight Show,* the duo took off with several hit albums and sold-out concerts. "We weren't political in any way then," Tom said. "We were kind of stupid and uninformed."

After flopping in a sitcom on CBS, the brothers were offered the *Comedy Hour,* and Tom—who was actually quite savvy, as he proved in his hands-on production of the show—insisted on creative control. Because the show was scheduled in the television kamikaze time slot opposite

NBC's ratings behemoth, *Bonanza,* CBS agreed to Tommy's demand, believing they had nothing to lose. But they had no idea what they were in for.

Much of the *Comedy Hour*'s humor remained wholesomely silly. The most oft-quoted lines are Tommy's helpless retorts in losing arguments: "Oh, yeah?!?" and "Mom liked you best!" The latter bit debuted in their act in 1961—

during their performances Dick would "just yell at Tommy," and one day that line popped into Tom's head. By the *Comedy Hour,* it was a polished Abbott-and-Costello-type argument, climaxing with Tom shouting, "Mom liked you best." Dick urged him, "Lower your voice," so Tom repeated the line in a deep voice to another round of laughter.

But the show also featured young up-and-coming writers like Steve Martin and Rob Reiner who had a hip political sensibility; meanwhile, Tommy was becoming increasingly socially conscious. The results were witty songs like the "Draft Dodger Rag," skits that simultaneously mocked Lyndon Johnson and Richard Nixon, and subversive bits laden with drug references, like the "Share a Little Tea with Goldie" skits, featuring the hostess greeting viewers with "Hi(gh)—and glad of it." (Tea was a Sixties code word for marijuana.)

The show's musical numbers also broke with tradition, appealing to young viewers, most famously when it incurred the wrath of CBS for letting blacklisted folksinger Pete Seeger perform his Vietnam War protest song "Waist Deep in the Big Muddy," and when the Who performed their truly explosive version of "My Generation." (Keith Moon illegally snuck explosives into his bass drum and set them off while Pete Townshend was smashing his guitar.)

But nothing struck a nerve as much as the mock presidential campaign hilariously unwaged by deadpan humorist and Smothers "editorialist" Pat Paulsen, whose slogan was "If nominated I will not run, and if elected I will not serve." Paulsen's editorials always stirred up a reaction, both because they made people laugh and because they made people think: "Now, we don't claim the draft is perfect, and we do have a constructive proposal for a workable alternative," Paulsen offered. "We propose a draft lottery in which the names of all eligible males will be put into a hat and the men will be drafted according to the head sizes. The tiny heads will go into the military service, and the fat heads will go into government."

Soon, Tommy recalls, "affiliates were demanding to see each show before it aired, and CBS caved in." Skits and songs were routinely blocked. In a funny response, the show ran a skit featuring a series of "censors" (each an actual writer on the show) laughing hysterically at a script while each tore out one page after another. The last in line hands the last single page to Tommy, and proudly proclaims, "There's nothing funny about this show."

Shortly after Richard Nixon was elected president, CBS canceled the highly rated show. "That was a shock," Dick recalls. "I didn't think they'd ever fire us." It was replaced with *Hee Haw,* the ultimate in play-it-safe comedy, a country-flavored variety show with corny jokes delivered straight from the cornfield.

But it was too late. For television there was no turning back. NBC had struck gold in 1968 with *Rowan & Martin's Laugh-In,* a show that featured nearly as many political zingers as *The Smothers Brothers*. But Dan Rowan once noted that *The Smothers Brothers* used comedy as a platform for politics while his show used politics as a platform for comedy, playing its controversial material as a reflection of the era's "anything goes" mentality, tossed off as one-liners accompanied by giggles or wacky music.

Catchphrases like "Look that up in your Funk and Wagnall" and "You bet your sweet bippy" made censors nervous, but NBC had been desperate for programming

and paid little attention until the first show was done. "They [the NBC brass] said the public won't understand this, but it went on the air because they had nothing else," recalls creator George Schlatter. And once it was a hit, the show could get away with anything—and often did.

Schlatter fused the offbeat zaniness of the underappreciated Ernie Kovacs, the topicality of the short-lived sketch-show pioneer *That Was the Week That Was,* and the dapper, smart-alecky personas of hosts Dan Rowan and Dick Martin (a comedy team since 1952) to create something entirely new and original. "I wanted to do a show that was reflective of the times," he says. "Until *Laugh-In,* television variety was like theater or a nightclub. Nobody had used the freedom television gave us."

Schlatter's "shotgun comedy show" moved as fast as the times. "The rules for *Laugh-In* were: it had to be short, it had to be political or it had to be whimsical, or it had to be crazy. We balanced between those."

The highlights included "The Cocktail Party" and the "Joke Wall," where lines flew by fast and furious and context no longer mattered. That freed the writers to toss out

risqué lines like Judy Carne's "All the kids in my school are really proud of the astronauts—imagine staying that high for that long," and guest Flip Wilson's "It's all in how you look at it—what you call riots, we call group therapy."

It helped that there were plenty of celebrities—from Billy Graham to Tiny Tim to Johnny Carson to Leonard Nimoy to TV-phobic John Wayne—and plenty of schtick and vaudeville-esque skits (like the ones featuring Arte Johnson's lecherous and punning old man). Goldie Hawn's giddy giggle generated plenty of innocent laughter, as did silly trifles like the recurring gag of marrying different names together: "If Queen Elizabeth married Steve McQueen she'd be Queen McQueen." The show, which gave new comic prominence to women and minorities, relied heavily on characters and catchphrases brought in by the talented cast, from Arte Johnson's German soldier ("Verrdy interesting") to Lily Tomlin's Ernestine the telephone operator ("One ringy-dingy, two ringy-dingy") to the most famous of all, "Sock it to me." (That old Count Basie phrase was most infamously performed by guest Richard Nixon; Schlatter still bemoans the fact that this self-effacing humanizing moment may have helped Nixon get elected.)

But even such silliness was often enlisted to score sociopolitical points. On one show, Ruth Buzzi's little old lady, Gladys, made a pass at guest James Garner, to much laughter. But later on, when Chelsea Brown, who is black, made her move on Garner, the camera cut to Johnson's soldier, who punctuated his "Verrdy interesting" by quipping, "But right now in Birmingham they're running a test pattern."

And Schlatter had Ernestine dial the phone with her middle finger so that when she dialed one "Jedgar Hoover," observant viewers would realize she was flipping the bird to the nation's powerful FBI director.

Being such a show of its time meant being a star that faded fast. After the first two years, only the addition of Lily Tomlin kept the show fresh. Yet it helped change television forever, and its influence is still felt today.

When *Laugh-In* first launched, a British comedy troupe swore out loud. "We were really worried about *Laugh-In,*" Eric Idle once said. "We went, 'Oh *%*$*, they're doing what we wanted, this madness.'"

taper off weakly, they would pursue what Jones once called a "chain of consciousness" effect: sketches could seem to end in the middle, often aided by Gilliam's far-out animation, or abruptly segue into other bits.

For instance, Jones and Palin were once writing a hilarious skit about a razor-wielding barber fighting his blood-lust but spent hours puzzling over a traditional ending. Finally they hit upon the line "I don't want to be barber anyway, I want to be a lumberjack" with a nonsensical segue into a musical number—and within a half-hour the now-famous "Lumberjack Song," with its cross-dressing lyrics, was complete.

The actor-writers had virtually no outside interference and placed none on their imagination. "There were absolutely no rules or limits," Michael Palin once said.

So, for Python's very first sketch John Cleese revived a skit, "The Frost Report," that had been rejected at his previous job for being too way-out and too silly: A tourist asks a shepherd why there are sheep up in the trees. "A fair question, and one that in recent weeks has been much on my mind," the shepherd replies. "It's my considered opinion that they're nestin'."

And yet that troupe, "Monty Python," managed to create something completely different—an entirely new, distinctively British form of madness, an unusual mixture of highbrow and lowbrow, often within the same sketch—with some hilariously destructive and occasionally naughty animated segments thrown in for good measure.

Even the name was funny. It had come about because the BBC insisted on the "Flying Circus" name for the show, so the troupe added an "owner," "Monty Python," whose name they thought sounded sleazy and a bit unpleasant.

Flying Circus, was far less topical and largely avoided the trap of relying on repeated catchphrases or favorite characters. Python members John Cleese, Terry Jones, Michael Palin, and Terry Gilliam (the show's animator) decided that to avoid having sketches go on too long or

It turns out the sheep believe they're birds, although "they do not so much fly as plummet." Where'd they get that idea? "From Harold. He's that most dangerous of creatures, a clever sheep. He's realized that a sheep's life consists of standin' around for a few months and then bein' eaten. And that's a depressing prospect for an ambitious sheep." But the shepherd won't remove Harold because of "the enormous commercial possibilities if 'e succeeds."

Flying Circus was clearly not political—it was revolutionary because it shattered expectations, presenting a world where nothing is what it seems and anything can happen at any time. Many of the laughs came from how far the troupe would go. (The troupe enhanced the absurdity by playing most women's roles themselves.)

In one bit, Mrs. Premise (Cleese) tells neighbor Mrs.

Conclusion (Graham Chapman) she spent four hours burying the cat.

"Yes," Premise says. "It wouldn't keep still."

"Oh—it wasn't dead, then?" Conclusion asks nonchalantly.

"No, no—but it's not at all well, so we were going to be on the safe side."

The troupe also delighted in skewering the stuffy upper class and mindless bureaucrats. Perhaps the most famous creation was Cleese's deadly serious "Minister of Silly Walks," a skit Michael Palin had struggled with before handing it off to Cleese and Chapman. But even at its silliest and most shocking, there was always a sophistication—often marked by a love of language—that elevated *Flying Circus* skits to comedy greatness. In "The Dead Parrot" skit, Cleese plays a customer trying to return a recently purchased but clearly dead Norwegian parrot. Palin, as the shop owner, cheerfully insists the bird is resting, and then that it's pining for the fjords of Norway. The towering Cleese, exasperated and angered, finally loses control.

"He's not pinin'! He's passed on! This parrot is no more! If you hadn't nailed him to the perch he'd be pushing up the daisies! He's off the twig! He's kicked the bucket, he's shuffled off his mortal coil, run down the curtain, and joined the bleedin' choir invisible!! *This is an ex-parrot!!*"

The indefatigable owner now says he'll replace it, but after a quick peek around he confesses he's "right out of parrots." Cleese's character bursts a few more blood vessels, but after a short pause Palin offers a sincere compromise: "I've got a slug."

The Smothers Brothers broke down the barriers, *Laugh-In* forever changed comedy sketches and their pacing, but *Monty Python's Flying Circus* managed to become an "exsketch show" at the right time, turning to movies like *Life of Brian* and *Holy Grail,* before combining their two interests with *The Meaning of Life*—a feature-length film of Python sketches.

· · ·

These television sketch shows captured the flavor of their era yet still resonate with every succeeding generation.

Just a few years later—in 1975—*Saturday Night Live* began its run to becoming an American comedy institution. *SNL* revived the controversial topicality of *The Smothers Brothers Comedy Hour* and *Laugh-In,* blending it with the brilliant sophomoric-but-sophisticated writing and ferocious performing of *Monty Python's Flying Circus.*

Although its creator, Lorne Michaels, adapted a more traditional sketch-show structure—hosts, self-contained skits, musical guests—he infused *SNL* with an anarchic energy and attitude that seemed compatible with the era.

However, even at its zenith, there was one major flaw in *SNL*'s world of humor—white guys overtly dominated it. With the exception of the incomparable Eddie Murphy, African-American stars weren't truly equal, and even Murphy was often playing stereotypes.

But that flaw opened the door for the next breakthrough sketch comedy show, *In Living Color.* Created by Keenen Ivory Wayans, this was also the first sketch show to rely on a black worldview for its humor. (Although Jim Carrey, who created manic characters like the overzealous and always endangered Fire Marshall Bill, became the biggest star.)

"I wanted the look, feel, and attitude of the show to be completely contemporary," Wayans said. "I wanted it to have an edge to it, to reach out and grab people right from the start. . . . They [Saturday Night Live] never had the ethnic makeup that we do, and I knew we could get away with things that they couldn't."

That pushed buttons, of course, and the show often got in trouble for negative stereotyping. One funny but harsh bit involved a brutish clown named Homey, who when asked to do anything he didn't want to do, would snap with "Homey don't play that," while another featured the Home Boy Shopping Network with two hoodlums selling stolen goods

The show was merciless in parodying everyone. In "Lassie '90," Jim Carrey played Timmy, a boy with a bloodthirsty pit bull with a penchant for pulling arms off anyone who comes too close. The "Hey Mon" skits portrayed West Indian immigrants as hard workers gone crazy—everyone has at least six jobs and the parents say a doctor isn't good enough for their daughter because "he has just one job."

And in the show's own *Star Trek* parody called "Wrath of Farrakhan," David Alan Grier as Louis Farrakhan incites insurrection aboard the *Enterprise* by saying the white Kirk is oppressing Uhura and Sulu. "My people have survived four hundred years of slavery, three hundred years of apartheid, and twenty-five years of *The Jeffersons* in syndication," Farrakhan declares before redirecting the *Enterprise* to Sylvia's, the famous Harlem soul-food restaurant.

But the show also had the credibility to make pointed comments about racism that no other show ever could. An ad for the "Equity Express Card" showed white shop employees and credit card company workers harassing a legitimate black customer, culminating in an unfair arrest. Then the credit card spokeswoman delivers the zinger: "Sure, he sued us and won, but it

from the back of a truck: "We got car phones, car stereos, car alarms—if you act now we can probably get the car, too."

Then there was the homeless wino named Anton who hosted *This Old Box,* a parody of PBS's *This Old House,* on the "Pavement Broadcasting System," with Anton stealing power from streetlights and adding a guest room—another box—held on with what he says mischievously is an "all-natural adhesive" as he sticks his finger up his nose.

Wayans believed it was important for blacks and whites to see blacks parodying themselves. "Making fun of stereotypes helps to defuse some of the power of stereotyping," Wayans said. "We're very conscious about who we make fun of, and we don't ridicule serious subjects."

was still fun to do." It was a line designed to make you think and even feel uncomfortable while you were laughing, and like the best of its predecessors, it pulled it off.

Although the fragmentation of today's television universe makes it more likely that new sketch shows will attract a cult following than become another national sensation. After all, before *The Smothers Brothers Comedy Hour, Laugh-In, Monty Python's Flying Circus, Saturday Night Live,* or *In Living Color* burst onto the scene no one had any idea a revolutionary new show was just around the corner. But there it was, every time, and as shocking as each new show may have been, we laughed.

THIS ISN'T YOUR FATHER'S SKETCH COMEDY SHOW

PLENTY OF SKETCH-COMEDY TELEVISION SHOWS have tried walking in the footsteps of *Saturday Night Live* and *In Living Color*, but none has achieved their longevity or legendary status, although several have conjured their fair share of laughs while puncturing society's sacred cows.

Second City TV

This classic parody of television itself launched almost as many careers as *Saturday Night Live*—John Candy, Eugene Levy, Rick Moranis, Dave Thomas, Andrea Martin, Catherine O'Hara, and Martin Short all got their breaks on this Canadian-based show.

There was John Candy doing Ben Hur as Curly from the Three Stooges and the *Leave It to Beaver* episode where Beaver (Candy) kills Eddie (Thomas), prompting Wally (Levy) to say, "You've really done it this time, Beaver."

Second City TV revolved mostly around the wacky characters of the fictitious television station, like the sleazy boss Guy Caballero (Joe Flaherty), who was healthy but stayed wheelchair-bound because "I get more respect that way"; the pompous boozer Johnny LaRue (Candy), who spouted nonsense like "I've got more talent in this little finger—than in this [other] little finger"; Yosh and Stan Shmenge (Candy and Levy), the polka players from Leutonia; the doofus McKenzie Brothers (Thomas and Moranis); and Ed Grimley (Short), who later took lines like "Completely mental, I must say" to even greater fame at *Saturday Night Live*.

Fridays

This cult favorite, which featured a couple of young unknowns named Larry David and Michael Richards, frequently tackled ambitious and lengthy conceptual skits, like its memorable "Moral Majority Comedy Variety Hour," "brought to you by the makers of milk and white bread." This "program" included "Whitestone the Illusionist," who made the one black audience member disappear, songs like "Three Cheers for the White, White, and White," and featured an ad for a book-burning event hyped in the style of Monster Truck or pro wrestling.

Mad TV

Fox's venture into Saturday night sketch comedy may not have the high-profile or star-making power of *Saturday Night Live*, but more often than not it holds its own laughs-wise against the NBC institution. The show's pop-culture parodies are often brilliantly twisted: "Malcolm X in the Middle" featured dead-on impressions of the hit sitcom's cast with a black insurrectionist trying to change society while getting yelled at by his overbearing white mother.

A send-up of the game show *Family Feud* featured the notorious Soprano family as contestants. Tony bumps off the host, chases off the opposing family, and then answers questions like "Name a feature you look for in a car" ("a roomy trunk"), all while feuding with his own, fractious, foul-mouthed family.

HOME IS WHERE THE HOWLS ARE

Throughout the 1930s and 1940s, the family comedy had become one of the most bankable commodities on radio. So it was not surprising that as the nation began turning to television for entertainment in the 1950s, comics and programmers pitched the domestic hearth as an ideal setting for schtick. With nearly 85 percent of American households wired by mid-decade, and parents and progeny together ingesting an average of five hours of small-screen sustenance each day, television was ripe for a home-to-home invasion.

And the invasion came. Over the past fifty years, a battery of fictional families has marched across the airwaves, firing off quips and wisecracks, stumbling over furniture, and gleefully yanking the chains of familial and marital loyalty. From the Kramdens and the Petries to the Huxtables and the Barones, these television families have become our loyal comic counterparts, playing out the dynamics of home life with a mixture of pathos and slaphappy lunacy, and—most important—giving us a glimpse of ourselves through the laughter.

When comic Jackie Gleason exhorted his *Honeymooners* writers, "Make it real, make it the way people live," he could have been giving a primer on family sitcoms in general. "If it isn't credible," he told them, "nobody's going to laugh."

Originally cooked up as a time-filling sketch for Gleason's *Cavalcade of Stars* in the early 1950s, *The Honeymooners*, thirty-nine half-hour comedic gems produced for CBS between October 1955 and September 1956, revolved around the contentious relationship between Alice (Audrey Meadows), an attractive middle-aged homemaker, and her bellicose husband, Ralph (Jackie Gleason), a portly mass-transit employee whose harebrained get-rich-quick schemes, aided and abetted by his moronic neighbor Ed Norton (Art Carney), backfired worse than his Brooklyn bus. It was a raw slice of urban, working-class comedy, full of cantankerous hollering, empty threats, and snappy putdowns, all delivered with machine-gun timing. "If you were only my size!" Ralph grumbles menacingly at one point to his disapproving spouse, to which the unflappable Alice replies, "If I were your size I'd be the fat lady in a circus."

According to *Cavalcade* writer Coleman Jacoby, *The Honeymooners* was also the only show where audiences got to see the real Gleason, whose gloomy, poverty-stricken childhood in Bushwick, Brooklyn—his father deserted the family when Gleason was eight, and his mother died ten years later—had undergone comic alchemy to become the stuff of great humor. "All that anguish and the bellowing and the bullying and pipe dreams, that was really part of

Gleason's early life," he said, "that's what made contact with millions of people. That plus one other thing—Carney, who gave it a note of originality and who took the edge off the brutal aspect of it."

If, as Gleason devotee Jerry Lewis has said, "Gleason's brilliance put every sketch comic on the planet back years to learn their craft," Art Carney helped him double that. As Ralph's dimwitted but perennially optimistic sewer-worker buddy and comic foil Ed Norton, Carney was the consummate scene-stealer, a bundle of jittery limbs and facial ticks crowned by a battered porkpie hat who was always spring-loaded with obtuse idiocies.

"The first time I saw the guy act, I knew I would have to work twice as hard for my laughs," Gleason said of Carney, who won an Emmy for his role. "He was funny as hell."

Whether hawking glow-in-the-dark wallpaper, engaging in fraternal intrigue at the Raccoon Lodge, or making fools of themselves as kitchen-utensil salesman on television, Carney and Gleason proved to be an unmatchable comic tandem.

"The Golfer" episode is a wonderful case in point. Eyeing a promotion at work, Ralph, in a typical display of ill-conceived braggadocio, informs his golf-crazy superior that he happens to be a first-rate duffer himself. Impressed, the boss insists Ralph join him on the links the coming weekend for an important game. Problem is, Ralph has never touched a club. In a panic, he and Norton retreat to the apartment with a tattered instructional manual to learn the sport and save Ralph's reputation.

The show's writers rarely missed an opportunity to have Carney and Gleason play off one another physically, and this scene surely ranks among the best in that regard. Norton begins in characteristic out-to-lunch fashion by reading aloud the book's dedication page before being urged by a bristling Ralph to get to the point. When he comes to the chapter on the proper way to "address the ball," Carney leans forward with eyebrows raised, waves enthusiastically at the practice pincushion, and shouts, "Helloooo, ball!" The studio audience exploded, but the best was yet to come.

Discarding the instruction manual's recommended golf swing, Norton instead devises an outrageous swivel-hipped spasm, which he convinces Ralph to emulate. As the beefy Ralph practices the "swing" with greater and greater gusto—getting bigger and bigger laughs—Norton becomes increasingly excited, stacking obstacles beneath Ralph's feet and suggesting he pretend to be playing up a hill, and then up a "really big hill." The combination of Carney's herky-jerky enthusiasm and Gleason's graceful girth brought the house down. To Ralph's good fortune, his boss unexpectedly canceled the date, thereby saving himself and his fellow golfers from the horror of witnessing Norton's creation.

Incidentally, Gleason unintentionally broke the prop club at the end of the scene, but by then it didn't matter, as the crowd probably couldn't see through the tears in their eyes.

To Gleason's credit, he never let his work with Carney become a competition. "He was a poor soul and a troubled man," said *Everybody Loves Raymond* star Brad Garrett, who portrayed Gleason in a 2002 biopic. "Talk about life imitating art—that's what made him a genius, because he was the first to play the Everyman, to play the down-and-out, to play the dreamer with schemes."

Whatever personal demons animated Gleason's Ralph, the public ate it up. The live filmings of the program quickly became an event, as upward of a thousand people crowded into the Adelphi Theater in midtown Manhattan each Tuesday and Friday night to see Gleason, Carney, Audrey Meadows, and Joyce Randolph work their comedic magic.

What the crowd didn't realize as they watched Ralph prance, pontificate, and perjure his way through his ridiculous misadventures was that Gleason had often memorized his lines just minutes before show time, if he had memorized them at all.

"He did not like to rehearse," remembered Meadows. "I kept saying to Art, 'When do we do the blocking?' And he said, 'You just did it.' I said, 'Well, are they going to do a camera run?' He said, 'You just did it.' I said, 'Well, what time is dress rehearsal?' And he said, 'You just did it.' I was in a state of panic. So I got through that first show, and then I got to love the fact of not rehearsing, because it's much better for comedy when you're not over-rehearsed." When it came to dialogue, Meadows claimed she would learn all Gleason's lines in addition to her own, so that when Gleason went blank—a fact he would indicate by patting his stomach—she could set him back on course.

Despite all their spats and misunderstandings, Ralph and Alice truly seemed to love one another. They had no kids (Gleason didn't trust their comic timing) and, regardless of Ralph's interminable financial scheming, little money—but they were clearly in it for the long haul. It's no wonder countless episodes ended with the two embracing

and Ralph intoning "Baby, you're the greatest" as the curtain fell.

In spite of the remarkable chemistry, Gleason pulled the plug after one season, claiming the show's quality couldn't be maintained. The breakneck production pace may have had something to do with it; churning out two full shows a week, from concept to final product, left things in a perpetual state of bedlam. Whatever the reason, *The Honeymooners* came and went quickly, a brief but brilliant chapter in the history of television situation comedies.

While Gleason cultivated comedy from his poor blue-collar background, a young New York comic actor was looking for comic fodder from his white-collar life in the suburbs. "I was getting sitcoms offered to me after *Your Show of Shows* ended," recalled Carl Reiner, who had spent a decade making a name for himself as a second banana on Sid Caesar's legendary variety program. "And *The Dick Van Dyke Show* came about because my wife said to me, 'You can write better than this!'"

The only trick was to find a subject. "I was on East River Drive at about Ninety-sixth Street," recalled Reiner, who at the time was living in New Rochelle, New York, with his family and commuting to Manhattan each day, "and I asked myself, 'What piece of ground do I stand on that nobody else stands on?' Then I said, 'That's it. I'll write about living in New Rochelle and working in New York, in variety.'"

The Dick Van Dyke Show didn't begin life as a hit; in fact, it didn't even begin with Dick Van Dyke. The original 1958 pilot starred Reiner in the role of Rob Petrie, the comedy writer and suburban family man whose life bore a striking resemblance to his own. *Head of the Family*, as the show was then titled, had been Reiner's labor of love, the result of a half-year spent feverishly pounding out scripts, assembling a cast, and begging for funding. Unfortunately, it was also a flop. With quiz shows and westerns proving to be reliable cash cows, networks simply weren't interested in the autobiographical musings of a former sketch-show performer.

But good material has a way of sticking around, and on the advice of executive producer Sheldon Leonard, Reiner stepped off-camera to become a producer and recast the program two years later with rising Broadway star Van Dyke in the lead.

"When I started writing the show, Rob Petrie was based on myself, a Bronx Jew," said Reiner. "But once we cast the show, we had Dick Van Dyke, who was a midwestern gentile. I didn't have to change the Rob Petrie character, because Dick processed Rob Petrie through his body and his work ethic and morality, which were similar to mine."

Finding an actress to portray Rob Petrie's wife, Laura, was a thornier affair. After a lengthy search, he finally tapped twenty-three-year-old unknown Mary Tyler Moore (whose highest-profile gig to date had been as a pair of legs on a TV detective show), simply because, Reiner recalled, "she said hello like a real person." Debuting on CBS in October 1961, *The Dick Van Dyke Show* ushered in a new era of sophisticated, adult-oriented family humor and proved that while real life wasn't always stranger than fiction, it was usually much funnier.

With the dawning of the Kennedy era, Rob and Laura emerged as comedy's answer to the first couple. They were handsome, stylish, intelligent, and apt to turn the most insignificant domestic snafu into a half-hour disaster. Bad dye jobs, sneezing fits, toes stuck in bathtub faucets, a sick child—it is a testament to the writing and to Van Dyke's and Moore's comic gifts—both won multiple Emmys during the show's five-year run—that such prosaic raw material consistently yielded such inspired camp and physical humor.

Writer Garry Marshall, who came to the show after a stint on *I Love Lucy*, felt that much of the show's genius stemmed from Reiner's unique scripting style. "Whereas on *Lucy* and numerous other sitcoms, writers would envision a funny final scene and work their way backward, *The Dick Van Dyke Show* went the other way. They took a little incident on page one and followed it along until it blossomed into a whole show."

To Reiner, who scripted most of the first two seasons, it was precisely these little true-life banalities—the "realies," as he called them—that provided the necessary spark for good comedy. "If the writers came up dry," he said, "I would ask, 'Anything happen in your family lately, to your wife, your kids, your partners—anything?' Things that actually happened to people made the best shows."

"Other sitcoms revolved around the battle of the sexes, where the husband and wife constantly played

against each other," said Reiner. *The Dick Van Dyke Show*—inspired by how I felt about my work and my wife—portrayed a husband and wife united against the world."

It also portrayed, in narrowly disguised form, Reiner's tenure with the *Show of Shows* writing coterie, which would spawn such future luminaries as Woody Allen, Neil Simon, and Larry Gelbart, in addition to Reiner himself. "*The Dick Van Dyke Show* would never have existed if I hadn't worked on *Your Show of Shows* in the writers' room," acknowledged Reiner. "The writers in that room, it was like going to college—there were so many different senses of humor and ways of approaching a joke."

Comedy vets Morey Amsterdam and Rose Marie filled out the roster as Rob's salty co-writers Buddy and Sally on the fictional *Alan Brady Show*. As loosely drawn stand-ins for *Your Show of Shows*, jokemeisters Mel Brooks and Selma Diamond, Amsterdam and Rose Marie infused the show with an edgy, urban comic sensibility that had all but disappeared from family shows by the early 1960s.

Reiner cast himself as the show's head honcho and namesake, a seldom seen and imperious comedy overlord patterned not on Caesar but on another variety-show giant, Milton Berle, whose tirades against his writing staff were legendary in showbiz circles. "He was always short-tempered and yelling at people," Reiner said. "I said, 'That's

a good guy to have.' It's wonderful to have a mean protagonist so that your hero has somebody to fight against."

Naturally, the collision of home life and work provided some of the show's funniest moments, most notably in the classic "Coast-to-Coast Big Mouth" episode when Laura, goaded by a fast-talking quiz-show host, confesses on national television that the famous head of Alan Brady was actually hiding beneath a hairpiece.

Writers Bill Persky and Sam Denoff, who would win an Emmy for the episode, didn't have to look far for inspiration. Their rug-topped boss occupied the office next door. His name was Carl Reiner. "The toupee was a pain in the ass for him," recalled Denoff, who had taken to heart Reiner's advice about using real-life situations in his scripts. "So we decided to do an episode about it."

It was a perfect opportunity for Moore to let her character's laughable neuroses hang out, and she played the guilt-ridden Laura to the hilt. Realizing she has endangered her husband's job with her scandalous revelation, Laura initially seeks to hide her gaffe but becomes increasingly flustered. As she tells the oblivious Rob about her experience on the game show, she is reduced first to uncontrollable stuttering, then to a series of incomprehensible squeals and pantomimes, before finally breaking down and admitting the truth. "That was Mary at her best," Persky said of Moore in the episode.

Reiner himself turned in a hilarious performance as the disparaged Brady. When Laura attempts to set things right by visiting his office to grovel for forgiveness, she finds the gloomy star surrounded by scores of now-useless toupees, which he insists on referring to as if they were old war buddies. When Laura enters the room he grumbles, "Fellas, there's the little lady who put you out of business."

"Coast-to-Coast Big Mouth," aside from being one of *The Dick Van Dyke Show*'s best-loved episodes, was confirmation of Reiner's philosophy that comic gold could, and should, be mined from individuals' personal idiosyncrasies. "Everybody's different," Reiner has said, "and if you can see where you are different from everybody else, you might have an original show."

Such advice was not lost on the freshman stand-up comic who paid an informal visit to *The Dick Van Dyke Show* set one day in 1963 and left the cast and crew gasping for air. "We didn't get a bit of work done that day, we were laughing so hard," Reiner recalls. "He did all of his act, and he was hilarious." Twenty years, a slew of television roles, and an untold number of Jell-O pudding commercials later, Bill Cosby would shoot to superstardom as the head of televisions Huxtables, an affluent African-American family whose day-to-day trials were culled largely from Cosby's own adventures in modern parenting.

As a father of five, raising kids was a subject Cosby knew something about and was regular fodder for his stand-up routine. And from his perspective, the sitcoms of the early 1980s were giving family entertainment a bad name. "I was watching television back then," Cosby said later, "and I noticed the children were brighter than the parents. And the laughs were coming because the parents really weren't parenting." Enter Dr. Heathcliff Huxtable, antidote to domestic disintegration, gynecologist, and purveyor of restorative comicality.

When Dr. Cliff, his wife, Clair (Phylicia Ayers-Allen), and the rest of the clan hit the air on NBC in the fall of 1984, they became an instant sensation. *The Cosby Show* returned family comedy to a gentler milieu, where not all kids were punks and ingrates and not all parents were hapless nincompoops. The five Huxtable children, while each with their own quirky traits, were exceedingly well adjusted and did their best to adhere to the dictum laid down by their stern but loving parents: study hard, fly right, respect your elders. In short, they were ordinary youngsters who kept their noses clean. And nothing was funnier in Bill Cosby's hands than the ordinary.

"Mr. Cosby is making the nation laugh," wrote John J. O'Connor of the *New York Times*, "by paring ordinary life to its extraordinary essentials." It was something the comic had spent his lifetime doing.

In essence, *The Cosby Show* was the most current extension of the stand-up routines that by the early 1980s had made Bill Cosby one of the most popular and respected comedians in America. Since his start twenty-five years earlier, he had earned a reputation as a consummate storyteller. "Cosby is the greatest monologuist that ever lived," said Carl Reiner. "You could give him a piece of paper and say, 'Do twenty minutes on this piece of paper,' and he could do it."

In fact, it was during a Cosby routine on parenting on *The Tonight Show* that then-president of NBC Entertainment Brandon Tartikoff hit on the idea of creating a family sitcom using Cosby's anecdotes as raw material.

The challenge for the *Cosby Show* writing staff was to create stories around Cosby's droll, sardonic comic personality. By eschewing hackneyed one-liners and wacky scenarios and focusing instead on everyday incidents, like the death of a goldfish, a visit from the grandparents, or a bad report card, they were able to trade on the qualities that had made the comedian such an icon.

"It is the most personal show I have been involved with," said original head writer Earl Pomerantz. "That is not just because Bill is the star, but because the show has to reflect his vision. It is also trickier to come up with material in harmony with what he wants to do."

But Cosby made sure they got it right, telling his writers, "I don't want sitcom jokes. I don't want jokes about behinds or breasts or pimples or characters saying 'Oh, my God' every other line. What we want to deal with is human behavior. If we can put it on paper and have it come to life through the actors, then we can have people identifying with us."

His vision paid off. Cosby's sharp wit and keen observations on parenthood played well on the small screen, and in a short time he became television's most beloved and amusing sitcom father. He was at his best when confronting

his children's behavioral problems, which were always minor but typical: Cliff doesn't like the boys his daughter Denise is dating, his son Theo doesn't understand the value of money, his knee-high daughter, Rudy, has developed a habit of biting objects, both inanimate and otherwise. Nothing couldn't be solved by an instructive, marble-mouthed monologue from Dad, which left the youngsters a little wiser and viewers splitting their sides.

In the episode "A Shirt Story," for example, Theo (Malcolm Jamal-Warner) arrives home from a shopping spree proudly clutching a ninety-five-dollar designer shirt with which he hopes to impress a date. Disturbed by this immoderate self-indulgence, and intent on teaching his son a lesson in humility, Cliff repossesses the shirt and suggests Theo take up his sister Denise's (Lisa Bonet) offer to tailor a replacement for one-third the price. "No boy should have a ninety-five-dollar shirt," Cliff tells Theo, "unless he is on stage with his four brothers."

Suspicious of his sibling's abilities but convinced by Cliff that blood is thicker than fashion, Theo consents. But

the resulting monstrous facsimile is enough to make even Poppa gasp. With one sleeve longer than the other, the collar askew, pockets sewn in the wrong place, colors clashing, Theo is inconsolable. When Denise suggests he tuck the shirt in for a better effect, Theo shoots back, "It's tucked into my *socks*!"

Cliff decides it's time for a pep talk. With Theo's date due to arrive in just minutes, he sits the boy down and tells him of a time when he was forced to don a hideous tie while addressing an important medical convention. The reason? The tie had been a gift from six-year-old Theo. "I think you've learned your lesson," he tells his son, informing him that he can now change into the original store-bought shirt, which Cliff has kept hidden upstairs.

The jubilant Theo makes a dash for the prize, but before he can lay his hands on it, he bumps into his date and friends, who have just shown up. Like a deer in head-lights, he freezes beneath their glare before glancing down at his court-jester's outfit, sucking it up, and announcing, "This is my shirt." His date immediately proclaims

Denise's creation fabulous, comparing it to top designer fashions, and a relieved Theo runs upstairs to congratulate his sister on her incompetence.

Cosby never shied away from promoting his message that family values did not have to come at the expense of good laughs. But as the show's appeal grew, so did the scrutiny. On one hand, it earned plaudits for its positive portrayal of upwardly mobile blacks who were educated, family-oriented, and about as distant from television's stereotypical dealers, pimps, and jive-talkers as Beaver Cleaver was from the South Bronx. Yet it was maligned for the very same reasons as a bogus depiction of black life in America, a sort of African-American *Father Knows Best* whose characters were just too quaint and guileless to be believed.

"Some people have said our show is about a white family in blackface," Cosby said. "What does that mean? Does it mean only white people have a lock on living together in a home where the father is a doctor and the mother a lawyer and the children are constantly being told to study by their parents?"

What couldn't be questioned, however, was the show's popularity. At a time when cultural prognostica-

tors were declaring the sitcom dead, *The Cosby Show* single-handedly resurrected the genre, and for four straight years of its eight-year run, from 1985 to 1989, remained the top-rated program on television. No other sitcom had been so consistently watched by so many. And since the 1950s no other had presented such a staunch vision of the traditional family.

So it wasn't surprising that, by the late 1980s, an anti-*Cosby* backlash of sorts materialized, as a crop of new sitcoms began picking away at the idealized veneer of family life that the Huxtables had done so much to promote. Programs like *Married . . . with Children* and *The Simpsons* reveled in family dysfunction and made a killing in the ratings. But it was a gum-chomping, wisecracking female comic with a penchant for controversy who, in 1989, finally knocked *The Cosby Show* off the ratings pedestal.

In her role as matriarch of the working-class Conner family on ABC's *Roseanne*, comedienne Roseanne Barr had been likened to a female Ralph Kramden—a paunchy working stiff with a chip on her shoulder whose barbed feminist rants were as hilarious as they were insightful.

This was no thrown-together television persona. *Roseanne* was based on its star's stand-up comedy, which was itself a reflection of her real life. After leaving home at the age of seventeen, Roseanne found herself, by age twenty-five, raising three kids out of a Denver mobile home, scrubbing dishes, and slinging hash to supplement her husband's motel-clerk income.

While blue-collar housewife-hood might not have been glamorous, it was rich grist for the comic mill, and by the mid-1980s Roseanne was chewing up the comedy-club circuit with cynical observations on husbands, housework, and family dynamics, delivered in her trademark adenoidal whine ("I ain't a housewife, I'm a domestic gaaahdess"; "We found a form of birth control that really works. Every night before we go to bed, we spend an hour with our kids").

After well-received appearances on *The Tonight Show* and HBO, Roseanne was approached by Matt Williams, a former *Cosby Show* writer who was developing a sitcom about working mothers, and in October 1998 the fictional Roseanne Conner was born.

"Shows are dominated by fathers who know best and their wives who are so enchanted with everything they do," Roseanne complained. "I wanted to be the first mom ever to be a mom on TV. I wanted to send a message about mothers and how much we do."

And at a time when the economy was slumping and many families found themselves living from paycheck to paycheck, she became America's working mother par excellence, slogging through a succession of low-paying jobs that earned her just enough to feed her intermittently employed husband and three kids, and cover the bills marked "Final Notice."

The premise resonated with viewers, one of whom wrote *People* magazine to declare, "There are a lot more Roseannes in the real world than there are Clair Huxtables." In that case, the world's genteel, well-heeled families were doomed.

The Conners were loud, sloppy, overweight, and generally obnoxious. They belched and bellowed, and fought over the TV remote.

But Roseanne worried that the easy gags and putdowns would obscure what she felt were the show's underlying feminist themes and her forthright views on sexism and discrimination—everything she had honed to perfection in her stand-up routine. And after years of writing her own material, she found it difficult to speak lines scripted by writers who, she felt, soft-pedaled her message.

"I knew they would try to homogenize the character I created," she said. "The question was how much. I wasn't prepared for the answer. It was hard for me to give ideas that weren't executed the way I wanted. That drove me out of my mind."

During the initial episodes, the producers and writing staff attempted to downplay the growing friction. "It's a rough transition from the total freedom of stand-up to the discipline of weekly TV, but she's been remarkable in adapting," said creator and executive producer Williams of Roseanne.

Perhaps a little too remarkable, as Roseanne managed to wrest control of the program from Williams just halfway through the first season and eventually performed a thorough housecleaning, prompting one departed writer to take out an ad in *Variety* announcing his plans to vacation "in the relative peace and quiet of Beirut."

The rancor behind the scenes was genuine, but on screen it belied an abiding affection that allowed *Roseanne* to transcend the standard kitchen-sink comedy. The Conners not only loved and appreciated one another, they displayed a refreshing open-mindedness toward outsiders and outcasts that was atypical of television's more prole-tarian folks, like Archie Bunker and Al Bundy.

For starters, *Roseanne* was one of the first sitcoms to regularly feature openly gay characters who weren't swishy stereotypes but normal, down-to-earth people, and it was the first to feature a woman-to-woman kiss (between Roseanne and actress Mariel Hemingway, who played a friend of Roseanne's lesbian co-worker). That memorable scene, from 1994's "Don't Ask, Don't Tell" episode, had to chart a difficult path past ABC censors, but when it aired it set the stage for a decade of thought-ful exploration into issues of alternative sexuality on net-work television.

While "the kiss" became a major source of publicity and controversy, it was a far less prominent peck that fueled one of *Roseanne*'s finest episodes. When the Con-ners' young son D.J. (Michael Fishman) refuses to kiss a girl in the school play because she is black, Roseanne and Dan are forced to confront the racism that has somehow been imparted to their children.

"White Men Can't Kiss" was a soul-searching tale that didn't pull punches or offer pat answers yet still delivered Roseanne's straight-talking, opinionated comic goods.

In the episode's best scene, Roseanne lays into D.J. about tolerance, shouting, "Black people are just like us, they're every bit as good as us, and any people who don't think so are just a bunch of banjo-picking, cousin-dating embarrassments to respectable white trash like us!"

It was classic Roseanne—outwardly caustic and at the same time humorously self-deprecating, a style of comedy that put everyone on equal footing by deflating the pompous without becoming too smug or self-important. "Believe me, that was a Roseanne-guided show," recalled writer Alan Stephan Blasband of the episode. "She is the one who chose the way it should be done. I think that's the beauty of what her show has done. I think if another sitcom did these issues it would lose the point."

Over its nine-year run, the show consistently broke new ground by dealing at length with other thorny issues, like divorce, abortion, domestic violence, and government

welfare policies, while continuing to hammer home the point that real mothers, warts and all, were a very powerful breed.

Perhaps nobody knows that better these days than stand-up comedian Ray Romano. As Ray Barone on CBS's *Everybody Loves Raymond*, Romano plays a Long Island sportswriter and father of three. He and his wife, Debra (Patricia Heaton), are kept in a perpetual state of siege by his adoring and overbearing mother, Marie (Doris Roberts), who lives across the street. Joining her in her intrusions are Ray's insolent father, Frank (Peter Boyle), and his dour, obsessive-compulsive older brother, Robert (Brad Garrett).

The interlopers treat Ray and Debra's house as an extension of their own, barging in unannounced, collapsing on the couch, and insinuating themselves into every corner of the couple's private life. For the elder Barones, "boundaries" is a word not yet invented. Caught in the middle is the laughably ineffectual Ray, who, despite Debra's insistent requests, is generally loath to confront his meddling mother and upset his status as the mollycoddled son.

The premise certainly isn't revolutionary—the show's creator and executive producer Philip Rosenthal has referred to *Raymond* as just "an old-fashioned, classic sitcom about family"—but the characters are so well drawn and the stories are so artfully constructed that the show maintains an honesty and authenticity, even in its hilariously skewed perspective that is uncommon in most domestic comedies.

And, in a sense, it should. Romano's life mirrors Ray Barone's in many ways. His brother, like Robert, is a policeman; he and his wife, like Ray and Debra, are the parents of twins; and in the early years of his marriage, he lived just down the road from his parents in Queens—all of which provided an endless source of inspiration for his stand-up act.

But after nearly a dozen years tramping across the country and delivering his deadpan offbeat observations, Romano began to despair that he'd ever get a shot at a television series.

Salvation came in the form of a 1994 appearance on the *Late Show with David Letterman* that so impressed the host that he decided to have his production company tailor a sitcom around Romano's family humor.

When *Everybody Loves Raymond* debuted in fall of 1996 with a veteran cast that had starred on stage, in film, and on television, Romano was the sole nonactor. "I was just so nervous that they were going to cancel it after the first week," recalled Romamo. "I was coming out of stand-up. I had never acted before."

"The fact Ray never acted before," joked Heaton, "didn't stop him from giving all of us notes during rehearsals."

But working with great actors raised the level of Romano's own performance. "It's like when you play golf," he said. "If you play with someone better, you become a little better."

And that skill comes through clearly in Boyle's and Roberts's portrayal of Frank and Marie, who are a fictionalized combination of Romano's and Rosenthal's parents,

albeit with a wicked nasty streak. When they aren't harassing Raymond and Debra, their life revolves around bickering, eating, and bickering some more. In one episode, Frank sells off his cemetery plot next to Marie's for a little pocket change, telling her, "Till death do us part, Marie, and after that, you're on your own." In another, when Frank tells Marie, "You are what you eat," she slides his food to him with the bon mot "Here's your order of miserable bastard."

"I think *Roseanne* broke ground in terms of the honesty in the way real families talk to each other and treat each other," said Rosenthal. "There's a certain open hostility on the surface. But you understand that there's love underneath. Also, their humor comes from these very old-fashioned wife-and-husband jokes that are from another time," Rosenthal recalls. "Those jokes never left my family, and yet they left television, it seems, for a long time. So now, when you see them, they seem so hysterical—and almost fresh."

And while Ray and Debra squabble frequently, although with less acerbity and a great deal more wit than

Frank and Marie, they are at their best when suffering through typical spousal insecurities. Ray worries that he isn't handsome enough, sensitive enough, tall enough (Debra lovingly presents him with shoe inserts to boost his height); Debra frets that she's too uninteresting and struggles with PMS. At one point, she becomes so obsessed with her own culinary ineptitude, and Marie's nagging criticism, that she breaks into Ray's parents' house to steal a prized meatball recipe.

The episode titled "Baggage" is a perfect example of what makes *Raymond* such a smartly written television series. There's a universal truth to it that anchors the episode, making it as compelling as it is funny. It's one of Phil Rosenthal's favorite episodes. "It actually won the Emmy Award [Best Writing—Comedy Series] for Tucker Cawley. . . . And to me this was a little miracle . . . to have something come up that's so relatable."

The setup of "Baggage" couldn't be simpler: Ray and Debra come home from a trip and, tired out, leave their suitcase on the landing on the staircase. In a silent dance of passive-aggressive stubbornness, neither will move it—for weeks. Ray thinks his wife should put it away because "I'm at work all day. . . . Debra's here, she's walking by it hundreds of times." Debra, we find out, hasn't moved it because in the Barone household, "If I don't do it, it doesn't get done." It's a classic connubial standoff.

"What better illustration of marriage could there be? It's literally baggage," Rosenthal says. "You can't ask for anything more in a metaphor."

To meddling father Frank, the suitcase isn't a metaphor, it's a challenge to Ray's manhood, and he offers him this tainted advice: "If you move that suitcase, you might as well put on a dress and change your name to Daisy-Mae Tinglepants."

Of course, in classic comedy fashion, things escalate. Hilariously. Ray, who's headed out of town, decides, in his customary juvenile manner, to retaliate (that'll show her!)

by stashing a wedge of extra-stinky Roquefort cheese in the suitcase. When the foul-smelling food is sniffed out by Debra and Marie, Marie, ever the archetypal mother-in-law, turns to her daughter-in-law (whose culinary skills she's always putting down) and says, blithely, "Debra, you can't keep cheese in a suitcase."

Finally, Ray, suffering guilt pangs over his bad behavior, returns home early. He confesses to Debra that he's had a disturbing revelation, one inspired by a piece of Chicago deep-dish pizza. "Cheese," he admits sheepishly. "I love it and yet I used it as a weapon."

With their fight seemingly resolved, the two kiss and begin to head upstairs for some "make-up action." All is bliss in Barone-ville—for about eight seconds. When the two pass the suitcase on the stairs, the fight quickly starts all over again. This time it gets riotously physical and ends with Debra clinging desperately to the suitcase while Ray has her by the ankles, trying to break her grip. In the marital wars, not even the promise of sex trumps the battle for upper hand. It's a moment of inspired lunacy, one that an audience can easily identify with because it's grounded, like all great comedy, in truth.

By 2004, *Raymond* had already collected twelve Emmys and been lauded in the *New York Times* as "the funniest, the smartest, the wisest, the most affecting, and most resonant comedy on television."

"I think *Raymond* is very honest about human relationships," said Heaton. "And what keeps it from being mean-spirited is that there's commitment to marriage and family. There's love, ultimately."

"Carl Reiner said he would get his writers together in the morning and say, 'What happened at your house yesterday?' And that's the greatest," asserts Rosenthal. "I thought that's how we should run this show, because we're talking about a family. We all have families. You can get a laugh doing almost anything. But in order to last longer than that second, it should come from a believable place."

Black or white, working class or wealthy, television's most celebrated clans managed to deftly capture the dynamics and devotion that exist in all families, regardless of their position in life. These classics have held a mirror to our world and given us a view of family that is somehow hysterical and yet unfailingly human.

CHAPTER 6

SITCOMS GET REAL

In the 1960s, sitcoms from *Green Acres* to *Gilligan's Island* to *The Brady Bunch* became increasingly formulaic and irrelevant. They failed to take in the massive societal changes happening all around them. The situation-comedy format simply fell behind the times. But in the 1970s something revolutionary happened—real life reenergized the sitcoms.

In 1969, pop culture was being transformed—America's youth were marching in the streets, the Rolling Stones and the Beatles were transforming music, and directors like Robert Altman, Mike Nichols, and Bob Rafelson were reinvigorating film. At the same time, the CBS comedy lineup included such lighthearted fare as *The Beverly Hillbillies, Mayberry RFD,* and *Hee Haw.* The network's dominant demographics were rural and decidedly older. In order to assuage nervous advertisers, CBS president Bob Wood systematically purged his schedule of thirteen shows and sitcoms in favor of programs that would attract a younger, more urban, more advertiser-friendly audience. A new breed of shows was born—shows that reflected all of life's issues while featuring superb actors and scripts that crackled with comic insight.

Though a battalion of talented professionals contributed to the success of these new shows, there was one man whose combination of creativity and chutzpah was the driving force behind much of this sitcom sea change—writer-producer Norman Lear.

Lear broke into television in the early 1950s writing for *The Colgate Comedy Hour,* NBC's challenge to *The Ed Sullivan Show.* In 1959, Lear joined forces with producer Bud Yorkin, forming the film company Tandem Productions. Together they had modest success with movies like *The Night They Raided Minsky's* and *Divorce American Style.*

By the end of the decade, Tandem was looking to expand into television production, and while in England, Lear saw the outrageous British comedy series *Till Death Us Do Part.* The show's lead character was the all-too-real Alf Garnett, a rude, perpetually angry, lower-class bigot who raved ceaselessly and offensively about everything under the sun—including TV taboos of the day like race and religion.

Alf was married to long-suffering Elsie (often referred to as "you silly moo," as in cow), and shared the household with his daughter Rita and her layabout husband, Mike, who was Alf's polar opposite. *Till Death Us Do Part*, which began in 1965, was both funny and controversial—a little "too real" for many. London's *Financial Times* called it "the rampaging, howling embodiment of all the most vulgar and odious prejudices that slop about in the bilges of the national mind." As Norman Lear judged so correctly, it was just the thing to shake up television in the colonies.

All in the Family, the Americanized version of *Till Death Us Do Part*, debuted on January 12, 1971. Lear had transformed Alf into loud-mouthed bigot Archie Bunker (Carroll O'Connor); Elsie became Edith (Jean Stapleton), Rita became Gloria (Sally Struthers), Mike became, well, Mike (Rob Reiner), and the location was now 704 Houser Street in a lower-middle-class neighborhood in Queens, New York. The names and location were changed to fit the hemisphere, but the premise was the same—Archie Bunker represented the viewpoint of the common man—the very common man.

Rob Reiner recalls, "I looked at the script and I knew what Norman was trying to do. And I thought, Well this is certainly gonna be the best thing that's ever been done on America television. There's no question about it."

The first show began with this timeless and, for the time, jaw-dropping, exchange between Archie and Edith:

ARCHIE: *If your spics and spades want their rightful share of the American dream, let them get out there and hustle for it, like I done. I didn't have no people marchin' and protestin' to get me my job.*
EDITH: *No, his uncle got it for him.*

CBS was understandably nervous about a show this edgy. It even tried to mitigate the show's controversial nature by introducing *All in the Family* as a series that would "throw a humorous spotlight on our frailties, prejudices, and concerns. By making them a source of laughter, we hope to show—in a mature fashion—just how absurd they are." Reiner recalls: "There was a big disclaimer that basically said, 'Don't watch this show.'"

CBS needn't have worried. Though they hired extra telephone operators to handle the expected backlash of an offended public, there were few calls, and most of those were supportive.

The critics were another story. For the most part they skewered the show, writing that it was "a plotless wonder," "a welcome breath of stale air," and "a flop." But *All in the Family* did have supporters in high places. *TV Guide* called it the "best show on commercial television," and the weekly *Variety* said it was "the best TV comedy since the original *Honeymooners*." The public debate among the critics was actually a good thing for the show. Its ratings had started out mediocre at best, but the media fuss got it a lot of attention among viewers, and during summer reruns, a lot more people tuned in to check it out.

In the first week of the second season, September 1971, *All in the Family* ranked number twelve. The very next week, the show leaped eleven notches to number 1 and stayed there, winning the TV ratings race for an astounding five years running, from 1971 to 1976—more than any show in television history. At its peak, it was estimated to have reached an average of fifty million viewers every week.

How could a show be this funny while traversing such potentially serious subject matter? Norman Lear thinks it was because *All in the Family* was "real people dealing with real issues." The best, most sustaining comedy always contains a kernel of universal human truth to it. This was new for sitcoms. Previous sitcoms had existed in a kind of unreal television universe, a sterilized place where cursing, bigotry, backbiting, and real consequences were verboten. Archie Bunker's world, though exaggerated and played for laughs, was someplace where real people, not TV people, lived.

The reality of the show came from people's lives—often the lives of the writers, the producers, and the actors. The cast was always encouraged to mine their own experiences for material. "Even though we were acting," Rob Reiner says, "many of the things we were doing were our own writing and improvisations—things that were extensions of how we saw things. Norman Lear encouraged that. So did Carroll O'Connor. Our own experiences would then form the characters. And that's, I think, what made the show so good."

Even something as simple as how you get dressed in the morning was fodder for the comedy mill, and an example of how the simplest, most mundane parts of life

can be funny and revealing and truth-telling. That's a bit Rob Reiner and Carroll O'Connor came up with themselves during rehearsal, and it remains one of Norman Lear's favorite memories of the show.

Lear recalls, "One of the great memorable moments was when Mike and Archie were getting dressed in the morning. And they were putting on their socks and their shoes. And Archie saw Mike put on a sock and a shoe and then a sock and a shoe. And he felt it should be a sock and a sock and a shoe and a shoe."

> ARCHIE: *Don't you know the whole world puts on a sock and sock and a shoe and a shoe?*
> MIKE: *I like to take care of one foot at a time.*
> ARCHIE: *That's the dumbest thing I ever heard of, you know that?*

"And they had a wonderful three minutes—I mean, glorious. And it was a surprise to each of the writers when we came to the run-through. All of that is part of the glory of working with enormously capable actors," said Lear.

Rob Reiner believes that the show succeeded on so many levels because of the very real complexity of the show's characters. *All in the Family*, he said, showed that "people can be ignorant and still have loving, human qualities." Beneath all the bluster, prejudice, and pigheadedness, Archie wasn't an *evil* man, just misguided.

In the show's third season there was an episode called "Henry's Farewell." Henry was Henry Jefferson, Archie's African-American neighbor. There was no love lost between the two, and when Henry announced that they were moving, the Bunkers threw the Jeffersons a party. At that party, Archie finds himself in conversation with Henry's pugnacious brother, George (Sherman Hemsley). It turns out that Archie and George Jefferson have a lot in common—they're both bigots, loudly and proudly contemptuous of anyone outside their own respective races. In fact, George Jefferson was Norman Lear's idea of the "black Archie Bunker." It was the first of Hemsley's highly popular appearances on the show, appearances that became stepping-stones to his own series.

All in the Family's second spin-off, *The Jeffersons*, was also produced by Norman Lear and Bud Yorkin and debuted in 1975. Upwardly mobile George Jefferson and

Though not as dominant in the ratings as *All in the Family*, *The Jeffersons* was nevertheless one of television's most popular shows, a cross-cultural smash that resided consistently in or near the top of the rankings for its ten-year run. *The Jeffersons* proved that America was ready, willing, and able to take to heart a sitcom that starred and was about black Americans—people who were a whole lot more real than the exaggerated stereotypes of *Amos 'n' Andy* or the watered-down homogeneity of Diahann Carroll's 1968 television series, *Julia*.

The Jeffersons, *All in the Family*, and two other Norman Lear series, *Good Times* and *Sanford and Son*, were largely responsible for revolutionizing how America portrayed its underclasses on television. Another of his series, *Maude*, did the same for the upper middle class.

Maude was the first spin-off from *All in the Family*, debuting in 1972 and featuring whiskey-voiced stage actress Bea Arthur in the title role. Maude Findlay was a middle-aged empowered woman—a strong-willed, strongly principled feminist who was (at least) her husband's equal. Maude and her distinctive silver-streaked coif made her first appearance on *All in the Family* playing Edith's outspoken, liberal cousin from the relatively wealthy suburb of Tuckahoe, New York. Maude was married to Walter (Bill Macy), her fourth husband, and had a divorced daughter, Carol (Adrienne Barbeau), and a grandson, Phillip (Kraig Metzinger / Brian Morrison), who lived with them.

his family were able to leave Archie and Queens behind and "move on up to the East Side, to a deluxe apartment in the sky" in Manhattan after his seven-store dry-cleaning chain became successful.

Louise "Weezy" Jefferson (Isabel Sanford) and their wisecracking maid, Florence (Marla Gibbs), took a lot less guff from George than Edith took from Archie. Florence, in particular, had no tolerance for her undersized, overbearing boss and would pass up no opportunity to go toe to toe with him. In fact, a good deal of the show's comedy emanated from them—the arrogant uppity boss who demanded deference from someone he'd *like* to feel superior to, and the employee who refused to let him forget from whence he came.

Surrounding the Jeffersons in their ritzy apartment building were eccentric Englishman Harry Bentley (Paul Benedict) and series television's first-ever interracial married couple, Tom and Helen Willis (Franklin Cover and Roxie Roker). Of course, for George their very presence was a constant source of irritation and a ready opportunity to pontificate on the evils of race mixing. When his son Lionel (Mike Evans, then Damon Evans, not related) got engaged to the Willises' "half-breed" daughter, Jenny (Berlinda Tolbert), George was nearly apoplectic.

Maude was as opinionated and as obstinate as Archie Bunker, but in a whole different arena. This was Norman Lear's outlet for social and women's issues. Hot-button topics like alcoholism, menopause, women's lib, birth control, face-lifts, vasectomy, and depression were dealt with for the first time within the confines of a network sitcom.

The subjects on *Maude* may often have been serious, but the show was always funny. A large reason was that *Maude*'s writing staff included Bob Weiskopf and Bob Schiller, two writers famous for their fabled work on *I Love Lucy*. The cast, which included comedy veterans Rue McClanahan

and Conrad Bain, meshed superbly. And like Archie Bunker with his "Meathead" and "Stifle," Maude had a trademark line whenever Walter or another character got a good crack in at her, she'd fire back: "God'll get you for that."

> MAUDE: *This is your home, and if you don't want my daughter and my only grandchild living here with us, just tell me.*
> WALTER: *And?*
> MAUDE: *And I'll rip your heart out.*

Maude's fusion of realism, provocative social matters, and humor resulted in some very controversial episodes. The one that caused the biggest commotion was "Maude's Dilemma," in which the matronly forty-seven-year-old discovers she's pregnant. After much discussion, Maude makes the heart-wrenching decision to have an abortion. When the double episode aired, some viewers picketed CBS, and the network received a number of complaints, but only a couple of affiliates refused to air the show. The letters that came in were six to one in favor of airing the subject matter and the way that "Maude's Dilemma" was resolved.

As on other Norman Lear series, the writers for *Maude* were encouraged to harvest their own lives for material for the show. Bob Schiller says that at one point in the series he and the rest of the writing staff were looking for an organic way to trigger a separation between Maude and Walter. They were stuck until Bob brought his own life to the writing table. "We used to plot things from our own lives—on *Maude*, particularly," he recalls. "And I came and I said, '[My wife] Sabrina is going to run for the state senate.' And one of the other writers said, 'If my wife did that, I'd divorce her.' Norman [Lear] said, 'Hey, we've been looking for a reason to split them up—' And we did. And we got five shows out of it."

Norman Lear's shows were some of the most innovative reality-based series in television, but they weren't the only ones. Another reality pioneer was *M*A*S*H*, initially written by TV veteran Larry Gelbart (pilot and ninety-one episodes) and produced by director Gene Reynolds. *M*A*S*H*, of course, was the television adaptation of celebrated director Robert Altman's Oscar-winning film of the same name.

When the show began airing in the fall of 1972, the United States was still enmeshed in the Vietnam War.

Although *M*A*S*H* was set in the Korean War, it was intended as an antiwar commentary on Vietnam in particular and war generally. The show told the story of the 4077th Mobile Army Surgical Hospital and its incredible cast of characters, led by Dr. Benjamin Franklin "Hawkeye" Pierce (Alan Alda), Dr. "Trapper" John McIntyre (Wayne Rogers), and later Dr. B.J. Hunnicutt (Mike Farrell)—brilliant surgeons forced into military service who'd rather be drinking homemade hooch, chasing nurses, or practicing their wedge shots than patching together teenage soldiers ripped apart by shrapnel. Their disrespect for and disregard of the Army's rules was a prime source not only of humor but also of conflict in the series. Hawkeye, Trapper, and B.J. were always a step ahead of their superior officers—and a heartbeat away from a court-martial.

The humor in *M*A*S*H* was as biting as the censors would allow. Interviews with hundreds of actual Korean and World War II era surgeons yielded not only the story lines for a majority of the shows but also information about how the medical teams kept their sanity in circumstances that were anything but sane. Humor—the blacker the better—was a tonic for these troops. The banter in the operating room was a drug against depression. Laughter really was the best medicine.

The ringleader was Benjamin Franklin "Hawkeye" Pierce, a skilled surgeon and unwilling soldier whose persona was that of a latter-day Groucho Marx. "I will not carry a gun," he once ranted in Groucho-like fashion. "When I got thrown into this war, I had a clear understanding with the Pentagon: no guns. I'll carry your books, I'll carry a torch, I'll carry a tune, I'll carry on, carry over, carry forward, Cary Grant, cash and carry, carry me back to Old Virginia, I'll even hari-kari if you show me how, but I will not carry a gun."

Senior Nurse Major Margaret "Hot Lips" Houlihan (Loretta Swit) was Pierce's khaki-clad Margaret Dumont. Houlihan and her undercover married lover, the strait-laced Dr. Frank Burns (Larry Linville), were often the butt of Hawkeye's beloved practical jokes, and it was only his surgical talent and the scarcity of doctors that prevented them from getting him booted out of the service.

Of course, there was one soldier who *wanted* to get the boot—the cross-dressing Corporal Max Klinger (Jamie Farr). Klinger was a Larry Gelbart invention, inspired, Gelbart acknowledged, by a Lenny Bruce routine on draft dodgers. Originally intended as a one-episode character, Klinger's Chanel and Army boots outfits were such a great comic visual that the character was drafted for the duration of the show's run. He never did get his sought-after "Section 8" and, ironically, after marrying a beautiful Korean woman, was the only member of the 4077th to remain "in country" after the war ended.

An episode titled "Adam's Rib" is an example of the reality/absurdity sandwich that was *M*A*S*H*. Driven to the brink of insanity (and nausea) by the Army's repetitive mess-hall slop, Hawkeye rants, "I've eaten a river of liver and an ocean of fish! I've eaten so much fish, I'm ready to grow gills! I've eaten so much liver I can only make love if I'm smothered in bacon and onions!" Desperate for a

taste—literally—of home, Hawkeye decides to "order in" a rib dinner from his favorite barbeque joint—in Chicago!

Though a Top 10 hit since its second season, *M*A*S*H*'s popularity peaked during the 1978–79 season. The show was so much in demand that CBS was airing new episodes each Monday during prime time and reruns during the daytime, as well as late at night on Thursdays. The two-and-a-half-hour finale, "Goodbye, Farewell, and Amen," which aired on February 28, 1983, remains one of the most-watched episodes in television history. It earned a phenomenal 77 share, which means that 77 percent of the people watching television that night were tuned in to *M*A*S*H*.

*M*A*S*H* and other cutting-edge sitcoms of the 1970s helped change series television forever. Getting "real" reenergized television, proving that the lives of real people are infinitely interesting and since time began, humankind's most compelling source of entertainment and humor.

KINGS OF LATE NIGHT

SATURDAY NIGHT LIVE has become the late-night comedy institution for Saturday. But during the week a different kind of late-night comedy rules the roost, where talk-show hosts deliver monologues, interview the famous and infamous, and perform comedy bits. The undisputed "King of Late Night" is Johnny Carson, who dominated the landscape for thirty years, but several crown princes before and after Carson have also provided plenty of late-night laughs. So now, Heeeeere's Johnny—and the others.

Steve Allen

The first *Tonight Show* host, Steve Allen, was a master of ad-libbing and willing to do anything for a laugh—he'd dive into a vat of Jell-O, get dunked in hot water with thousands of tea bags tied to his clothes, or simply go outside and talk to strangers on the street. He'd hail a taxi and throw a giant salami in the back, saying, "Just take this to Grand Central, and hurry." When a guest showed up with a few live ducks in a wading pool, Allen jumped in for a dip along with them. He was there only for two short years, but he set the standards—just ask David Letterman, who openly acknowledges lifting large parts of Allen's act for his own.

Jack Paar

The most serious and cerebral of late-night hosts, Jack Paar was often a straight man for his show's kooky characters like Charley Weaver, played by Cliff Arquette, who when Paar asked "Did you ever go up behind your wife when she's working at the kitchen sink and surprise her with a little hug or tickle from behind?" replied that he did it—once. "Don't ever do it when she's cleaning a turkey," he deadpanned. Paar's most memorable quip came when, angry about NBC's censoring a joke, he quit for a month. Upon his return, he opened his monologue by saying dryly, "As I was saying . . . "

Johnny Carson

The smooth-talking charmer with the perfect comic timing, for more than three decades Johnny Carson was America's last laugh before bedtime. And he got his laughs in many different ways.

The monologue
Carson was America's political barometer, and his Watergate jokes helped seal Nixon's fate: "Egyptian President Sadat had a belly dancer entertain President Nixon at a state dinner. Mr. Nixon was really impressed. He hadn't seen contortions like that since Rose Mary Woods."

But Carson knew that to endure in late-night television he had to be bipartisan in his pokes.

"In the papers was a picture of Ross Perot, George Bush, and Dan Quayle. I couldn't get this image out of my mind—the millionaire, the Skipper, and Gilligan."

The silly gags
Carson had plenty of running characters, from Art Fern (of *Tea Time Movie* fame) to Floyd R. Turbo to the most famous of all, Carnac the Magnificent. This quirky seer from the East would hold an envelope up to his head and mystically ascertain an answer: "Sis Boom Bah." Then he'd open the envelope and read the question: "What is the sound of a sheep exploding?"

The ad-lib
When Carson failed to make a proper pretzel, the lady doing the demonstration gave him a new strip of dough, saying, "Try this piece. I don't think yours is long enough." To which Carson cracked, "Yes, I think I've heard that before."

Jay Leno

At its best, Jay Leno's monologue is filled with a biting political wit, where even something as minor as the death of the president's dog can be ammo for a whole round of targets: "Some sad news: President Bush's lapdog passed away. Gee, I didn't even know Tony Blair was sick. And then, "The Bush family dog, Spot, had to be put to sleep. Well, he was fifteen years old, and President Bush said he had to be put down because of a series of heart problems over the years. Well, that's gotta make Dick Cheney kinda jumpy. Actually, he was the second-most famous Spot in the White House that wasn't considered evidence."

David Letterman

Although David Letterman is an amalgam of those who came before him, unique to him are his Top 10 Lists. Here are the Top 10 ways David Letterman transformed late-night comedy:

10. Letterman's mom: Who else would even think of getting laughs by sending their mother to Norway to cover the Olympics?

9. Dropping ojects off the roof: Letterman connected with viewers by doing silly stuff they wish they could do. One guy asked him to drop a bowling ball off a roof. Done. A piñata filled with baked beans. Done. An onslaught of watermelons. Done.

8. Larry "Bud" Melman: A nonactor, Calvert DeForest, playing a late-night character who doesn't seem to know he is one, Melman never even held his microphone in the right place when interviewing people and was defined by his off-kilter cackle that came at perfectly inappropriate times.

7. Letterman's refusal to take the talk-show format seriously: Letterman once did an entire show with dentist chairs replacing the host's seat and guest's couch—he even spoke as if he'd just inhaled nitrous oxide, and he persuaded the usually dignified NBC newswoman Jane Pauley to play along.

6. The Late Night Monkey Cam: As if this mockery of show-biz gimmickry wasn't funny enough—just watching the monkey skitter about was always as much of a laugh as his camera's viewpoint—Letterman eventually parodied himself with the Late Night Tiger Cam, in which the "tiger" wearing the camera "mauled" bandleader Paul Schaefer.

5. Chris Elliott: "The Guy Under the Seats," "The Regulator Guy," and especially "The Fugitive Guy" were priceless characters, but their zany story-lines were enhanced by Elliott stepping out of character to trade verbal spars with Letterman.

4. Reviving Steve Allen's humor: Letterman had his body covered with Velcro, then jumped on a trampoline and stuck to a giant Velcro wall; he also had himself covered with Alka-Seltzer and then lowered into a nine-hundred-gallon tank of water.

3. Letterman's honesty about show biz: "What the hell is the deal?" he once asked famed Cadillac spokesman Ricardo Montelban. "Is there anything that really is fine Corinthian leather?" Montelban confessed, with a laugh, that the term was meaningless. When a young Michael Jordan appeared with his black-and-red Air Jordan sneakers banned by the NBA "because it doesn't have any white in it," Letterman quipped: "Well, neither does the NBA."

2. Taking every concept way, way over the top, like "Late Night Baby"—honoring a baby born during the course of a ninety-minute anniversary special and pitting prospective parents at two New York hospitals in competition with each other ups the ante. But what truly made the segment classic is that Letterman got sportscaster Bob Costas and WWF host Vince McMahon to be the on-site correspondents at each hospital, reporting back to Letterman as if this were a breaking news event of great import.

1. The Top 10 Lists: In the early days, the Top 10 Lists were brilliant bits of whimsy, largely divorced from the headlines of the day.

Conan O'Brien

O'Brien was not a performer, but he had impeccable comedy credentials, writing some of *The Simpsons*' funniest, zaniest episodes before getting his own show. He brought that same freshness, that same knack for intelligent silliness and sophisticated juvenile humor, to *Late Night*, where he once stuck his staff of writers inside a homemade Trojan horse and sent them over to where Letterman was taping his show for CBS.

While many talk shows travel to other cities as a sweeps-ratings gimmick, O'Brien instead did "*Late Night*'s Time Travel Week," traveling to ancient Greece, the Civil War, and even a postapocalyptic future.

Like Letterman, O'Brien is willing to trust his comedic instincts and go overboard on a joke—when the show's writers couldn't reach the agent for Whitman Mayo, who played Grady on *Sanford and Son*, O'Brien began "Gradyhunt" and started a "Find Grady" hotline that logged tens of thousands of calls over several weeks before an Atlanta cable repairman tipped off the actor's mother that *Late Night* was looking for her son.

And O'Brien has developed his share of recurring bits that stack up well with the best of Letterman and Carson. For example, "Triumph the Insult Comic Dog," a hand puppet who has generated laughs and controversy with withering attacks during interviews of everyone from Eminem—who tried to attack it—to fans dressed in costume for a *Star Wars* convention. ("I think Eminem should relax a little. I mean, my mom's a bitch too, but I don't sing songs about it," Triumph once said.)

That type of humor always seems to work best late at night.

CHAPTER 7

WHEN FRIENDS BECOME FAMILY

The late 1960s were marked by a seismic cultural shift that reverberated through nearly every aspect of American life. As women left home, joining the work force in droves, the traditional family structure changed—and the traditional television situation comedies changed too. More and more shows discovered that unattached friends or work colleagues offered a more current reflection of reality and fresh laughs, compared with the traditional family sitcoms of the 1950s and early 1960s. After all, we all have a Reverend Jim, a Cliff Clavin, a Kramer, or a Joey in our lives.

Perhaps no show highlighted the sitcom's dramatic change of focus from family to friends more than *The Mary Tyler Moore Show*. Before its debut in 1970, the show's star and namesake was primarily thought of as Laura Petrie,

the faithful and adoring wife from *The Dick Van Dyke Show*. Moore was so popular in the role that she won two Emmy Awards for Lead Actress in a Comedy Series for the program's final two seasons.

However, as its very title suggested, *The Mary Tyler Moore Show* would put the leggy future queen of sitcoms in a completely different light. Instead of the sidekick wife of the show's star, Moore's character of Mary Richards was the star of the show.

Even more startling for the times was the revelation that the show's creators had originally planned to have the program's protagonist be a woman who struggles to regain her own identity following a recent divorce. But CBS nixed the idea, fearing that America wasn't ready to laugh at the trials and tribulations of a divorcée. The network brass

feared that viewers would also remember Moore as Laura Petrie and would assume that she had recently divorced Dick Van Dyke.

That Girl, starring Marlo Thomas, similarly focused on a young single woman during its run from 1966 to 1971, before *The Mary Tyler Moore Show* hit the airwaves. However, viewers found *Mary Tyler Moore* easier to relate to and more realistic. Thomas's Ann Marie was an actress-model looking for work while experiencing various high jinks with her boyfriend. *Moore*'s Mary Richards was a thirty-year-old single woman who moved into the more common town of Minneapolis and the less glamorous profession of associate producer of a low-rated TV news program.

Rather than milk everyday family situations for comic fodder, James L. Brooks and Allan Burns, creators and executive producers of *Mary Tyler Moore*, focused instead on Mary's interaction with her best friend and fellow thirty-something single, Rhoda Morgenstern, played by Valerie Harper, and the assorted characters that inhabited the WJM newsroom. That crew included the hard-nosed boss Lou Grant (Ed Asner), the likeable dim-witted news

anchor Ted Baxter (Ted Knight), and nice-guy news writer Murray L. Slaughter (Gavin MacLeod).

During its seven-season, 168-episode run, the show mixed humor with serious issues—even death, in the unforgettable episode "Chuckles Bites The Dust."

In that episode, Chuckles, the beloved WJM kid-show clown, dressed as a peanut, is killed while marching in a parade. After hearing the news that Chuckles's death was caused by "an elephant trying to shuck him," Lou comments, "Lucky more people weren't hurt. Lucky the elephant didn't go after anyone else!" And Murray adds, "That's right. After all, you know how hard it is to stop after one peanut." Later Murray quips, "Can you imagine the insurance claim? Cause of death: a busted goober."

While *Mary Tyler Moore* focused on career instead of family, in one poignant episode the show's writers made it quite clear that—for many single, adult Americans—co-workers were becoming surrogate families. "I get to thinking that my job is too important to me. And I tell myself that the people I work with are just the people I work with," Mary admitted to Lou Grant. "But last night I thought, what is *family* anyway? It's the people who make you feel less alone and really loved," she sobbed, "and that's what you've done for me. Thank you for being *my* family."

Over the years, the show's characters actually developed and grew with the audience, rather than remaining one-dimensional cartoon-like cutouts. One of the funniest moments of the series came during its very first episode. During Mary's interview for the associate producer job at WJM, her future boss, Lou Grant, smiles and tells Mary, "You know, you've got spunk!" Mary humbly thanks him, before Grant bluntly adds, "I *hate* spunk!" The show's creators credit that brief exchange with eliciting the longest laugh the show ever received from their studio audience.

Like *The Mary Tyler Moore Show*, *Taxi* focused on the workplace rather than the home, and it also shared some of the *Moore* show's creative visionaries. A year after the end of *Mary Tyler Moore*, the show's co-creator James L. Brooks found himself in a similar role with *Taxi*. Again like *Mary Tyler Moore*, a mix of sharp-witted writing and fine comic acting fueled *Taxi*. But there were major differences. While *Mary Tyler Moore* occasionally relied on an eccentric personality for its laughs, more often than not the show's girl-next-door namesake was the center attraction. The cast of lunatics who called the Sunshine Cab Company's garage in New York City their workplace drove *Taxi*.

Leading the charge was Judd Hirsch's Alex Rieger, the most well-adjusted character of the bunch, who was actually content with his career as a cabbie. Yet beyond Rieger's character, normalcy grinds to a screeching halt. Danny DeVito's Louie De Palma was the grouchy dispatcher who never pulled punches. Marilu Henner was cast as the divorced mother of two and object of Louie's lustful desires, Elaine Nardo; Tony Danza played the punch-addled wannabe boxer Tony Banta; and Jeff Conaway's Bobby Wheeler was an aspiring actor. The show's most eccentric and entertaining characters were Andy Kaufman's transplanted immigrant Latka Gravas and Christopher Lloyd's drug-damaged Reverend Jim Ignatowski. The latter was introduced in a hilarious episode titled "Reverend Jim: A Space Odyssey."

A particularly funny exchange came in a scene in which Bobby Wheeler was helping Reverend Jim fill out an application. "Mental illness or narcotic addiction?" asks Bobby, before Reverend Jim quips, "Now that's a tough choice."

At times, *Taxi* also tipped its hat to the great comedians of all time—including the Marx Brothers, in this exchange between Louie and Latka: "What's this?" Louie asks. "It's a kebble," Latka responds. "What's a kebble?" Louie asks. "One hundred and ten kebble make a lithnitch," Latka responds. "What's a lithnich?" Louie asks. "Two hundred seventy lithnich make a matta," Latka responds. "What's a matta?" Louie asks. "I don't know," Latka responds, "what's the matter with you?"

Taxi was so beloved that it was not easily moved into the TV junkyard of canceled sitcoms. After its fourth season, with its ratings dipping to an embarrassing fifty-third place, ABC decided to axe the show, even though it had won three consecutive Emmys for Best Comedy Series.

Even with it headed down the highway to syndication, *Taxi* continued to pick up accolades. The September after its final cancellation, the show was honored once again with a carload of Emmy Awards. At the ceremony, Hirsch, who also picked up the award for Best Actor in a Comedy Series, quipped, "Don't they know we've been canceled?"

If viewers welcomed a TV newsroom and a taxicab garage as settings for two of the most beloved sitcoms of the 1970s, surely a neighborhood bar where everybody knows your name would serve as the perfect backdrop for a hit show.

Like *The Mary Tyler Moore Show* and *Taxi*, *Cheers* relied on a similar mix of quirky personalities brought together in the workplace. "We wanted to do an ensemble show, like *M*A*S*H* or *Taxi*, rather than a family story," *Cheers* co-creator Glen Charles explained.

Cheers too shared creative ties to its predecessors. Glen Charles and his brother Les broke into show business as writers and later as producers on the ill-fated *Mary Tyler Moore* spin-off *Phyllis*. During that stint, the brothers met James Burrows, another talent from the *Mary Tyler Moore* stable, who directed episodes of *Phyllis*, the other *Mary Tyler Moore* spin-off *Rhoda*, and *The Bob Newhart Show*.

When the future *Taxi* creative brain-trust of James L. Brooks, Ed Weinberger, Stan Daniels, and David Davis left

The Mary Tyler Moore Show to set up their own shop, they recruited Burrows and the Charles brothers to come along for the ride. All three were involved heavily in *Taxi*, writing, directing, or producing the majority of the show's first three years, but it wasn't long before Burrows and the Charles brothers began craving their own vehicle to showcase their talents. They found it in *Cheers*.

With the on-again off-again relationship between Ted Danson's saloon-owning ladies' man Sam Malone, and Shelley Long's snobbish waitress Diane Chambers, serving as the show's main focus, *Cheers* kept viewers returning to the bar.

Perhaps no scene captured the volatile relationship between Sam and Diane better than this classic exchange:

"You are the nuttiest, the stupidest, the phoniest fruitcake I ever met," Sam says.

"You, Sam Malone, are the most arrogant, self-centered—," Diane says.

"Shut up! Shut your fat mouth!" Sam responds.

"Make me," Diane says.

"Make you? My God, I'm—I'm gonna—I'm gonna bounce you off every wall in this office," Sam threatens.

"Try it and you'll be walking funny tomorrow, or shall I say funnier," Diane counters.

"You know—you know—I always wanted to pop you one. Maybe this is my lucky day, huh?" Sam adds.

"You disgust me," Diane says. "I hate you."

"Are you as turned on as I am?" Sam asks.

"More," Diane says.

Long left the show in 1987 and was replaced by Kirstie Alley in the role of Rebecca Howe, to whom Sam sells the bar after his relationship with Diane hits the skids.

Like its predecessors, *Cheers* employed a similar "friends as family" blueprint; it was much more than a comedy centered on a romance. A cast of quirky regulars, including Rhea Perlman as hard-boiled waitress Carla, Kelsey Grammer as the neurotic psychiatrist Dr. Frasier Crane, George Wendt as the rotund and jovial bar regular Norm, and John Ratzenberger's mama's boy, know-it-all mailman Cliff Clavin, kept viewers laughing between Sam's romantic follies.

In fact, Norm's mere entrance into the bar was heralded by a chorus of all patrons shouting *"Norm!"* followed by a comic twist. In one such entrance, Sam asks, "What are you up to, Norm?" Norm replies, "My ideal weight if I were eleven feet tall."

In another, Cheer's bartender, Coach, asks, "Draw you a beer, Norm?" Norm's reply: "Naw, I know what they look like, just pour me one."

Although often referred to as "the show about nothing," *Seinfeld* was another in the distinguished lineage of sitcoms with a family of friends. "*Seinfeld* was a show that was created by two guys who are very true to comedy, Jerry Seinfeld and Larry David"—so says the show's executive producer and the namesake's manager, George Shapiro. If nothing else, *Seinfeld* was a show about the life of a stand-up comedian where comedy was king.

The real-life Jerry Seinfeld was primarily known as a stand-up comic before the debut of his landmark sitcom.

Jerry's one previous stint on a sitcom, as a character named Frankie on the *Soap* spin-off *Benson*, lasted a mere four episodes in 1980–1981. After he was axed from the show, he vowed he would never appear on a sitcom again unless he had more creative control.

That opportunity came in 1989 in a pilot known as *The Seinfeld Chronicles*. Co-written by Seinfeld and David, the pilot included future *Seinfeld* regulars Jason Alexander as George Costanza and Michael Richards, but in this early episode Richards's lanky goofball character was known as Kessler rather than Cosmo Kramer. Julia Louis-Dreyfus, who would later have a key role in the series as Elaine, was absent from the pilot.

Like its predecessors *Taxi* and *Cheers*, *Seinfeld* earned notice for its fine writing and great cast of oddball characters. Stand-up comic and *Seinfeld* writer Carol Leifer referred to the show's incredible cast as the "X factor." "That's such a wildcard," she said. "When you look at all the classic shows like *Seinfeld*, you have Jerry, but you have these satellites, these other characters who are so, so

buying tomatoes she comes out of the swimming pool topless. Everyone saw her half-naked except George."

That wasn't the only lowlight in the episode for the unfortunate Costanza character. Later, Jerry's girlfriend accidentally walks in on George just as he is pulling off his swimming trunks. As she begs his forgiveness her look of shock and embarrassment quickly gives way to smirks and giggles. 'I was in the pool! I was in the pool!' George shouts in his defense.

Mortified by the emasculating encounter, George desperately explains his dilemma to Jerry. "Well, I just got back from swimming in the pool. And the water was cold," George explains.

"Oh, you mean—shrinkage?" Jerry asks.

"Yes. I mean, if she thinks that's me, she's under a complete misapprehension. That was not me, Jerry," George pleads. "That was not me."

Later in the same episode, Elaine got in on the gag, offering a women's perspective.

"Do women know about shrinkage?" George asks.

"What do you mean, like laundry?" Elaine asks.

"No," George explains. "Like when a man goes swimming—afterward—"

"It shrinks? Why does it shrink?" Elaine asks.

"It just does," George says.

"I don't know how you guys walk around with those things," Elaine quips.

"Friends" certainly wasn't the most original name for a sitcom that focused on the friendships of three females and three males living in New York City, but then again, it perfectly summed up the show.

Friends co-creators and real-life friends Marta Kauffman and David Crane began their collaboration in college. They spent their twenties living in New York, for the most part single, with "a tight group of friends hanging out," experiencing life. After moving to Los Angeles to pursue their careers writing for television, it occurred to Kauffman and Crane that their life and friendships in New York would make for an interesting show.

"And at first we're like, well, maybe they all work in a restaurant," Crane recalls as he and Kaufman were settling on the show's foundation. Then they thought, "What if it's just about six friends who hang out . . . some of them can live together maybe, but it's not a workplace comedy." The simplicity of the premise made it instantly relatable, and millions of twentysomethings flocked to watch the show

uniquely talented and just made the character their own." Leifer added that finding one person with that X factor is like sifting "through grains of sand in the desert," but "to get six people like that" is unheard of.

Also key to the show's success was the ability of Seinfeld and David to come up with fresh sitcom ideas that spawned such memorable catchphrases as "the puffy shirt," "yada yada," and "Soup Nazi." According to Leifer, the credo for *Seinfeld* writers was to come up with ideas that "you could never see on another show."

An episode titled "The Hamptons" gave new meaning to the word "shrinkage." For executive producer Shapiro and millions of *Seinfeld* fans, it remains a favorite. "This is when they saw the ugly baby and they went out to the Hamptons," Shapiro recalls. "George brought a girlfriend whom he'd never slept with before but who agreed to go away with him for the weekend. Then while George is out

about a group of fictional twentysomethings sharing their lives, relationships, and everyday struggles. *Friends* became one of the most successful television situation comedies of all time.

But *Friends* did have some family ties, which became a bit more tangled during its decade-long run. *Friends'* familial elements include the fact that Courteney Cox's character of Monica Gellar Bing was the sister of David Schwimmer's Ross Gellar. In season one, Ross's wife leaves him for her lesbian lover but later gives birth to his son. In season two, Lisa Kudrow's Phoebe character divorces her husband, Duncan, whom she thought was gay, but who turns out to be straight. Phoebe meets her birth mother in season three. The next season, Ross marries Emily but mistakenly says

"Rachel," the name of Jennifer Aniston's character, while reciting his wedding vows. In season five, Phoebe becomes the surrogate mother of triplets, and Emily divorces Ross, setting the stage for his wedding to Rachel. A season later, the pair divorce, but Monica proposes to Chandler Bing, played by Matthew Perry. The following season, the pair wed and Rachel finds out she's pregnant. In the show's eighth season, Rachel gives birth to a baby sired by Ross during a one-night stand. Later, Matt LeBlanc's Joey proposes to Rachel, but by the start of the ninth season the proposal is off. In the tenth and final season, Phoebe marries Mike, Rachel and Ross vow never to have sex again, Monica and Chandler's adopted twins are born, and Rachel ditches a plane and job offer in Paris to be with Ross.

The ability of the show's creators to find humor in such romantic turmoil was evident from the start, in the very first episode:

"Sometimes I wish I was a lesbian," Chandler announces, adding: "Did I say that out loud?"

Later Ross says, "I don't want to be single. I want to be married again," as Rachel runs in wearing a wedding dress.

"And I want a million dollars—," Joey interjects.

Later in the same episode, as Joey attempts to console the heartbroken Rachel, Monica says, "Joey, stop hitting on her. It's her wedding day."

"What?" Joey asks. "Like there's some rule or something?"

"Every episode of *Friends* had to utilize all six characters in some significant way," says the show's co-creator David Crane, "which was a real challenge. That's why most of the episodes have three story lines." According to Crane, finding the three compatible story lines wasn't easy. "We had big boards in the writer's room, with lists of stories, and you'd go, well, how about this? 'This story takes place in an afternoon, but that story takes place over three weeks. So they can't go together."

Friends certainly contained a bit of fantasy—with its incredibly good-looking cast and sometimes unrealistic story lines. In fact, critics complained that it rarely featured ethnic characters, even though it was set in racially mixed New York City. Nonetheless, *Friends* also included some realistic episodes that endeared it to fans and ironically helped it stave off reality-TV juggernaut *Survivor* in its final four seasons.

One such episode—and a particular fan favorite—was titled "The One with the Prom Video." Crane recalls the episode presenting a particular challenge, "because we'd spent the first season keeping Ross and Rachel apart, and that was a trick in and of itself, trying to throw obstacles in their way. Finally," after watching the home video of their prom night, "Rachel discovers that Ross has loved her. And then we took it away in the next show. It was the most frustrating thing for an audience ever."

The episode was based in part on writer-producer Alexa Junge's own experience. "That had a tremendous amount of personal meaning to me, because I stole some parts of my own life and put them in it, to my then-boyfriend's, now-husband's chagrin," Junge says. "Don't take things your boyfriend tells you and put them on television is really the lesson."

Junge's future husband compared his relationship with the television writer to a couple of lobsters. It was Kudrow's Phoebe character who delivered the lines Junge borrowed for the show. In the episode, Phoebe comforts Ross by telling him that Rachel is his "lobster." At first he doesn't understand, until she explains. "It's a known fact that lobsters fall in love and mate for life," she said. "You know what? You can actually see old lobster couples walkin' around their tank, you know, holding claws."

While sharing such intimate thoughts may have initially upset Junge's significant other, time healed those wounds, especially when it became one of the best-received *Friends* episodes ever.

Another key element of that episode was that it made the almost-too-perfect "friends" seem human. Rachel is shown, before plastic surgery, with a rather large nose, while Monica is captured as an overweight teen in the faux video clip that had Courtney Cox donning a fat suit for the scene. "I felt like it would help make her become a more interesting character to know that she had been a different person at one point," Junge says. "And, especially 'cause they were all so good-looking, you wanted to feel like they had some realness in their past."

It was that sort of reality that made comedies centered around friends—both at home and in the workplace—some of the most memorable sitcoms of the last three and a half decades. America had changed tremendously since the days when the Ricardos and the Nelsons ruled the TV roost. For many Americans, friends were the new family—both in their daily lives and on their televisions—and we turned to them to find humor in the mundane occurrences of everyday life.

"LIVE FROM NEW YORK"

A Tribute to *Saturday Night Live*

• • •

By the time you get on the air on *Saturday Night Live*, you're so tired, you can't even remember why you wanted to be a comic, or what you ever thought was funny. But when you get that first huge laugh in this famous place and there are literally millions of people watching and you're affecting what they do that night, you can't get higher. It can't be better.

—Darrell Hammond, *Saturday Night Live*

By 1975, the last U.S. troops were leaving Vietnam, Richard Nixon had resigned, and sex, drugs, and rock 'n' roll were a permanent part of the American social landscape. On Saturday, October 11, a new sketch-comedy show shook up the late-night TV landscape, opening with a bizarre skit in which an English teacher (writer/actor Michael O'Donoghue) taught his chubby Eastern European student (John Belushi) an absurdly comic but menacing English phrase: "I would like . . . to feed your fingertips . . . to the wolverines." This offbeat skit defied traditional rules of mainstream television sketch comedy, but it had a certain energy and freshness to it. In other words, it was a perfect example of what *Saturday Night Live* (originally titled *NBC's Saturday Night*) would bring to television.

"Research had shown that people wouldn't be home on Saturday nights, so it was a very low-stakes game," *SNL* creator and executive producer Lorne Michaels said. "Because of that, there was this sort of intoxicating freedom, in terms of both being able to write and being able to create an environment in which, on and off the air, people could play."

And doing it live from New York meant there was no safety net, which was quite a rush for performers who were new to television, according to Michaels. "At the beginning, we were doing the show for ourselves, and I think the fact that we were making it up as we went along was thrilling," he said.

Once, fifteen minutes before showtime, guest host Louise Lasser panicked and locked herself in her dressing room, saying she couldn't perform; Chevy Chase got ready to don a wig with pigtails and do her lines. Another time, Belushi accidentally sliced host Buck Henry's forehead with his Samurai prop sword; Henry appeared in the next sketch with a Band-Aid on the laceration, and for the remainder of the show, all the cast members donned similar bandages on their heads.

While the show has provided laughs for longer than any of its predecessors, nothing has ever matched the fevered comic intensity of the original Not Ready for Prime Time Players and writers. No show has ever created so many household names—Chevy Chase, John Belushi, Dan Aykroyd, Bill Murray, Gilda Radner, Jane Curtin—or contributed so much to pop culture. So many of *SNL*'s greatest bits have passed into comedy lore that even a roll call of their most beloved catchphrases and characters induces chuckles: the Coneheads, the Samurai, Nick the lounge singer, Lisa Loopner and Todd DiLaMuca, Emily Litella, Roseanne Roseannadanna, Baba Wawa, the Bees, Father Guido Sarducci, Mr. Bill, the "Cheeseburger" restaurant, "I'm Chevy Chase and you're not," "Jane, you ignorant slut," "We are two wild and crazy guys," "But noooo . . . ," "Never mind," and "Bay-za-ball's been beddy beddy good to me."

The show, which nabbed four Emmys in its first season, relentlessly parodied pop culture with skits like "Land Shark," which transformed *Jaws* into a conniving and deadly door-to-door salesman, and the *Star Trek* satire,

with Chase as Mr. Spock and Belushi brutally overacting as Captain Kirk.

Belushi also memorably portrayed an obese and insatiable Elizabeth Taylor choking on chicken while Dan Aykroyd's Julia Childs cut her finger but kept instructing as a steady stream of blood gushed out. These scenes were complemented by the lampooning newscast "Weekend Update" and commercial parodies mocking consumer culture: the Royal Deluxe II, a sedan "so smooth a rabbi can perform a circumcision in the backseat"; Mel's Char Palace, "Where you find your own cow! You cut your own steaks! We give you the saw!"; and the Super Bass-O-Matic 76 blender: "Yes, fish-eaters, the days of troublesome scaling, cutting, and gutting are over, because Super Bass-o-Matic 76 is the tool that lets you use the whole bass with no fish waste." It also pushed the boundaries of taste, managing to get an ad for "Pussy Whip"—the first dessert topping for cats—past the censors.

The early days were a whirlwind of behind-the-scenes hilarity, drug use, creative tensions, bruised egos, love

affairs, and hard work—lots of it. The cast and writers essentially lived in the offices at Rockefeller Center. "The better part of the first season, we were in a bubble," Michaels remembered, "always up until three or four in the morning. We dealt with organizational problems, network problems, then scripts. . . . It was exhilarating."

"It's great when you're twenty-five," recalled original writer Tom Schiller. "Only later do you begin to realize you have no life."

By 1980, the breakneck pace and internal struggles had taken a toll. All of the original cast had departed, along with Michaels. Helmed by producer Jean Doumanian, the show slipped and was nearly canceled. But by 1981, *SNL* rebounded under the leadership of producer Dick Ebersol, fueled primarily by the arrival of a young comic named Eddie Murphy.

Although *SNL* has never regained the consistency or revolutionary status of its early days, Murphy's charged, unique comic vision energized the show with memorable characters like Little Richard Simmons, a hilarious hybrid of the flamboyant 1950s rocker and the effeminate 1980s exercise maven ("Good golly, Miss Molly, you look like a *hog*!"); pimp Velvet Jones hawking how-to books like *I Wanna Be a Ho*; film critic Raheem Abdul Muhammed pondering why Jimmy "J.J." Walker was overlooked for the lead role in *Elephant Man*; and dead-on impressions of Bill Cosby, Stevie Wonder, and Mr. T.

Most famous of all were his satires of television itself—his live-action Gumby selling items like Galactic Prophylactics, "Mr. Robinson's Neighborhood" (parodying Mr. Rogers with lines like "Can you say 'scumbucket,' boys and girls?"), and a grown-up Buckwheat from *The Little Rascals* ("I have a little sister named Shredded Wheat, a sister who's a prostitute named Trix, an older brother who's gay, Lucky Charms, and a mentally retarded brother, Special K.")

"The most talented impressionist I have ever seen, bar none, is Eddie Murphy," says current *SNL* impressionist master Darrell Hammond. "James Brown, Jackie Gleason, Michael Jackson, Mr. T.: I've seen him do thirty or forty of the best impressions I've ever seen anywhere."

Then came the 1984 season with polished pros Billy Crystal, Martin Short, Christopher Guest, and Harry Shearer, which brought characters like Crystal's send-up of actor Fernando Lamas ("You looook mah-velous") and Willie the masochist ("Did you ever thread your tongue into a self-winding movie projector? I *hate* it when that happens"), and Short's psychotically nerdy Ed Grimley ("Kind of mental, you know?"). The group also added inventive short films like Guest and Crystal's affectionate parody of Negro League ballplayers ("Rooster was so fast, he once hit a line drive to center field and got hit in the head at second base"), and Short and Shearer's "Lifestyles of the Relatives of the Rich and Famous," in which Shearer played a Robin Leach–type interviewer and Short played Katharine Hepburn's cousin Nelson, a hot dog vendor in Central Park with a dead-on Hepburn vocal tremor.

As times changed, the audience changed and so did the comedy. The gags became a little less risqué, the satire less rebellious. "We were in our late thirties, our sensibilities were a little less angry than the first group," said Crystal of

his mid-'80s tenure on the show. "We were a kinder, gentler *Saturday Night.*" Every few years, it seemed, the show would experience a short dip in quality before a new generation of stars and memorable characters would rescue it from the brink.

Following Michaels's return as producer in 1985 came Dana Carvey as the "Church Lady" ("Oh, isn't that special?"); "Master Thespian" Jon Lovitz, who also played compulsive liar Tommy Flanagan ("Yeah, that's the ticket"); the incredibly versatile Phil Hartman; and Kevin Nealon, Dennis Miller, and Nora Dunn. Over the next twenty years, the pattern would repeat itself: in the late 1980s and early 1990s with Mike Myers ("Wayne's World"), Chris Farley, David Spade, Chris Rock, and Adam Sandler; in the late 1990s with Will Ferrell, Darrell Hammond, Tracy Morgan, Cheri Oteri, Molly Shannon, and Colin Quinn; and most recently with Jimmy Fallon, Tina Fey, and Rachel Dratch.

While the cast experienced frequent turnover, there was little change in the show's legendary pressure-cooker mechanics: the writing and rewriting early in the week, the read-throughs and readjustments on Thursdays and Fridays, and the mad rush to the zero hour on Saturdays, hampered by late scripts, arguments with network censors, and the antics of unpredictable cast members and guest hosts. "It was like final exams every week," said Martin Short. "And that got to you."

Dana Carvey recalled developing his own process for dealing with the high-stress demands of weekly live television. "I'd try to be bad at read-through, bad in rehearsals," he said. "Sometimes the writers would go, '*What* are you doing?' Even trying at dress rehearsal not to do it *too* well, so that when you're on air you're discovering where its limits are, right as the camera's rolling."

For the hundreds of comics who have passed through *SNL*'s Studio 8H at Rockefeller Center, and for the millions of viewers who have tuned in over the years, that moment when the cameras start rolling and those famous words—"Live from New York"—ring out has come to symbolize some of the most innovative and spontaneous humor on American television.

Still, *SNL* has had a tough road. Over the years, it has been lauded as a revolutionary force in comedy and criticized as reactionary comic boot camp, where women and minorities have been given short shrift and little airtime. It has been attacked as being too subversive and disparaged for having satire duller than a butter knife. But through all the social, political, and artistic changes of the last three decades, the program has managed to reinvent itself time and again, and, most importantly, it has endured. Today, what Lorne Michaels once called the "little, dinky late-night show" has become a venerable cultural institution.

"LADIES AND GENTLEMAN, THE PRESIDENT OF THE UNITED STATES!" (OR A REASONABLE FACSIMILE THEREOF)

EACH GENERATION has had impressionists who mimic our leaders—Vaughn Meader's 1962 comedy album *First Family* aped President John Kennedy and other members of the Kennedy clan and sold two and a half million copies. But for presidential impersonations (and presidential hopefuls), nothing can match *Saturday Night Live*, which has created lasting images of the presidents (and hopefuls) it mocks.

Richard Nixon

Richard Nixon was already disgraced when Dan Aykroyd parodied the former ex-president's final days, depicting a raging, paranoid, delusional anti-Semite that may have been, like all great humor bits, uncomfortably close to the truth. Nixon rants at paintings of former presidents, telling Abe Lincoln, "Well, Abe, you were lucky. They shot you. Come on clot. Move up to my heart. Kill me!" and yelling at John Kennedy, "They're gonna find out about you, too. The president. Having sex with women within these very walls. That never happened when Dick Nixon was in the White House."

Gerald Ford

Chevy Chase didn't try to look, sound, or even act like President Gerald Ford. In fact, during one bit, a graphic appeared, reading: "This is not a good impression of Gerald Ford, but Rich Little won't work for scale." Chase just took a few physical and mental gaffes and transformed this former college football star into a bumbling idiot of epic proportions. He sneezed into his tie, heard a phone ring and "answered" a glass of water ("Nelson? I can't hear you. Where are you—in the pool?"), and even told a stuffed dog to "roll over." Asked a question about the economy and unemployment at a debate, Ford responded, "It was my understanding there would be no math." Chase's portrayal badly hurt Ford's image and was the first mark of *Saturday Night Live*'s cultural power.

Jimmy Carter

Dan Aykroyd nailed Jimmy Carter's worst flaw—his penchant for micromanaging—in a skit called "Ask President Carter." The "president" (Aykroyd), accompanied by Walter Cronkite (Bill Murray) took phone calls from ordinary Americans. Most memorable was the one in which the "president," after explaining that he disapproves of drugs, talks down a seventeen-year-old caller named Peter who admits to being on a bad acid trip. After learning the pills were orange and barrel-shaped, the know-it-all "president" tells Peter he did some "orange sunshine." "Everything is going to be fine," Carter assured the caller. "Try taking some vitamin B complex, vitamin C. . . . If you have a beer, go ahead and drink it. . . . Just remember you're a living organism on this planet, and you're very safe. You've just taken a heavy drug. Relax, stay inside, and listen to some music, okay? Do you have any Allman Brothers?"

Ronald Reagan

Phil Hartman's Ronald Reagan seems docile with the general public but behind the scenes is really on top of every detail of his illicit covert operations, a nonstop dynamo who wears out his staffers and speaks Arabic and other languages to foreign leaders. His best line: "I'm the president. Only I need to understand."

George H. W. Bush and Michael Dukakis

Dana Carvey's impression helped make George H. W. Bush famous. His crowning achievement came in a mock 1988 debate when Bush had nothing of substance to say and tried to give back his allotted time before being reduced to a series of empty catchphrases: "On track. Stay the course. A thousand points of light. Wouldn't be prudent. On track . . . " When asked for his rebuttal, Michael Dukakis (Jon Lovitz) summed up much of the problem with America's electoral process by blurting out: "I can't believe I'm losing to this guy."

Bill Clinton

Phil Hartman captured the wonky, lovable but amoral and gluttonous Clinton in a fast-food restaurant where the candidate mingled with ordinary folks, explaining his policies and charming them, all while picking at their food and finally grabbing it away, shoving huge handfuls into his mouth. His funniest line: The Secret Service says, "Sir, we've only been jogging for three blocks. Besides, Mrs. Clinton asked us not to let you in any more fast-food places." To which Clinton (Hartman) responds, "There's gonna be a whole bunch of things we don't tell Mrs. Clinton. Fast food is the least of our worries."

Ross Perot

Dana Carvey again, this time as the daffy third-party candidate, proposing to cut energy consumption and increase productivity with a national curfew of 8:45 P.M. and a "National Wake-Up Siren" at 4:45 A.M., and to reduce waste by suggesting if "every American could wear the same style shoe, we could save over $18 billion the first year alone! Now, you might ask, where does such a shoe come from? Well, it's already been designed by the volunteers. [Holds up shoe.] Here it is. This unisex, water-resistant shoe is handsome, stylish, and comes in all three sizes—small, medium, and large! Case closed."

Bob Dole

This 1996 presidential nominee was brilliantly captured by Norm McDonald in a parody of MTV's *Real World,* which stuck the grumpy, stubborn, and old-fashioned Dole in a house full of twenty-somethings, where he's reduced to complaining. "Nobody eats Bob Dole's peanut butter without asking."

George W. Bush and Al Gore: The 2000 candidates' debates again provided easy fodder. Darrell Hammond's Al Gore spoke slowly and ponderously, punctuating everything with heavy sighs. He answered every question with a reference to the "lockbox" that the real Gore had mentioned incessantly regarding the protection of Social Security. "There would be two different locks in my lockbox. . . . This lockbox would also be camouflaged—as a leather-bound edition of the *Count of Monte Cristo.*" Meanwhile, Will Ferrell's squinty-eyed, uninformed, and immature George W. Bush responded either by "passing" on questions as if he were on a game show or with nonsensical answers like "I don't know what that was all about, but I do know this: Don't mess with Texas," or when asked about foreign leaders, "I'm not going to pronounce any of their names, it is not in our national interest."

PART 2

FUNNIEST MOMENTS FROM STAND-UP

9

FROM THE BORSCHT BELT TO THE BIG TIME: THE PIONEERS

• • •

I just got back from a pleasure trip. I took my mother-in-law to the airport.

—Henny Youngman

"I'd like to show you something you probably haven't seen in a long time," Buddy Young Jr. tells his gorged Catskills audience. "Your feet!" As the room erupts in wheezes and groans, the tuxedoed comic calmly puffs his cigar and waits to deliver his next zinger.

The joke—old-time schmaltz. The delivery—pure borscht belt. The comedian? Actor Billy Crystal playing an aging joker in *Mr. Saturday Night,* his 1992 homage to the corned-beef cutups and one-line wizards who in the decades just before and after World War II carved out the comedic styles that would dominate American stand-up for years to come.

Crystal's "Buddy" might have been a creative fiction, but he was an amalgam of some of the best-known comic personalities from that golden age when performers like Shecky Greene, Don Rickles, Alan King, Buddy Hackett, Jackie Mason, Jan Murray, and Rodney Dangerfield ran riot from the Catskills to the Vegas strip. Most were first- and second-generation Americans, sons of Russian and Polish Jews or Italians who had grown up in Depression-era New York. They had cut their teeth in neighborhood talent contests and local clubs, then graduated to the resorts of upstate New York's borscht belt, where they plied their stock-in-trade mother-in-law quips, ethnic jokes, raunchy asides, and barbed insults to vacationing East Coasters.

In time, the best and the blessed became regulars on television variety shows and headliners in New York, Miami, Chicago, Los Angeles—and of course Las Vegas. "They're amazing characters," said Crystal, who, like so many stand-ups of subsequent generations, learned his craft from observing and, to some extent, emulating these comedy pioneers. "They're really show business to me."

And without a doubt, Henny Youngman was the god-father of them all. Known as the King of the One-Liners, he was the first postvaudeville comic to build an entire career on stand-up comedy. While many of his contempo-raries—Milton Berle, Jack Benny, George Burns—moved from radio to television in the 1950s, Youngman remained a club-bound gun for hire, ready to hop on a bus or plane at a moment's notice and deliver his barrage of well-honed wisecracks.

"I can go anywhere, play any date, for any kind of people," he used to say. And for a performer whose per-sonal motto was *nem di gelt* (Yiddish for "get the money"), no gig was too cheap, no venue too obscure. Once, after playing to 6,500 people at New York's Waldorf-Astoria Hotel, Youngman got off at the wrong floor on his way to the lobby, saw that a bar mitzvah party was under way, and inquired about doing a quick, fifteen-minute set. "I made an extra $150," he recalled. "Ah, what a night!"

Born in London and raised in Brooklyn, Youngman never intended to become a professional joker. His artistic aspirations were musical, and as a teenager in the early 1920s he played violin in a nightclub band, working days as a printer. ("If things went sour in comedy," he would later say, "I could always get a job printing. Or I could be out of two jobs at once.") But in 1927 fate intervened in the form of a New Jersey club owner who convinced the twenty-one-year-old fiddler, known as an inveterate back-stage ham, to fill in for a comic who had called in sick. Youngman killed, and music's loss was comedy's gain.

Over the next seven decades, his routine never varied, and his assembly-line joke assault—also used to great effect by Bob Hope and George Burns—would come to be seen as the quintessential old-time stand-up style. "I miss my wife's cooking—as often as I can," he quipped with a half-smile, pausing momentarily to scratch out a few bars on his ancient "Stradivaricose" violin. "I told my mother-in-law, 'My house is your house.' So she sold it. What good is happiness? It can't buy you money. When I was born, I was so ugly the doctor slapped my mother." The jokes came so fast and furious that Youngman was once clocked delivering 250 punch lines during a forty-five minute set.

Occasionally the one-line king veered outside his nat-ural oeuvre to offer *two* lines: "A guy goes to a psychia-trist, and the psychiatrist tells him, 'You're crazy.' 'I want a second opinion,' the guy says. 'Okay,' the psychiatrist tells him, 'you're ugly too.'"

His philosophy was simple: keep it quick, and keep it visual. "If a joke is too hard to visualize, what the hell good is it?" he asked.

After ten years of playing borscht belt resorts and any dump along the eastern seaboard that would chuck him spare change ("I played in places where the checkout girl's name was Rocco and the owner would stab me good night"), Youngman was introduced to a wider audience through *The Kate Smith Hour* radio program in 1936. Orig-inally slotted for a six-minute routine, Youngman steam-rolled through ten minutes and had so much material left over that he was asked to be a regular.

During one performance of that show, he uttered what is perhaps the most famous one-liner in comedy his-tory. When his wife, Sadie, arrived late to the theater, Youngman grabbed her and steered her to an usher. "Take my wife—please!" he said innocently, hoping to find her a seat. The usher was so amused that Youngman began using the line in his act.

With radio fame came bigger and better jobs. Young-man appeared frequently in Las Vegas in the 1950s, 1960s, and 1970s, and also landed small parts in Hollywood films, like Mel Brooks's *History of the World, Part I* and Martin Scorsese's *Goodfellas* in the 1980s and 1990s. But he was never above taking small-time stand-up work to beef up his paycheck. Well into his eighth decade, the peripatetic comedian performed more than one hundred times a year, booking his own gigs and traveling around the world.

Even offstage, he never lost his penchant for the one-two punch. Three years before his death in 1998 at the age of ninety-one, Youngman summoned the press to a New York restaurant to read his last will and testament. "To my nephew Irving," he began, "who still keeps asking me to mention him in my will: Hello, Irving!"

While Youngman was breaking up Catskills showrooms in the early 1940s, teenager Leonard Hacker was earning summer money bringing blintzes to the patrons. The son of a Brooklyn furniture upholsterer, Hacker himself—after a rechristening as Buddy Hackett—would become one of the borscht belt's biggest draws in the early 1950s and 1960s,

known as much for his ribald, profanity-laced humor as for his quick wit and impish, roly-poly mien.

Described by a *New York Times* critic as "a large, soft, messy comic with a glib tongue," the dumpy Hackett could get laughs just by raising an eyebrow. His moppy haircut, bulbous nose, and cock-a-hoop mouth—"a face like a plate of mashed potatoes," one paper remarked—pegged him as a promising candidate for Fourth Stooge (he was even asked to replace Curly Howard when the latter suffered a stroke in 1946, but declined), and his high-pitched Brooklynese delivery only added to the comic effect.

When he broke into the New York City and Catskills clubs in the mid-1940s, Hackett used a typical setup joke style ("Two guys and a duck walk into a bar . . ."), but soon added longer tales and impressions, including his now-famous surly Chinese waiter: "You don't know whatsa fly lice?" the agitated server asks his confused white customers. "Fly lice is fly lice! Whatsamata, can't you speak Engrish, round-eye idiot?!"

As his act evolved, much of his schtick tended to center on being fat, funny-looking, and Jewish. In one perennial bit, the comic has an uneasy encounter with two chiseled Austrian ski instructors ("blond hair, blue eyes, tan skin, high cheekbones—you know, freaks!") during his first, and only, time on the slopes.

"'I am Klaus und zis is Sandor,' the guy says. '*Jew* vish to ski?' I told 'im, 'I don't do nothin' with Klauses and Sandors. If you ain't got a Herbie, I ain't goin'.'"

In another, he meets an ailing Jewish acquaintance at Lourdes. "I says, 'Herbert, what are you doing here? This is for Catholics.' He says, 'Well, where are *we* supposed to go?' I says, '*Putz*, you're a Jew. You call a cousin who tells you about a specialist.'"

The irrepressible goofiness and rubber-faced, side-of-the-mouth drawl that seemed tailor-made for the nightclub stage translated well to other mediums, and throughout the 1950s and 1960s, aside from being a frequent guest on the late-night shows of Jack Paar and Arthur Godfrey, Hackett starred on Broadway (*Lunatics and Lovers*), in films (*It's a Mad, Mad, Mad, Mad World*, *The Love Bug*), and on television—most notably opposite Carol Burnett in 1956's *Stanley* and as Art Carney's replacement on *The Jackie Gleason Show* in 1958.

As Hackett's stock skyrocketed in the 1960s, the raconteur's routines became a little saltier, the ad-libs more obscene. "When you're filling the room," he said, "you can do what you want." He once reportedly took the stage at a Lake Tahoe hotel in 1970 wearing nothing but a large pendant that covered his privates, and during his packed Vegas performances, often advertised "For Adults Only," he laced his act with raunchy sexual anecdotes, pausing intermittently to embarrass the attendees.

"Do you know what I mean when I talk about the *member*, young lady?" he'd ask a blushing woman stageside. "The dick, yes, that's correct." Chastising a man whispering to his wife, he'd say, "Just look at *me*, okay? You can play with her tits later."

In the hands of another comic, the off-color jokes and profanity might have seemed crude and overly aggressive, but coming from a baby-faced teddy bear, they were simply good-naturedly mischievous, if a little perverse—and the audience couldn't help laughing along. He even joked that he used swear words only to keep other comedians from stealing his act on television.

Hackett continued to headline clubs in Vegas and Atlantic City throughout the 1970s and 1980s. In the Catskills, where he was revered as a comedy king, the Concord Hotel kept a suite open for him year-round. And although he retired from stand-up in 1996, he took small parts on television (including comedian Jay Mohr's 1999 *Action*) and called old Catskills buddies like Louis Nye and Jan Murray daily to exchange jokes, until his death in 2003.

"He was the most creative comic I've ever seen," said legendary Vegas entertainer Steve Lawrence. "[He was] a groundbreaker with a lot of taboos we grew up with. But he always did it in a way that was hysterical."

If breaking taboos and inducing hysteria were the marks of a good comic, Don Rickles had success in a headlock. Funny, because the comedy legend never had any success telling jokes.

"I'm not a big one for jokes," he once admitted. "I can't tell a joke, believe it or not. If you gave me a thousand bucks and said, 'Don, get up at a party and tell a joke,' I'm the worst."

Fortunately, Rickles discovered his Achilles' heel early in his career while playing strip joints and small clubs in New York and the Catskills during the late 1940s. When his canned gags fell flat and audiences began aggressively voicing their displeasure, the spurned comic turned on them with a fury. Surprisingly, they laughed, and Rickles began taunting his way into comedy history.

He wasn't the first insult comic of the time. "Fat" Jack Leonard, who predated Rickles by a decade, had built a

career blistering both the low and the lordly and was known to commence his nightly slamfests with a brusque "Good evening, Opponents." But where Leonard's stage persona evoked the air of a mild-mannered salesman, Rickles was pure raving crank—frothing, swearing, and squawking splenetically at the objects of his derision—a heart attack waiting to happen.

There was something irresistibly amusing about watching the bald-headed, wide-mouthed Rickles work himself into a lather over the most innocuous transgressions. A lady in a fur coat irks him. "Lady, you look like an old beaver in heat," he snarls, leaning to a nearby male patron and confirming, "That was a good one, wasn't it, queer?" A hefty man is targeted: "What do you eat for dinner? Furniture? You hockey puck!" Nobody was safe but, hilariously, it was Rickles's blood pressure that always seemed to get the worst of it.

Most understood the artifice. "If I were to insult people and mean it," Rickles once said, "that wouldn't be funny. There is a difference between an actual insult and just having fun."

In 1957, Rickles was having fun with his audience at a Hollywood club when Frank Sinatra popped in. The thirty-one-year-old comic, who had yet to catch a big break, didn't miss a beat. "C'mon in, Frank," he greeted the volatile star. "Make yourself at home—hit somebody!" Sinatra doubled over laughing, and the Chairman's seal of approval helped catapult Rickles to stardom.

By 1959, Hollywood celebrities were flocking to Rickles's Las Vegas performances for the honor of being humiliated by the "King of Zing," and for the next forty-five years he was happy to oblige. "Oh my God, look at you," he told Ernest Borgnine. "Anyone else hurt in the accident?" When Bob Hope appeared, he shouted, "Bob Hope's so popular, when he was in Vietnam they were shooting at him from both sides!" "Who picks out your clothes?" he asked David Letterman. "Stevie Wonder?" There wasn't a name in show business—from Bob Newhart to Orson Welles—that didn't sustain a good drubbing.

As his popularity grew in the 1960s and 1970s through regular appearances on *The Tonight Show* (Johnny Carson facetiously dubbed him "Mr. Warmth") and Dean Martin's celebrity roasts, Rickles, who had once trained as a dramatic actor, was offered plum roles on television and in films like *The Rat Race* and *Kelly's Heroes.* But with the increased exposure came censure from some who took offense at the caustic racial and ethnic humor that had by then become a staple of his stand-up act.

He would regularly single out members of the audience for a tirade. "I'm a Jew and you're a Mexican," he'd tell a patron. "I say this from the bottom of my heart: A black guy can move into my neighborhood. You can't!" Or, "This Pollock here thinks we're in a bowling alley." Even Sammy Davis Jr. was a mark: "You can't get Negro help like *that* anymore. Wow, to have a guy who can sing, dance—and dust!"

Such material remains part of his act to this day, albeit slightly toned down, and Rickles, who prides himself on being an equal-opportunity offender, has always looked at the issue philosophically. "God put us on this earth to laugh," he said. "We're human beings—Jew, gen-

tile, Irish, Negro, Puerto Rican. Laugh at bigotry—bigots and morons and dummies."

As recently as 1998 a *Los Angeles Times* reviewer wrote; "Rickles still does jokes about ethnic groups . . . but everyone sees through the ruse. In fact, the act is a celebration of diversity, of the melting pot mentality at the heart of the American dream."

Rickles might be championing the American dream, but as such dreams go, Rodney Dangerfield must be counted as one of the most hilariously pathetic casualties. His miserable lament (or at least that of his stage persona)—"I don't get no respect"—has over the last forty years become the comedic rallying cry for every sad-sack *schlub* forced to drag himself out of bed each day to face a cruel and merciless world.

"Hey, I had a rough childhood, let me tell you," Dangerfield quips on stage, characteristically adjusting and readjusting his tie. "I was an ugly kid—they tried to make me the poster boy for birth control. My mother never breast-fed me—she told me she liked me better as a friend. My uncle's dying wish was to have me sit on his lap—he was in the electric chair. No respect, I tell you."

It's not difficult to imagine Dangerfield as an easy Rickles scapegoat, with his hallmarks that made him the archetypical set-upon Everyman of the 1960s: the bulging eyes underlined by deep, gray bags; the cheap suit; the slumping, defeated posture, as if he'd just been canned from his umpteenth job.

"Comedy is a camouflage for depression," Dangerfield once said, and he spoke from experience; over nearly seven decades, his life and career saw more ups and downs than a Coney Island roller coaster.

Born Jacob Cohen in New York, Dangerfield followed in his comedian father's footsteps and by the age of fifteen was writing jokes professionally. At age eighteen, he stepped out on his own, playing neighborhood dives under the name "Jack Roy" and working as a singing waiter and fish-truck driver. But in 1949, after ten years of professional disappointments and meager paychecks—and with a wife and two children to support—he decided to shelve his show-business dreams and took a job selling aluminum siding.

"I used to do a joke about it," Dangerfield said, "that I was the only one who knew I quit."

But even then, things didn't work out quite as he'd planned. A dozen years later, divorced, twenty thousand dollars in debt, and living alone in a cheap Manhattan

Playing the ultimate loser, he bombarded audiences with snappy one-liners about unhappy marriages ("Last week my house was on fire. My wife told the kids, 'Be quiet, you'll wake up daddy'"), failing libidos ("At my age, making love is like trying to shoot pool with a rope"), and, naturally, a general lack of respect ("When I get in an elevator, the operator takes one look and says, 'Basement?'").

A successful spot on *The Ed Sullivan Show* in 1965 earned Dangerfield a heap of high-paying, high-profile jobs and a stint in Vegas that would last more than twenty years. His film roles—including 1980's *Caddyshack* and the self-penned *Back to School* in 1986—brought him more acclaim and further boosted his stand-up career.

By the 1980s and 1990s, the idea of a senior citizen making a living reeling off one-liners might have seemed an anachronism, but Dangerfield kept plugging, often playing to adoring crowds in their twenties and thirties. An explanation for his continuing popularity may lie in the words of Jack Benny: "Rodney, I'm cheap and I'm thirty-nine, that's my image, but your 'no respect,' that's the soul of everybody. Everybody can identify with that."

Today, as much of the humor pioneered in the golden age of stand-up fades into memory like a distant rim-shot, there is a tendency to view the old-time jokes as hopelessly cornball, the products of an era whose concept of comedy bears little resemblance to our own. Few modern comics would agree. Through the routines of Billy Crystal, who considers the borscht belt clowns his comedic godfathers; and Chris Rock, who grew up on Friar's Club roasts and still records every Don Rickles TV appearance for lessons on comic timing; and the work of the late Sam Kinison and Jim Carrey, whose careers owe much to the inspiration and encouragement of Rodney Dangerfield, the spirit of the great early comedians continues to thrive, and to keep us laughing.

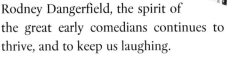

hotel, the former comic decided to give stand-up one last shot. On the advice of a club owner, he became Rodney Dangerfield ("I was depressed enough to keep the name") and began forging a routine that would play on the failures and frustrations in his own life.

"At forty-four, I finally had an image and something to say—that nothing goes right," Dangerfield recalled. "And people identified with it."

Unlike many younger comics coming up at the time—Woody Allen, Mike Nichols, and Bill Cosby, who were pioneering a more conversational style—Dangerfield hewed closely to his old-school borscht belt roots. But if the form was Henny Youngman, the content was pure Rodney.

THE CATSKILLS, CASINOS, AND THE RISE OF STAND-UP

IN THE SALAD DAYS OF STAND-UP, during the 1950s and 1960s, there seemed to be a pipeline that pumped comic talent directly from upstate New York to the Las Vegas Strip.

At its source was the borscht belt, a string of resort hotels and bungalow communities scattered throughout New York's Catskill Mountains that served as a vacation destination for thousands of middle-class, mostly Jewish, families seeking to escape the congestion and summer heat of New York City.

By 1960 there were more than five hundred such resorts, including Kutscher's, The Pines, The Windsor, and The Raleigh, accommodating close to a million tourists a year. The biggest and most luxurious—The Concord and Grossinger's—were de facto towns, equipped with their own lakes, summer camps, post offices, and airports. Here, professional athletes like boxer Rocky Marciano came to train, crooners like Jan Peerce and Eddie Fisher stretched their vocal cords, and of course every comic from the Bronx to Boston crawled in from the city's bars and nightclubs to sling his latest routine.

Countless aspiring comedians—among them Buddy Hackett, Alan King, and Shecky Greene—made their way to the hotels as teenagers, working as busboys, waiters, and bellhops, before becoming *tummlers*, or paid jokers, whose job it was to entertain guests after dinner.

And those borscht belters who hit it big usually ended up in the promised land of Las Vegas, where, by the late-1960s, comics like Hackett, Greene, and Don Rickles were regularly pulling down one hundred grand a week playing to gambling vacationers and Hollywood royalty.

Vegas arose out of the desert in the 1940s, not long after gambling was legalized in Nevada, and the hotel-casinos that sprang up over the next decade—like the Sahara, the Sands, the Stardust, the Dunes, the Tropicana, and the Flamingo (built by soon-to-be-whacked mobster Bugsy Siegel)—played host to some of the biggest names in show business.

It was a freewheeling city, where the mafia laundered its money, Frank Sinatra and the Rat Pack caroused the Strip with showgirls and strippers, and comics worked in round-the-clock lounges where anyone could stop in and catch a few laughs for the price of a drink.

"We did five-o'clock-in-the-morning shows," recalled Rickles of those early years. "There he is, Don Rickles, up there with two drunks and a guy eating spinach."

Over time, the adventures of Vegas's most famous comics became legendary—Jackie Mason being shot at and having his nose broken by a thug who told him to stop doing Sinatra jokes; Rodney Dangerfield suing a hotel after claiming he received first-degree burns on his eyelids in their steam room; and Shecky Greene smashing his Cadillac into the fountain at Caesars Palace, responding to police who knocked on the car window, "No spray wax, please."

Clearly, in their journey from the Catskills to the Wild West, the boys from the borscht belt never lost their sense of humor.

REBEL YELL:
THE OUTLAWS OF COMEDY

• • •

It's the duty of the comedian to find out where the line is drawn
and to cross it deliberately.

—George Carlin

For the most part, stand-up comics are a reputable bunch, content to toil within society's accepted laws and limits. But every now and then a performer casts a defiant shadow across the landscape of American humor, and the old troublesome questions start flying. Can he *say* that? Isn't that *illegal*? Is that creep wrestling a woman on stage?

Over the last half-century, a handful of these brazen misfits have succeeded in redefining the comic terrain. Unsatisfied with the fogyish conceit that a comedian should stand before an audience and deliver tasteful jokes with pleasant punch lines, they risked their careers—and occasionally their freedom—for the right to challenge, offend, and antagonize the powers that be. Whether it was Lenny Bruce and George Carlin breaking society's taboos on "dirty" language and religious vituperation, or Sam Kinison primal-screaming past the edge of political correctness, or Andy Kaufman outraging everyone from feminists to professional wrestlers with his provocative performance

art, the changes wrought by comedy's outlaws forced us to examine humor in a new light and pointed the way for generations of comic renegades to come.

In the late 1950s, those changes were just beginning to be felt. While the snappy one-liners and mother-in-law jokes popularized in the prewar years were still the rage among the masses, outside the cozy confines of Eisenhower-era popular culture, comedy was growing teeth. In jazz clubs and gin joints across the country, upstarts like Mort Sahl and Dick Gregory were forging a new brand of stand-up that spotlighted progressive politics and social criticism—long considered off-limits by old-guard jokesters—and doing it in a style that owed more to Beat poetry and bebop than to Bob Hope or the borscht belt. With Americans increasingly divided over the Cold War and the burgeoning civil-rights movement in the South, the emergence of a rebellious, confrontational vein in comedy was seen by many as a welcome and exciting change.

But not everyone was ready for Lenny Bruce. While his colleagues were busy castigating Joe McCarthy and J. Edgar Hoover, the iconoclastic former strip-club emcee declared war on hypocrisy and pretense in all forms, skewering everything from white liberals and the Catholic church to Hollywood films and the sex lives of the upper crust. Bruce cursed. He raved. He got naked on stage. He made hardened hipsters blush. And, naturally, he got busted.

Yet to see Bruce as merely a foul-mouthed noncon-formist—he was nailed fifteen times for obscenity in a two-year span—is to overlook the fact that his "shock" techniques and four-letter words were more a means of cutting through the apathy and prejudice that he felt muddied the waters of clear thinking than they were an end in themselves. "The issue is not obscenity," he once complained, "but that I spit in the face of authority."

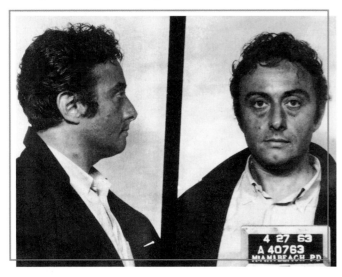

And in the staid atmosphere of 1958, his anti-authoritarian satire had the force of blasphemy. Thirty years before the televangelist scandals of the 1980s, Bruce was performing his controversial "Religions, Inc.," a pointed spoof on organized religion in which the spiritual leaders of the Western world—portrayed here as the crassest of Madison Avenue hucksters—convene to discuss their annual financial schemes, including marketing a multidenominational cigarette lighter and placing Pope John XIII in an ad for Viceroy tobacco. The meeting concludes with Pentecostal preacher Oral Roberts on the phone to the pope: "Johnny baby, uh, Billy [Graham] wants to know if you can get 'im a deal on one of them dago sports cars."

When his attacks on religion brought heat, particularly from predominantly Catholic big-city police forces,

Bruce responded with typical chutzpah. "Show me your average sex maniac," he joked, "the one who takes an eight-year-old girl, *schtupps* her in the parking lot, then kills her, and I'll show you a guy who's had a good religious upbringing."

But the guardians of piety and order weren't Bruce's only targets. One of his most searing routines, "How to Relax Your Colored Friends at Parties," goosed even those high-minded liberals who were his biggest fans with its portrayal of a white man whose latent racism seeps out after a few cocktails with a black acquaintance. The closet bigot goes from cordial to blasted drunk, hitting every racial stereotype in the book before blurting out, "Hey, I heard you guys got a really big wang-on. Now whip out that roll of tarpaper and let's see whatcha got there, Chonga!"

In 1962 the thin ice cracked, and municipal burghers began hauling thirty-six-year-old "Dirty Lenny" into court for uttering the vernacular equivalents of fellatio, genitalia, and excrement, among other profanities. But Bruce remained undaunted. If anything, his experience with the judicial system spurred him to explore language and forbidden words with an etymologist's passion.

Why is "derriere" acceptable while "ass" is not? he asked. What makes a D. H. Lawrence love scene legally palatable and a dime-novel depiction of rough sex inde-cent? What gives racial epithets like "jigaboo," "wop," "kike," "spic," and "chink" their uncanny power to offend?

"Are there any niggers here tonight?" he began one memorable improvisational routine attended by black comic Dick Gregory. As the house squirmed, Bruce argued that such terms were insulting precisely because they had been suppressed. If everybody used them in daily conver-sation, he claimed ("If President Kennedy said, 'I'm con-sidering appointing two or three of the top niggers in the country to my cabinet'"), within six months the words would be meaningless. The crowd ate it up.

"This guy is the eighth wonder of the world," the stu-pefied Gregory told Bruce's publicist. "You have to go back to Mark Twain to find anything remotely like him. And if they don't kill him or throw him in jail, he's liable to shake up the whole country."

By late 1964, Bruce had been deported from Britain, banned in Australia, and unoffi-cially barred from playing most American cities. Bankrupt and facing possible prison time in New York, he spent the majority of his days buried in legal books. On the few occa-sions he did perform, he would often appear clutching a thick stack of court transcripts, declaring, "I'm sorry if I'm not very funny tonight, but I'm not a comedian—I'm Lenny Bruce." It was a clear statement, on one hand, that patrons looking for laughs in his monoma-niacal ramblings on the sanctity of the First Amendment might just as well finish their drinks and skedaddle. But it was also a self-conscious assertion that there was no one else like him.

When Bruce died of a heroin overdose in 1966 at the age of forty, he had broken almost every commandment in the comedy rulebook, and his freewheeling, shoot-from-the-hip style had become the blueprint for a new generation of performers intent on shaking up the system. "Lenny led the way," said comic George Carlin, whose own spiel on "dirty" language would result in a landmark legal decision in 1978. "The greatest gift I derived from knowing him was the importance of honesty, in the words and on the stage."

Carlin hadn't always been a public rebel. In fact, the former deejay had begun his stand-up career playing it straight as a suit-and-tie man and dishing his witty—if unchallenging—observations at Las Vegas nightclubs and on network television. But as the late 1960s counterculture blossomed, the thirty-year-old comedian found himself struggling to maintain an image that was at odds with his defiant nature. "I was completely out of place entertaining people I didn't like or agree with socially [or] culturally," he recalled.

He opted for a dramatic makeover and reemerged in 1970 with a new look—long hair, scraggly beard ("It hides my pimples"), blue jeans—and an irreverent new attitude, and he was promptly canned from a lucrative Vegas gig

for saying "shit" in his act. The one-time company man had suddenly become straight society's hippest critic, and whether the topic was dog doo and deodorant or bennies and birth control, Carlin delivered his square-bashing monolgues with a tongue-in-cheek acidity and the jaundiced eye of a cynic.

Disillusioned with a political process that limited voters to a choice between bad and worse, he told audiences: "On election day, I'll be doing the same thing you folks are doing, except that when I'm finished masturbating, I'm going to have a little more to show for it."

An avowed atheist, or, as he occasionally liked to boast, a "Frisbeetarian" ("When you die, your soul goes up on the roof and gets stuck"), the Catholic-school dropout said bluntly he "would never want to be a member of a group whose symbol is a guy nailed to two pieces of wood." "Who says life is sacred?" he asked in one routine. "God? Hey, if you read your history, God is one of the leading causes of death."

Carlin's harangues against America's sacred cows might not have had the sting of sacrilege they did in Bruce's day—an intervening decade of psychedelic drugs, free love, and liberalized social attitudes had seen to that—but there were still some areas where performers were not permitted to trespass. And Carlin made sure he found them. "Seven Words You Can Never Say on Television," which examined the colloquial use of curse words ("You can prick your finger, but you can't finger your prick") and laid out an unofficial list of terms prohibited by the broadcast media, had become one of the comedian's most popular bits by 1972. "Shit, piss, fuck, cunt, cocksucker, motherfucker, and tits— those are the heavy seven," he said. "Tits doesn't even belong on the list, it's such a friendly sounding word. It sounds like a nickname. 'Hey, Tits, come over here!'"

He took it a step further with 1973's "Filthy Words," an augmented index of expletives that further explored the acceptable-unacceptable boundaries of language ("Remember the first time you heard about a *cockfight*? 'What? Huh? Naw. It ain't that! Are you stupid, man? It's chickens'") and included an extended riff on figurative uses for the word "shit": "Get that shit out of here, I don't want to see that shit anymore, I think you're full of shit," and so on.

Carlin had been pinched for obscenity during a concert in 1972 after authorities determined his vulgarity was corrupting minors in the audience (the charges were later dropped), but the political excrement hit the fan when Paci-

fica radio affiliate WBAI in New York aired "Filthy Words" in 1973 as part of a program on language and society. The Federal Communications Commission deemed the broadcast "indecent" because of its possible harmful effect on children and sanctioned the station. Pacifica brought the matter to court. The case eventually reached the Supreme Court, where in 1978 a plurality ruled in favor of the FCC, stating that although Carlin's act "does present a point of view . . . that our attitudes toward [dirty words] are 'essentially silly'" and that "there are few, if any, thoughts that cannot be expressed by the use of less offensive language."

Carlin was not directly implicated in the legal battle (WBAI had played a recording of his act), but the ensuing hullabaloo ensured his status as a counterculture hero and contributed to his growing popularity as Saint George, slayer of the repressive, the hypocritical, and the small-minded.

After being essentially shut out of network television following his 1970 transformation, Carlin was seen with increasing frequency on hip, anti-authoritarian sketch-comedy shows like *Saturday Night Live*, whose inaugural episode he hosted in October 1975. That evening's program, in addition to Carlin's monologues and musical sets by Billy Preston and Janis Ian, featured one of the oddest comedic performances ever seen on television. Following a skit by *Saturday Night Live*'s regular players, a man in a black ascot and sport coat stepped on stage, dropped the needle on a battered record player, and stood stock-still as the scratchy theme from *Mighty Mouse* blared. Each time the chorus rolled around, he animatedly lip-synched "Here I come to save the day!" before returning to his rigid state. His name was Andy Kaufman.

"I first heard about Andy Kaufman, coincidentally, from two people on the same day," recalls comedy impresario and Kaufman's manager George Shapiro. "Carl Reiner was telling me about this comedian that he saw at Catch a Rising Star. And Carl, who has total audio recall, did his whole act with the accent. And then Bud Friedman, the owner of the Improv, called me."

"I love when people put one over on me," says Friedman. "Andy shows up as the foreign man. 'Ha-lo, I am Andy Kaufman,' and I look and I say, 'Well, hello. Where are you from, kid?'

"'I am from an island in da Caspian Sea.' Well, I didn't realize there were no islands in the Caspian Sea. I really think he's a foreigner and so does the audience," Friedman admits. "And he goes on stage and there's some titters. We don't know what to think. Then he says, 'Well, thank you very much,' and I knew I had been had and I fell in love with him then."

"He just blew me away. I did have one concern," Shapiro also recalls, "that he might be insane."

Like Carlin, Kaufman would become a regular fixture on the late-night TV scene during the late 1970s and early 1980s, logging more than a dozen appearances on *Saturday Night Live* and on ABC's *Fridays*. But as his behavior grew increasingly outlandish and aggressive, audiences began to question his sanity. Things came to a head on February 20, 1981, when a fistfight erupted on the *Fridays* set after the thirty-two-year-old Kaufman broke character during a live sketch about marijuana, declared that he "felt stupid" acting high, and hurled a glass of water at a cast member.

The brawl seemed real enough to viewers, but rumors soon began circulating that it had been staged. It wouldn't have been the first time Kaufman, by then best known for his role as the unclassifiably foreign mechanic Latka Gravas on the sitcom *Taxi*, had pulled a fast one. Although generally considered a stand-up comic, Kaufman never felt comfortable with the label, and his career in comedy

read more like a bizarre experiment aimed at undermining every commonly held notion about entertainment than a typical joker's résumé.

"Every comedian has a fear of bombing on stage. But Andy would say, 'I'm going to do my bombing routine now. He'd do jokes that were terrible. I would cringe from them and people would walk out of the club. But I couldn't talk him out of it. Andy's comedy came from his heart and whatever muse he followed, he was true to," Shapiro explains.

"I just want real reactions," Kaufman said of his act. "I want people to laugh from the gut, be sad from the gut, or get angry from the gut." And often it seemed he was prepared to take one in the gut. Perhaps no other comedian has had such a contentious relationship with his public; indeed, no other comedian took such pains to rankle audiences with behavior that veered so wildly from the absurd to the downright belligerent. Comics told jokes and stories—they didn't wash their soiled underwear on stage or lie motionless in sleeping bags, they didn't spend forty-five minutes reading aloud from *The Great Gatsby*, and they certainly didn't taunt and wrestle female patrons in the aisles. At least not with a straight face.

But Kaufman was no ordinary entertainer. From the moment he hit the stand-up scene in the early 1970s, he charted new territory, befuddling fans and club owners with his strange stunts and assortment of oddball identities. Sometimes he appeared as the cantankerous lounge singer Tony Clifton, who, after being driven from the stage by debris hurled by outraged audience members, would frequently reappear in riot gear to finish his act. At others, he was Foreign Man, a timid Central Asian immigrant whose stockpile of dreadful one-liners and mangled impressions ("Archie Bahnker: 'Me-meat-meathead, get out of chair.' Tank you veddy much") never failed to incur the heckles of dissatisfied patrons who believed Kaufman truly *was* a bumbling foreigner.

Occasionally, he'd reveal the con by capping his routine with a spot-on Elvis impersonation and an unmistakably American "Thanks, everybody, you've been great," leaving crowds to scratch their heads at what they'd witnessed. Just as often, his stage personas spilled over into real life. When Kaufman was hired for NBC's *Taxi* in 1978, he demanded—and received—a separate contract for Clifton to appear as a guest in several episodes. When the drunken, heavily made-up crooner arrived on set with a couple of hookers and was forcibly removed by studio security, Kaufman, who had been away on "vacation" at the time, expressed shock and disbelief.

"Whenever I play a role, whether it's good or bad," the comedian once said, "I believe in playing it straight to the hilt." And in 1979, Kaufman took on his most notorious role, as the self-proclaimed intergender wrestling champion of the world. Over the next three years, he would grapple with hundreds of women in nightclubs and on television, spewing misogynist insults and offering a thousand dollars to any female challenger who could defeat him.

"I believed in his talent. He's an artist, you know. And you make a little room for their eccentricity," says Shapiro. "But there were certain things that I warned him about, like wrestling women on television. It was great at the colleges . . . with everyone rooting against him. And

he played the bad guy wrestler, which was a dream of his. But I said, 'You know, Andy, it's not going to work on television.' I knew there'd be a backlash. And later on he admitted that it was a mistake."

By 1982, the act, which appeared to have become a personal obsession, was wearing thin, and many of those who were once eager to ride Kaufman's zany roller coaster of high jinks now found him tiresome. That year, he was dropped from his semi-regular spot on *Saturday Night Live* after an audience call-in vote, and he began assembling his mountainous piles of hate mail for publication as an antitribute book. "He played the ultimate bad guy," said friend and fellow comic Elayne Boosler of those years, "and he played it well, judging by the way people felt about him."

Was it a put-on? Like no other comedian, Kaufman blurred the divide between showmanship and real life. Whether he was treating his entire Carnegie Hall audience to milk and cookies following a 1979 concert, or working part-time as a delicatessen busboy at the height of his success, it was never quite clear where his eccentric performance art ended—if, in fact, it ever did—and his "authentic" existence began. In the end, it seemed fitting that even his untimely death from lung cancer at the age of thirty-five was interpreted by many as just one more in a series of elaborate hoaxes.

With Kaufman's 1984 passing, the world's women might have breathed a sigh of relief, but it would have been premature. In 1985 a new heavy stepped up to shamelessly vilify the fairer sex—not to mention homosexuals, starving Africans, Arabs, teetotalers, the disabled, the diseased, and anybody vaguely connected with organized religion. Frothing with apoplectic outrage and equipped with a scream that could shatter beer mugs, Sam Kinison seethed and bellowed beneath his trademark beret and trench coat, ripping the punctilious, cursing the politically correct, and gleefully mashing the sacrosanct into the ground.

"I think people get anger out of their system by seeing me—I give them a vicarious thrill," he said. "You can't ignore the anger." And neither could the various anti-defamation groups that regularly picketed his gigs, the critics who deemed him "reactionary, infantile, [and] pre-verbal," or his own record label, which took the unprecedented step of affixing disclaimers to his albums, distancing the company from his controversial views.

It wasn't difficult to understand the horrified reaction. Much of Kinison's material was fantastically raunchy, odious, and abusive. On marriage: "I don't worry about terrorism—I was married for two years!" and "I don't condone wife-beating, but I *understand* it!" On condoms: "Because a couple of fags fucked some monkeys in the jungle and bring us back the Black Plague of the fuckin' Eighties, they want us to wear fuckin' rubbers?!" On AIDS: "Heterosexuals die of it too? Name one!"

His supporters insisted that Kinison's crude, visceral rants, whether one agreed with them or not, offered a sort of cathartic release; that in the free rein he gave to his deep sense of betrayal and frustration with society and his life, audiences could recognize their own suppressed vitriol. While other comics might address similar themes from a cute, ironic, and therefore more acceptable distance, they argued, Kinison was the first one to let it all hang out.

"Sam Kinison was absolutely fearless," said comic Robin Williams. "Most people go to the edge and then stop. Not Sam. He'd see the edge and just keep on going. He couldn't stop saying the things that everyone else might think but was afraid to say."

Such reckless abandon was a far cry from the restrictive

atmosphere of his youth. Growing up the son of a Pentecostal minister in Peoria, Illinois, Kinison was expected to follow in his father's footsteps; and true to form, after a short spell in Bible college, the future wild man of comedy spent seven years preaching the Good Word as an itinerant evangelist before turning to stand-up in 1978, at the age of twenty-five. While working a club in Houston, he was spotted by Rodney Dangerfield, who gave Kinison his big break when he featured the comic on his 1985 HBO *Young Comedians* showcase.

Kinison's ministerial experience, and his ultimate disenchantment with the ecclesiastical establishment, was to have a profound effect on his comedy. Kinison's brother and manager, Bill, also a former preacher, recalls, "He'd only been doing comedy about six weeks. And this guy comes backstage at the club and he goes, 'Man, that's a tough crowd.' Another one comes back after he's performed and goes, 'Man, that's a rough crowd.' And so finally, Sam goes, 'You guys don't know what a rough crowd is. If all I have to do is go make these people laugh, that's nothing.' He said, 'Let me tell you what a tough crowd is. A tough crowd is going to a morning service and you got six people there and you gotta pay your house payment. That's a tough crowd.' And that's how Sam always looked at it."

While his style may have been rock 'n' roll trash, his manic energy was 100 percent evangelist, and throughout his career, he reserved a special place in his act for religious satire.

Many of those bits dealt with a hilariously humanized Jesus—one who, after being crucified and resurrected, must shuffle home and explain to his skeptical wife where the hell he'd been all weekend; whose miraculous birth caused his father untold misery ("You *better* be the son of God, lit-tle mister—and you better be the *only* son of God!"); and whose fish-and-loaves wonderworking was exploited by his dimwitted fellow carpenters ("Uh, Jesus, I forgot my lunch again. Can you make me a sandwich?"). Coupled with his high-decibel drubbing of the Bakkers, the Swaggerts, and the Robertses of the world, Kinison's religious jokes raised the hackles of many in the fundamentalist community, who saw him as an anti-Christian demagogue.

"He was a strong believer," insisted Bill Kinison. "His unhappiness was with religion and never with his commitment to God."

And it was precisely Kinison's unhappiness—be it with religion, women, safe sex, or gay necrophilia—that elevated his performances from vulgar slamfests to brutally honest, soul-baring experiences. Kinison didn't parse or edit his emotional anguish; he shared it with the crowd. "I guess they're tough jokes," he said of his more-offensive routines, "but there's lots of things you either laugh or cry at. And you just can't cry."

Kinison had mellowed considerably by the early 1990s in an effort to go mainstream, cutting down on his legendary drug and alcohol intake, and apologizing to gay groups for some of his earlier tirades. But his transformation came to an abrupt end in 1992, when the thirty-eight-year-old comic was killed by a drunk driver on a lonely stretch of California highway.

"Every generation has someone who steps outside the norm and offers a voice for the unspeakable attitudes of that time," Kinison once said. "I represent everything that was supposed to be wrong, everything that's forbidden."

It has been said that one generation's revolutionary is the next's conservative, and perhaps there's some truth to that in comedy. What couldn't be uttered in the 1950s was easier to get away with in the 1970s. By today's standards, many of those cultural bugaboos can seem rather quaint, and a visit to a comedy club or a quick glance at cable television—where drug comedies, hard-hitting political satire, and profanity-laced spoofs on sex and religion run opposite presidential speeches and televised masses—might seem to be definitive proof that the very success of yesterday's outlaws has made their struggles obsolete. But the spirit of rebellion and defiance they embodied lives on.

REBEL REINFORCEMENTS

IN OUR FRAGMENTED MULTIMEDIA UNIVERSE, where it seems all the rules have already been broken, it's hard to imagine comics becoming iconic rebels on the level of Lenny Bruce or George Carlin. But each generation finds its own ways to push the boundaries, and in recent decades Cheech and Chong, Bill Hicks, and Denis Leary have pushed hard, but with a touch deft enough to inspire the love 'em or hate 'em reactions of all great rebels.

As the 1970s drug culture's wacked-out answer to Abbott and Costello, the stand-up team of Richard "Cheech" Marin and Tommy Chong took reefer madness to a whole new level. Dope in school, dope in court, dope behind the wheel—anywhere the bong bubbled, the pair could be found unleashing comic mayhem and stymieing the forces of law and order.

To be fair, not all their routines reeked of pot fumes. Teaming up in 1969, the duo began fashioning the musical comedy and raunchy skits that remained part of their act for years. Bits like the canine-spoofing "Ralph and Herbie," in which the comedians scuttled around on all fours, sniffing each other's crotches and discussing the exigencies of lawn-defecation and car-chasing, earned them a reputation for outré humor and offbeat stage antics.

But it was their unapologetic forays into narco-comedy that made them outlaws—and later, film stars—cheered by dope freaks and free spirits, and reviled by conservatives, cops, and frantic parents everywhere. The pair's "Let's Make a Dope Deal," a kooky send-up of TV game shows, featured an LSD-addled contestant forced to choose between three doors—one hiding the grand prize (a brick of hashish), the other two concealing federal agents. Drug-taking schoolchildren were parodied in routines like "Sargent Stadanko," during which Catholic-school students gleefully begin informing on one another to a visiting police officer, initiating a stampede to the bathroom to discard the contraband.

But nothing epitomized Cheech and Chong's commitment to drug recreation better than the inane adventures of Pedro and

Man, a couple of harebrained dope-hounds whose sole occupation seemed to be low-riding, smoking torpedo-sized joints, and unintentionally outwitting the Keystone narcs who pursued them. With their idiotic banter and who's-on-first-style gags, Marin's frenetic East L.A. Chicano and Chong's bedraggled hippie quickly became the poster boys of potdom, celebrated as much for their endearing stupidity as for their pro-marijuana principles.

A typical routine found the two stalled on the side of the road, lost in a drug haze. As Pedro struggles beneath the hood, the spaced-out Man repeatedly misinterprets his requests for assistance. Ordered to turn the key in the ignition, Man honks the horn. Asked to release the brake, he shoots a stream of wiper fluid in his associate's eyes. Finally, a desperate Pedro suggests that they ask the police for help. "Hey! Hey!" Man bellows at a passing patrol car. "Can you pigs give us a push?"

As insidious as dope might have been—and the subject was a matter of heated debate as illegal drug use peaked in the 1970s—Cheech and Chong managed to sweeten the whole *Sturm und Drang* with a heaping spoonful of comic sugar.

Equally revered and reviled in his time was Bill Hicks, who died of pancreatic cancer at age thirty-two in 1994. The angry but philosophical Hicks ranked among the all-time great rebel comics, and an entire generation of musicians swore by his rock 'n' roll mentality—Radiohead dedicated an album to him, while other 1990s bands worked Hicks into their lyrics. Hicks loathed how big business had co-opted music: "Which is my favorite New Kid [on the Block]? *The first one that dies!*" but he would tackle any topic from his radical viewpoint.

He went after fundamentalists for clamping down on pornography by attacking the Supreme Court for reducing the definition of pornography to something that has "no artistic merit and causes sexual thought" by quipping, "Hmm, sounds like every commercial on television."

After President Bill Clinton hit Baghdad with missiles in response to an alleged assassination attempt on Former President George H. W. Bush, Hicks railed, "Six innocent people in Baghdad were dead and the U.S. had spent upward of sixty-six million dollars. What we should have done was get rid of Bush ourselves—and that way there would have been no loss of innocent life."

Hicks's jokes often had less obvious punch lines, like his declaration that the country was run by an elite group of industrial capitalists who controlled even the president. Whenever a new president is elected, Hicks explained, they'd take him into a smoky room and show him footage of the Kennedy assassination, "from a new angle—from the grassy knoll," then simply ask, "Any questions?"

So much of his material seemed rebellious that his twelfth (and final) performance on Letterman's show was completely deleted by censors for jokes like "These pro-lifers—you ever look at their faces? [he twists his face and speaks in a bitter, pinched voice], 'I'm pro-life'—boy, they look it, don't they?" and "I'm quitting

stand-up because I finally got my own TV show. It's called 'Let's Hunt and Kill Billy Ray Cyrus'" and "Why do Christians wear crosses around their necks? You think when Jesus comes back, he's ever gonna wanna see a cross?"

But many of Hicks's seemingly extremist takes on religion sound, a decade later, merely prescient, now copied by other more mainstream comics. After the government destroyed the Branch Davidian compound at Waco, he asked: "If child molestation is actually your concern, how come we don't see Bradley tanks knocking down Catholic churches?"

Like Hicks, Denis Leary launched himself into a full-fledged attack on just about every politically correct stance imaginable. (There was a semi-rivalry there. Leary credited Hicks as an influence, but Hicks dissed Leary as Donovan to his Dylan.)

His grunge-rock song "I'm an Asshole" mocks suburban Americans who "like football and porno and books about war," tucked cozily inside their "average house with a nice hardwood floor." He links conspicuous consumption from the suburbs to the inner city as a distinctly American problem, but he does it in a startling way that makes people laugh while driving home the point: "Only in America would a guy invent crack. Only in America would there be a guy that cocaine wasn't good enough for—one guy walking around New York City back in 1985 going, "You know, that cocaine's pretty good, but I want something that makes my heart explode as soon as I smoke it, okay? That's the problem in this country. People are never satisfied with stuff the way it is."

A furious smoker, the perpetually manic Leary also makes a half-serious, half-mocking defense of cigarettes. "Know what I'm gonna do? I'm gonna get one of those tracheotomies, so I can smoke two cigarettes at the same time. I'm gonna get nine tracheotomies all the way around my neck. He can smoke a pack at a time! He's Tracheotomy Man!"

He also taunts those pushing for bigger cigarette warnings. "You could have cigarettes that come in a black package with a skull and crossbones on the front, called "Tumors," and smokers would be lined up around the block. They're a drug, we're addicted, okay!?"

Like Hicks, Leary goes after religion and pop-culture icons with a twisted glint in his eye. "Somebody should've walked up behind Elvis in '57 with a .44 magnum, put the barrel of the gun right up to his brain stem, and just pulled the trigger—so you can remember Elvis in a nice way. You know how you remember Elvis. He was found in the toilet with his pants around his ankles and his big fat hairy sweaty king of rock 'n' roll ass exposed to the world! Creepy!"

And, like Hicks, Leary was years ahead of the media in taking on the Catholic church over its handling of abusive priests, saying he's starting his own church where "if you so much as look at an altar boy the wrong way you don't get transferred to some distant parish in Nova Scotia, you stand naked in the middle of Times Square with a big neon sign that says 'I carry a torch for kids who carry candles.'"

CHAPTER 11

SASS, BRASS, AND CLASS: THE WOMEN OF COMEDY

• • •

The thing women have got to learn is that nobody gives you power.
You just take it.

—Roseanne Barr

In the 1950s, comedienne Jean Carroll laid out the recipe for success in the male-dominated arena of stand-up comedy. "In addition to good material," she wrote, "[the female comic] has to knock down the wall of resistance built up in the minds of men that women aren't funny; and more important, that women shouldn't be funny." She might have added that they also needed *cojones*—big ones.

Not that bold, brassy woman were in short supply at the time. Throughout the decade, burlesque-inspired saucy ladies like Belle Barth and Pearl Williams worked the blue lounges and after-hours clubs with a ribaldry that matched Redd Foxx, and their bawdy "party" records sold by the truckload. On television, Lucille Ball was crowned as comedy's queen. But away from sitcoms and stand-up's red-light district, success was harder to come by. Mainstream audiences, unaccustomed to lone female performers who didn't warble or cha-cha, habitually turned a deaf ear to anyone in heels—besides Milton Berle.

It fell to stalwarts like Carroll and Phyllis Diller to drag them kicking and screaming—and, by turns, shaking with laughter—into the modern age. But blazing a trail isn't easy. "A lot of people give up because they can't stand the total rejection," Diller once said of her female colleagues. "If you can take that, then you can make it."

For Diller, comedy was as much a financial imperative as it was a passion. With five children and a chronically unemployed spouse to support, the thirty-seven-year-old housewife figured to parlay the quick wit she had honed as a part-time advertising copywriter into a few extra bucks on the nightclub stage. "We ran out of money, and somebody had to go to work," she recalled matter-of-factly. "So I went to work."

Armed with a bevy of machine-gun one-liners and a freakish wardrobe that blended Big Bird with *haute couture*, Diller debuted at San Francisco's Purple Onion in 1955 (an engagement that would eventually run for two years) and proved to audiences what her husband and co-workers

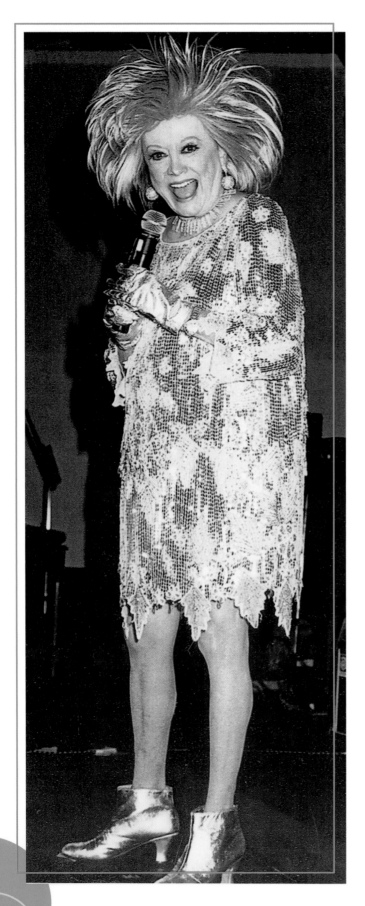

had been telling her all along—that she could be just as funny, if not funnier, than her male counterparts.

In a profession where women were still a peculiarity, patrons might have expected a female joker to step lightly, but not Diller. She bulldozed through routines, appearing in fright wigs and garish makeup, delivering lines with rat-tat-tat fury, and punctuating each quip with a wicked cackle. She took obvious delight in slamming her doltish husband, "Fang" ("Fang's idea of a seven-course meal is a six-pack and a baloney sandwich"; "Fang is so lazy he called into work *dead* today") and in lamenting the plight of the harried housewife, but the primary target of her caustic cracks was herself. "I've turned many a head in my day—and a few stomachs," she joked. "I went to this plastic surgeon. He took one look at me and wanted to add a tail. He said my face looked like a bouquet of elbows. My foot doctor sent me to a blacksmith."

In 1960, after several lean years on the road during which she was buoyed by the encouragement of her idol, Bob Hope, Diller landed on *The Jack Paar Show*, followed by an appearance on *The Ed Sullivan Show*, and her career took off. The *New Yorker* dubbed her "the thinking man's chatterbox," and she was frequently introduced as "the first lady of laughter." Suddenly she was everywhere—in films, on television sitcoms, touring with Hope for the USO, performing piano recitals of Bach and Beethoven (she had been trained as a classical pianist), and recording albums of well-known pop tunes.

But the ubiquitous Diller always returned to stand-up, packing houses from New York to Vegas and constantly tightening her delivery to the point that she merited a mention in *The Guinness Book of World Records* as the only comic to bang out twelve punch lines in a minute. "My timing is so precise," she once said, "a heckler would have to make an appointment just to get a word in."

The bankroll Diller earned in the 1960s and early 1970s allowed her to indulge more conspicuously in one of her favorite pastimes—plastic surgery—and the subject of her supposed anatomical deficiencies remained the taproot of her act for years. "I went to the beauty salon the other day," she told audiences. "I was there for five hours—and that was just for the estimate!" But as the women's movement gathered steam in the mid-1970s, she was publicly criticized by feminists who felt that her act disparaged women.

"Some of those women got after me because they didn't want me to say self-deprecating things," Diller once said.

But she shrugged off the objections as facile misinterpretations by those who couldn't discern humor from real life. "That's all comedy is—bitching," she remarked. "But there's a way to bitch, and it's called mock hostility. If it's real, it isn't funny."

By the time Diller retired from the stage at the age of eighty-three, she had gone from penurious homemaker to international comedy icon, and, despite changing tastes and the occasional flak over her material, her drawing power had hardly wavered. "I'm a natural," she said of her nearly five decades of success. "I was born to do it."

If anybody *wasn't* born to do it, it was Joan Molinsky. The second daughter of a wealthy physician from New York, she had graduated Phi Beta Kappa from Barnard College in 1954 and was biding her time as a secretary while awaiting her big break as a dramatic actress.

"And someone told me, instead of typing your heart out, you can make six dollars a night in a club performing as a comedian," she recalled. "I thought, I can do that. I did it as a means to an end."

To the horror of her well-heeled family, that end never came, and their princess ended up humping through a succession of sleazy strip-club gigs as the perkily named comic Pepper January before upgrading to Greenwich Village cabarets, where she would make her mark in the early 1960s, after another name change—to Joan Rivers.

"There were very few women in those days," Rivers said. "When a woman walked out on stage, it was like 'Why?'" Starting out, she stuck closely to Diller's tried-and-true format, carping in one-liners about being the black sheep ("My parents said, 'Why can't you be like the girl next door?' We lived next to a cemetery") and the ugly duckling ("A robber broke into my house and said, 'One bark and you're dead!'"). But unlike Diller, whose outrageous costumes and stage persona marked her as a wacky caricature, Rivers preferred a stylish, understated approach. "I wanted to be pretty on stage," she said. "I broke that barrier."

"Joan is not grotesque," a *Newsweek* critic commented at the time. "She is chic, blonde, and pretty, hip, intellectual, and restrained." That restraint, however, did not always carry over to her material. While she was frequently compared to Woody Allen for her neurotic spiels about personal inadequacies, her hero was Lenny Bruce, and like Bruce she eventually developed a strain of off-color, let-it-fly humor that sometimes got her into trouble with the guardians of taste.

When she appeared on *The Jack Paar Show* in 1964, her routine, which featured a quip about Italian women possessing an inordinate amount of facial hair, met with a bitter rebuke from the host. "I hope you realize a lot of Italians watch our show," the dour Paar told Rivers on air before sending her packing.

Bowed but unbroken, the thirty-one-year-old comic returned to the nightclub circuit, where she continued to infuse her self-deprecating act with risqué comments on adultery, pregnancy, and her gynecologist. In 1965, Johnny Carson gave Rivers a second shot, and her energetic performance on *The Tonight Show*—a program on which she would appear dozens of times and guest host for two months in 1983—validated her ticket to stardom. "In that instant," she recalled in her autobiography, "I put my

dreams of legitimate acting on the shelf and became the hot girl in town."

Over the ensuing years, Rivers would supplement her monologues with barbed bits about marriage and motherhood, telling audiences, "I'm a double-bagger. Not only does my husband put a bag over my face when we make love—he puts one on his own in case mine falls off." "Having my daughter, I screamed for twenty-three hours straight," she claimed. "And that was just during conception."

But she became best known for her hoarse signature line, "Can we talk?" and her merciless skewering of celebrities. "Elizabeth Taylor is so fat, when she pierces her ears gravy comes out," she zinged at one of her favorite targets. "Willie Nelson is so dirty he wears a Roach Motel around his neck."

Rivers's pit-bull attacks on the rich and famous—and her ability to continue laughing at herself amid the carnage ("My body is falling so fast my gynecologist wears a hard hat")—garnered the comedienne a loyal following that supported her through even the toughest times, including her acrimonious public spat with Carson in 1986, the cancellation of her talk show in 1987, and the suicide of her husband that same year. "My audiences are my group therapy," Rivers confessed.

Therapeutics aside, some weren't so enamored of her bullying approach. "When she started doing Elizabeth Taylor fat jokes, that upset me," comic Roseanne Barr told an interviewer in 1987. "I do not like fat jokes by skinny people." She then added, "What I would say to Joan is, 'Yeah, I eat the same as you. I just don't puke when I'm through.'"

Barr had never had a problem being blunt. The chunky mother of three and former cocktail waitress had taken the stand-up world by storm in the mid-1980s with her trenchant observations on husbands and housework, and by decade's end she had earned a place alongside Ralph Cramden and Archie Bunker as one of comedy's premier blue-collar loudmouths.

"I do offensive things," she boasted. "Like I belch at the audience and swear and fart and stuff. That's who I am. That's my act." In truth, burps and flatulence played a rather limited role, but her act was no less controversial for its insistence that disgruntled housewives—particularly those who were overweight, indolent, and obnoxious—had nothing to be ashamed of. "I'm the real American woman," Barr declared. "I schlep through my housework, I yell at my kids, and I ignore my husband. That is a real woman."

On stage, the self-proclaimed "domestic goddess" chomped gum, whined adenoidally, and regaled audiences with vignettes from her unedifying trailer-park existence: "My husband comes home and says, 'Roseanne, don't you think we should talk about our sexual problems?' Yeah, like I'm going to turn off *Wheel of Fortune* for that! Then he says, 'Well, do you think maybe you'll wash a dish this week?' 'Get real,' I said. 'What's the matter—is Lemon Joy like kryptonite to your species?'"

Turning the tables on men was a skill Barr had polished to perfection. It began in 1981 when, during a visit to a Denver comedy club, the twenty-eight-year-old working mom hopped on stage to deliver an impromptu rebuttal to the chauvinist male comics she had seen. "I thought it was about time there was a woman up there that says the other side," Barr recalled.

Her guerrilla-style tongue-lashing didn't bring the house down, but it did convince Barr that stand-up was in dire need of a hard-hitting feminist transfusion. If her female predecessors had mocked their own supposed shortcomings as women, Roseanne would revel in them. "I will clean house when Sears comes out with a riding vacuum cleaner," she snarled. "If the kids are still alive when my husband comes home, I've done my job." And in a profession where a woman's appearance often became the springboard for self-disparaging humor, Barr was unapologetic about her girth. "You're looking at one happy fat bitch," she announced.

By 1983, Barr had won the Denver Laff-Off competition and was chewing up comedy clubs in Los Angeles with her trash-talking, stereotype-slamming routines. An impressed Johnny Carson (who predicted that Barr would be "the biggest woman comic ever") booked her twice for *The Tonight Show* in 1985, and after a 1987 HBO special, Barr landed a network sitcom—*Roseanne*—which featured her as the ballsy, opinionated matriarch of a working-class family much like her own.

The critical and commercial success Barr enjoyed with *Roseanne*, however, did nothing to blunt her sharper edges, and while she played very few stand-up dates, she managed to bring her outrageous and provocative humor to the public in other ways. Her now famous *pièce de résistance* of performance art—a caterwauling, crotch-grabbing rendition of the National Anthem at a 1990 San Diego Padres game that prompted cries of "disgusting" and "disgraceful" from the White House—overshadowed her more mundane mooning episodes, sham three-way marriages, and butt-tattooing, but they all contributed to Barr's growing legacy as a wild woman who couldn't be hemmed in by convention or traditional ideas of femininity.

As Barr's sitcom wound toward its finale in 1997, another female comic-turned-television-star was grabbing headlines with her own scandal of sorts. "Yep, I'm Gay," trumpeted the April 14 *Time* magazine headline, just above a smiling Ellen DeGeneres. The announcement—and the news that DeGeneres's character on her sitcom *Ellen* would also come out in an upcoming episode—capped months of speculation in the media and among her fans about the private life of the thirty-nine-year-old performer.

For a comedienne as unpretentious and demure as DeGeneres, the resulting brouhaha—the cheers and denunciations, the network advertising controversies, the gallons of tabloid ink spilled, and ultimately the dumping of her show from ABC's lineup—all seemed a bit too much. "Let's get beyond this," she implored the public at the time, "and let me get back to what I do."

What she did was get back to her roots in stand-up, and over the next half-decade DeGeneres would reacquaint audiences with her homespun brand of quirky observational humor. Whether parodying the 800 advice-line on the back of a shampoo bottle ("Um, I'm gonna stop you there. Did you wet your hair first? Sure, you're welcome"), discussing why people videotape their lovemaking ("There is one of two reasons people videotape their sex. They're either thinking 'We are hot!' or they're looking at it like football players trying to improve for the next time—'Where'd you come up with that technique, did you make that up? I thought so. Don't do it'"), or visiting God's house (where a snapshot shows Jesus in a top that reads 'My Parents Created the Universe and All I Got Was This Lousy T-Shirt'), DeGeneres's new material displayed the same winsome style and unwavering eye for offbeat details that had made her a stand-up star more than fifteen years earlier.

While in her early twenties, the New Orleans native had been casting about for direction, trying her hand at oystershucking, house painting, bartending, and selling vacuum cleaners before giving comedy a chance. The choice proved to be an auspicious one, and in 1982, just a year after her first open-mic appearance, she was selected by the Showtime network as the Funniest Person in America following a nationwide talent search.

In her routines, DeGeneres psychoanalyzed supermarket customers based on their purchase items, questioned how water gets *on top* of toilet seats, called God and got put on hold. Her roundabout storytelling and flustered, halting delivery drew comparisons to Bob Newhart and Woody Allen and endeared her to audiences who saw the rosy-cheeked, towheaded comic as the natural heir to those celebrated surveyors of life's amusing oddities.

But with her early success came a backlash from other comics who felt DeGeneres's Showtime honor was undeserved and that the rookie comedian was getting an easy ride. During one appearance, a belligerent club emcee incited the mostly male crowd to turn their backs during her performance. When the demoralized DeGeneres left the stage mid-routine, he jumped to the mic and shouted, "Let's hear it one more time for the Funniest Person in America!" "I was crying," she recalled. "I wanted to go home and get out of the business."

But her perseverance paid off when in 1986 she was asked to deliver a monologue on *The Tonight Show* and became the only female comic to be invited to sit and chat with Johnny Carson after her first performance. Carson's approval, and the public's newfound appreciation for DeGeneres's idiosyncratic humor, led to a series of small roles in television and films in the late 1980s and early 1990s, culminating in the 1994 sitcom that would make Ellen a household name—and a rather reluctant gay icon.

It is perhaps ironic that as one of the few women in stand-up whose act featured almost no overt references to sexuality or gender issues, DeGeneres's sexual orientation came to occupy center stage in her career. "My comedy got lost and my sexuality overshadowed it," she remarked several years after her coming-out. But if her recent resurgence—and a new daytime talk show—is any indication, her comedy has triumphed, and she has come to be seen much less as a "lesbian comedian" than as a talented female performer who happens to be gay.

DeGeneres might never have achieved that level of acceptance, however, had it not been for her predecessors—

comics like Diller and Rivers, who first opened the door; and Barr, who ripped it off its hinges—asserting that the house of humor wasn't meant to be a stodgy old-boys' club.

Comedy has long been considered a bellwether of social and cultural change, the shifts and innovations behind the mic heralding—and at times creating—transformations in society at large. And for women, that role has had a double significance; not only have female comics over the years created brilliant material that both reflected their times and pointed the way to new attitudes, but their very presence on stage (from an odd handful in the 1950s to a flourishing worldwide sorority today), and their dogged determination to stay there, changed the terrain of stand-up itself. It is no longer just a man's game.

CHAPTER 12

VERY STRANGE BEDFELLOWS

Will Rogers, like his contemporary, Franklin Delano Roosevelt, was a larger-than-life figure. In fact, the twentieth century's first great political humorist was in many ways even more beloved than the first modern president. Rogers had a knack for the one-liner that may have seemed timely but that has since proved timeless—a rare feat in political humor. Since then, politics and comedy have successfully mixed only sporadically in the stand-up world. But in recent years, as politics and entertainment have become increasingly entwined, political humor has again risen to prominence, with politically minded stand-ups like Dennis Miller, Bill Maher, and Jon Stewart taking Will Rogers's mantle and bringing to the masses via television.

Rogers was an unlikely candidate to become America's political wit, the twentieth-century heir to a tradition tracing back through Mark Twain and Ben Franklin. He was born in 1879 in Indian territory to parents who were part Cherokee, dropped out of school in tenth grade, and became a cowboy. He landed in *The Guinness Book of World Records* for throwing three lassos, simultaneously looping a horse's neck, its four legs, and the rider. He added jokes to his cowboy tricks and toured the vaudeville circuit, which led to the Ziegfeld Follies. In 1915, he decided the constant repetition of performing in the follies was mak-

ing his jokes feel stale, so his wife, Betty suggested he look to the newspapers to develop topical humor. That proved to be sage advice, for the news of the day provided constant fodder. As Rogers later wrote, "Most people and actors appearing on the stage have some writer write their material. I don't do that—Congress is good enough for me. They have been writing my material for years."

Rogers's popularity soared as he came to be thought of as the common-sense common man commenting on the foibles of those in power. Although he only occasionally commented on the plight of Native Americans, his Cherokee heritage gave him keen insight into life on the bottom of the pile, and no matter how successful he

became, he forever remained the voice of the underdog and the powerless.

He went on to appear on Broadway and in seventy-one movies while writing four thousand syndicated columns and six books; he also became a renowned radio commentator. He crisscrossed the nation, pouring out nuggets—some plain funny, some more wry and astute. Many from the latter category seem to weather the test of time particularly well:

"If you ever injected truth into politics you'd have no politics."

"If we ever pass out as a great nation, we ought to put on our tombstone 'America died from a delusion that she has moral leadership.'"

"Diplomacy is the art of saying 'Nice doggie' until you can find a rock."

But Rogers prized the laugh as much as if not more than the lesson, as his commentary on the invention of Presidents' Day reveals. He points out that there are weeks in honor of everything—"Apple Week, Smile Week, Don't Murder Your Wife Week"—and someone realized that "if prunes are worth a week then a president ought to be worth something. They couldn't give them a week, but they could give a day."

While his folksy, rambling delivery and gentle humor often lacked the attacking needles of modern political humor, much of his material seems positively modern: "I belong to no organized party. I am a Democrat." Some even seem downright edgy by contemporary standards: "There ought to be one day—just one—when there is open season on senators" and "My jokes don't hurt anybody—you can take 'em or leave 'em —but with Congress, every time they make a joke it's a law."

After Rogers's tragic death in a plane accident, there was a void at the top until Bob Hope came along. Like

Rogers, Hope was more movie star than a stand-up comedian. (He even had his stable of writers pen witticisms for him to break out at private dinner parties.) Still, Hope was an unstoppable force—America's most honored entertainer (though he was born in England) was, like Rogers, filled with eminently quotable, bipartisan pokes at politicians of all stripes. Hope's urbane persona and Hollywood glamour, along with his laudable devotion to performing for the troops decade after decade and his never-ending run of specials on NBC, gave him a sense of permanence on the American comedy landscape. Hope's monologues were peppered with clever ribbing dished out evenhandedly to whoever was in power.

When Senator Joseph McCarthy was threatening to expose Communists from every corner of the nation, Hope quipped: "I have it on good authority that [Senator Joseph] McCarthy is going to disclose the names of two million Communists. He has just got his hands on the Moscow telephone directory."

"Eisenhower admitted that the budget can't be bal-
anced, and McCarthy said the Communists are taking over. You don't know what to worry about these days—whether the country will be overthrown or overdrawn."

But most of his political humor played it safe and light. When the youthful John Kennedy was running for office, Hope joked: "A few months ago Kennedy's mother said, 'You have a choice. Do you want to go to camp this year or run for president?'"

While he continually made light of Kennedy's age, when it came to Nixon he also took aim at the political practices of self-mythologizing and reinvention: "Nixon lives here in Whittier, California. They're so sure he's going to be president they're building the log cabin he was born in."

But Hope, with his pro-Vietnam stance, was also a golfing buddy of the presidents and was too firmly entrenched in the establishment to be too strong a political comedy voice. Yet even before Vietnam, a new voice arrived, an independent thinker, ready to wield his jokes like weapons. Mort Sahl was a groundbreaker, a man who helped shape the culture. He was willing to probe for the

"A conservative is someone who believes in reform. But not now."

"Two hundred years ago we had Jefferson, Washington, Ben Franklin, and Tom Paine, and there were four million people. Today we have 220 million, and look at our leaders—Darwin was wrong."

But Sahl, who was called "Will Rogers with fangs," was much more scathing than Rogers. He ruthlessly mocked political heavies like Joseph McCarthy and the House Un-American Activities Committee Communist witch-hunts with lines like "Joe McCarthy doesn't question what you

truth, to tilt at windmills, and the fact that he studied politics beyond the front-page headlines gave his humor a savvy edge that others lacked.

Sahl wanted to avoid the vaudevillian "wife and mother-in-law" jokes, and he found his comic identity as a guy with a sweater, a newspaper in his hand, and a head brimming with ideas. In the 1950s, before comedy clubs, Sahl broke onto the scene in the San Francisco nightclub "Hungry i" and made his name opening for Count Basie and others, before recording the first-ever stand-up comedy record. By 1960, Sahl was lauded on the cover of *Time* magazine as the leader of a new generation of comics, influencing and liberating the likes of Lenny Bruce, Woody Allen, and Dick Gregory.

"Will Rogers used to come out with a newspaper and pretend he was a yokel criticizing the intellectuals who ran the government. I come out with a newspaper and pretend I'm an intellectual making fun of the yokels running the government," Sahl said by way of introduction. His rapid-fire monologues earned him the nickname "Rebel Without a Pause."

Some of Sahl's humor can trace its lineage directly to Rogers:

say so much as your right to say it" and "HUAC's enacting a new policy. From now on, every time the Russians throw an American in jail, we throw an American in jail."

After the U-2 spy plane was shot down and President Eisenhower publicly fretted that there were Soviet spies in America, Sahl sniped, "If we get lucky they'll steal some of our secrets and then they'll be two years behind." But although Sahl was a liberal, he went after everyone: "Liberals feel unworthy of their possessions. Conservatives feel they deserve everything they've stolen."

He even mocked hard-core affirmative-action efforts with his quip "I went to my dressing room between shows and an attorney for the NAACP was waiting for me. He wanted to know why I don't have any Negroes in my act."

This tendency earned the wrath of Joe Kennedy. He had invited Sahl to write jokes for his son during the 1960 presidential campaign, which Sahl did, but after John Kennedy became president he too became a target for Sahl's wit. But, allegedly under Joe Kennedy's direction, Ed Sullivan refused to let Sahl do Kennedy bits on his show, and Sahl's bookings fell off; after Kennedy's assassination, Sahl became obsessed with conspiracy theories and refused to let go even as the public moved on and his popularity plummeted.

Still, the cynicism aroused by the Vietnam War led people to again pay heed to this witty truth-teller. Although he never again wielded national influence, his sword remained sharp. During Watergate he enunciated Nixon's credo as "If two wrongs don't make a right, try three," and during the Iran-Contra scandal he opined, "George Washington couldn't tell a lie, Richard Nixon couldn't tell the truth, and Ronald Reagan couldn't tell the difference." But he kept applying his old standards to both sides, accusing the left of selling out too: "The country today is 50 percent Republican and 50 percent left-wing Republican—buying a ticket to hear Barbra Streisand sing doesn't make you a liberal."

In recent years, the best and brightest of political stand-ups have found their way to gigs on late-night television, where their shows have gone far beyond Leno and Letterman in terms of comic commentary. Political humorists like Dennis Miller, Bill Maher, and Jon Stewart have satirized the powerful and pushed the boundaries as hard as Sahl, but because this humor now has real currency in our bitterly partisan but entertainment-crazed country, they reach a far wider audience than Sahl ever did.

First came Miller, who translated a successful stand-up persona into gigs on *Saturday Night Live*'s "Weekend Update," HBO, *Monday Night Football,* and then the cable news network CNBC. Miller blended his politics with a love of obscure cultural references: "We need anything politically important rationed out like Pez: small, sweet, and coming out of a funny, plastic head."

Miller originally targeted both sides. He pointed out that Walter Mondale was such a loser "he made McGovern look like William the Conqueror. He spent forty million dollars, . . . and I almost tied him," but then fretted that the winner, President Ronald Reagan, was seventy-seven years old "and he has access to the button. You know, my grandfather is seventy-seven and we won't even let him use the remote. There's no more frightening image in the world than the finger having access to the button having a string tied around it."

But it wasn't all easy jibes—often Miller dove straight to the heart of the policy debates with his stinging remarks. A joke about the first President Bush was really an attack on any hypocrite who proclaimed the sanctity of life only when it suited their needs: "Now let me get this straight—Bush is anti-abortion, but pro–death penalty. I guess it's all in the timing, huh?"

And Miller pointed up the absurdity of whining about the Brady Bill and the five-day waiting period to purchase a handgun. "What's the big deal about a five-day waiting period? You have to get on a waiting list to buy *Aladdin* at Blockbuster Video."

Miller's "rants" began espousing increasingly hard-edged, get-off-my-back libertarian politics—"If somebody wants to shoot up and die in front of you, more power to them. The herd has a way of thinning itself out."

Finding the right balance is always tricky, as Bill Maher learned after 9/11. The stand-up was host of the cable-then-network television series *Politically Incorrect*, in which he'd bat around hot topics with an eclectic collection of guests—one night might feature gay playwright Harvey Fierstein and Watergate conspirator G. Gordon Liddy, the next might have *Jeopardy*'s Alex Trebek and Guns N' Roses guitarist Slash. Even while doing the show, Maher drew fire for politically incorrect jokes made during stand-up gigs, like the time he told a crowd of Washington politicos that D.C.'s drug-troubled mayor Marion Barry "had promised to get drugs off the street, one gram at a time," that Senator Phil Gramm's campaign slogan was "Gramm: For people who think Dole isn't mean enough," and that Gramm "was so tough on immigration he was going to deport his wife." (Gramm's wife is Asian-American, and Maher was not slurring her but slamming the politician's support of anti-immigration laws like Proposition 187.)

The prickly Maher went too far in the minds of government officials and advertising executives after 9/11 when he said the suicide bombers were not cowards compared with American bomber pilots who kill from a safe distance. Following a firestorm of criticism and even threatening statements from the White House that people "need to watch what they do," Maher apologized for the

wording, but ABC, in large part because of advertiser reaction, canceled his show anyway.

Still, Maher was not silenced, returning to stand-up with his show "Victory Begins at Home." But while he went after the Bush administration, he made it clear that he held everyone responsible: "I think people hate us around the world because they perceive that we waste when we could share. And they're not totally wrong about that. We have a holiday where we stuff food into other food. I mean—Thanksgiving is really typical of how we think about third-world indigenous people. We celebrate the one nice moment we ever had with the Indians. It'd be like a date rapist saying, 'Let's concentrate on the nice dinner we had early in the evening.'"

Maher simultaneously attacked President Bush's handling of the post-9/11 situation and the American public's blind willingness to go along with it: "Ladies and gentlemen, on September 11, 2001, America was attacked by a squad of Saudi Arabians, working out of Germany, Pakistan, and Afghanistan. And by that I mean, we were attacked by Iraq." Maher then did a double-take, punctuating his statement before adding, "Yes, the true axis of evil in America is the genius of our marketing combined with the stupidity of our people."

Also in the decendancy of Will Rogers and Mort Sahl is Jon Stewart, a stand-up comic who earned a cult following on several short-lived talk shows before becoming a political comedy superstar as host of the faux newscast *The Daily Show*. Less acerbic than Miller and Maher, Stewart satirizes politicians of every stripe, and the media, with unerring accuracy. But he became a media darling and political force because he did it all—much like Rogers—with a mischievous twinkle in his eye.

Even before taking over *The Daily Show*, Jon Stewart had a penchant for astute comments on the foibles of politicians and the excesses of the press, along with a knack for remaining self-deprecating and absurdist. At the height of the Monica Lewinsky scandal, he wrapped all that up in one quip: "I know more about Bill Clinton's penis now than I do my own, which says something about the media or just something really sad about me."

After taking over *The Daily Show* from Craig Kilborn, whose smug, frat-boy approach minimized savvy political humor, Stewart shifted its direction. The show took flight with its "Indecision 2000" coverage—which featured not only Stewart and his team of correspondents headed by the brilliant Stephen Colbert, but also regular guest commentators, like former presidential candidate Senator Bob Dole.

Within a few short years, Stewart was being heralded on the cover of just about every magazine as the funniest political commentator in America. The show has been cited as a source of news for many college students and twenty-somethings and as must-see TV for Washington's chattering classes—former Senator Bob Kerrey, who took time off from the 9/11 commission to appear as a guest, confessed to TiVo-ing the show, while Senator John Edwards announced his candidacy on the program. The show keeps its humor fresh by mixing it up, veering from clever wordplay to over-the-top silliness, from deadpan delivery to true outrage, from satirizing the Republicans to poking fun at the Democrats. And every step of the way, it takes on the folks in the real media and the American citizens who buy into the pack mentality pushed by the government and much of the press.

Stewart often plays directly off news clips to highlight deceit and hypocrisy. On a day when insurgents were fiercely attacking American troops, President George W. Bush declared with willful obliviousness, "I think we're welcomed in Iraq," to which Stewart added slyly, "Apparently the rocket-propelled grenade is the Iraqi equivalent of 'aloha.'" (Mocking the news networks love of dramatically named stories, the show calls the Iraq conflict "Mess-o-potamia.")

While Stewart leans to the left, he tolerates foolish behavior from no one. So when Democratic presidential nominee John Kerry attacked the phoniness of President Bush's now infamous "Mission Accomplished" flight-suit politically orchestrated photo-op, Stewart ripped Kerry back by offering subtext for that speech during which the wealthy Bostonian tried appearing genuine and down-to-earth: "As I stand here in my borrowed work jacket in front of a sign saying 'The Real Deal'. . . "

But sometimes wry remarks don't do the trick, and Stewart is ready to show genuine outrage when the situation warrants—especially if it will help nail the joke. After White House correspondents began pressing the president hard on his National Guard record from the 1970s, an incredulous Stewart let loose, fuming, "I have just one question for you guys. Where the *#$& have you been? All of a sudden you've got questions—and it's about his Vietnam service. Guys, you're like eight wars behind."

Stewart also provides a big-picture perspective missing from most news shows and newspapers. After the 2004 New Hampshire primary, Stewart asked Colbert about the attitude of Democrats. "Well, Jon, I'd say that they have an attitude of anger," Colbert pontificated. When Stewart asked whether the anger was directed at the president, Colbert's deadpan remark highlighted the problem with America's media and electoral process. "No, Jon, toward me. Me and the other reporters."

Perhaps no bit sums up the show's inventive look at the issues of the day as well as a "debate" that Stewart moderated between President George W. Bush and Governor George W. Bush. Stewart spliced together the clips brilliantly to use the president's words as a candidate in 2000 to demonstrate just how disingenuous Bush had been as a candidate and in the rush to war in Iraq.

> PRESIDENT BUSH: *We must stand up for our security, and for the permanent rights and hopes of mankind. The United States of America will make that stand.*
>
> STEWART: *Governor, do you agree with that?*
>
> GOVERNOR BUSH: *I'm not so sure the role of the United States is to go around the world saying "This is the way it's gotta be."*
>
> STEWART: *Let me just get specific, Mr. President, why are we in Iraq?*
>
> PRESIDENT BUSH: *We will be—um—changing the regime of Iraq, for the good of the Iraqi people.*
>
> STEWART: *Governor, then I'd like to hear your response on that.*

> GOVERNOR BUSH: *If we're an arrogant nation, they'll resent us. I think one way for us to be viewed as the Ugly American is for us to go around the world saying, "We do it this way, so should you."*

At the end, Stewart wonders aloud where he could store this historic debate when suddenly Al Gore's image appears on the screen, decreeing, "I think it should stay in a lockbox—lockbox, lockbox, lockbox."

Finishing with a bipartisan poke, a jab at the man who could have been president, is a fitting reminder that no one has all the answers even if they think they do. It's that kind of touch that makes Stewart a true descendant of Rogers, Hope, and Sahl and keeps political humor center stage on the comedy landscape in the twenty-first century.

LIFE UNDER A MICROSCOPE: THE OBSERVERS

Observational comics are a highly inquisitive group who find fodder for comedy in life's nooks and crannies, digest it, then regurgitate it—making the mundane magnificent and the everyday extraordinary. Through them we see such ordinary events as a missing sock, a visit to the dentist, a fishing trip, or the misery of a blind date with fresh eyes—and big laughs.

The roots of observational comedy lie in the late-1950s, in a group of comedians who left "mother-in-law" and "she's so fat" jokes behind. They developed material that was topical, literate, and grounded in real events. In the forefront of this evolution were envelope-pushing performers like Lenny Bruce, Mort Sahl, Mike Nichols and Elaine May, and Shelley Berman, who spawned a generation of comics free to be themselves on stage, observing the world around them through their own personal filter.

But the seeds of that shift were sown when comedian Jonathan Winters hit the nightclub scene with the force of a comic hurricane. The former disc jockey could blow away a room with his sound-effects, impressions, rapid-fire transformations into and out of characters, and his mastery of improvisation. For anyone under the age of forty, the easiest way to explain Winters is to say that he was Robin Williams before Robin Williams was Robin Williams.

The son of an alcoholic banker and a mother busy with her own radio program, as a boy Winters was forced to entertain himself. "I didn't understand them," he said of his parents, "so consequently it was a strange kind of arrangement. They didn't understand me. And I'd be in my room. Being an only child, I'd talk to myself, interview myself. I would be a general, I would be a war hero or something—whatever I wanted to be."

Those childhood impersonations would figure prominently in his comic future. Winters began his stand-up career relying heavily on celebrity impressions—Boris Karloff, James Cagney, John Wayne, Bing Crosby—but soon turned to more observational humor. "Did you ever undress in front of a dog?" one stand-up bit went. "A bird doesn't count, or a cat. But a dog," he says with a sudden grimace, "they really stare."

At seventeen, Winters joined the Marine Corps, serving two and a half years in the South Pacific before returning to Ohio and enrolling in the Dayton Art Institute. "I thought I was a pretty good observer to begin with, but studying art really taught me how to become a darn good observer," Winters recalls. "I try to paint pictures, verbal pictures."

Winters also began creating a menagerie of memorable characters culled from his youth in Dayton, Ohio, including the hard-drinking, lascivious grandmother Maude Frickert (inspired by his Aunt Lou); Maude's UFO-sighting stepson Elwood P. Suggins; and various other hayseeds, kids, and codgers. When he was given his own series on NBC in 1956, Winters often played several roles at once, embroiling his characters in outlandish situations—like Maude and Elwood's ill-fated foray into aviation:

> "He was always a little 'off'—I think is the term. One day he said to me, 'Maudie, I'm gonna fly.' We went up to Willard's Bluff and he Scotch-taped a hundred forty-six pigeons to his arms. He was airborne for a good twenty seconds, then some kid came outta nowhere, threw a bag of popcorn in the quarry, and he bashed his brains out."

"I took—and I still take—from everything around me," Winters once said of his comedy. "I mean, life—and it's pretty funny out there, these characters."

Winters's characters didn't even have to be human. In one famous bit that melded his knack for observation with his flair for sound-effects and character transformation, he portrayed Fred and Alphonse, two large bass critiquing the inept fishermen trying to catch them. By the bit's end, Winters was switching rapidly among the two fish and the two men, never missing a beat.

"He is every character in the scene," said comic actor Eugene Levy, "and he has a mind so entrenched in characters that you actually believe each one is different. This is not only a comic genius at work—this is the epitome of character acting."

In 1959, Winters, who would later be diagnosed as a manic-depressive, was arrested in San Francisco after climbing the rigging of a boat at Fisherman's Wharf and screaming that he had just arrived from outer space. Another breakdown in 1961 led to an eight-month hospital stay. Returning to stand-up, with his condition under control, Winters appeared as a frequent guest on *The Andy Williams Show* and *The Tonight Show with Jack Paar*, where he worked

his improvisational magic like a virtuoso. Williams would hand him a pile of hats, and Winters would go to work, riffing one character after another. Paar passed him a stick, and suddenly Winters was a lion tamer ("Send in the big cats!" he yelled, and followed it with a tremendous roar—"Uh, send in the smaller ones"), a flute player, a fly-fisherman, a violinist, and half a dozen other characters.

Performances like those prompted Paar to remark, "If you were to ask me who were the twenty-five funniest people I've ever known, I would say, 'Here they are: Jonathan Winters.'"

Although he retired from stand-up in the late 1960s (performing only periodically over the next forty years), Winters continued to work in television and movies, starring in films like 1963's *It's a Mad, Mad, Mad, Mad World*, hosting his own programs in 1967 and again in 1972, and portraying Mearth, the son of Mork, on the Robin Williams television hit *Mork and Mindy*.

At one point during filming with Williams, Winters told the young comic to stop referring to him as his mentor. "I said that's a bad word," Winters recalled. "Idol is better." And for many of the observational comedians who followed in his wake, Winters was nothing less than a comic godfather; he infused the everyday with new life through his ingenuity and originality.

When Bill Cosby made his first appearance on *The Tonight Show* back in 1963, he was—like Winters—something unique. In the time of the civil-rights struggle, Cosby was a black man who was colorless—his message was inclusive, not divisive. "I don't think you can bring the races together by joking about the differences between them," he explains. "I'd rather talk about the similarities, about what's universal in their experiences." In this way, he established himself as an Everyman, someone who represented his family, your family, the family of man.

He did it by establishing his persona with the public as a clean, clever comedian who mined his family background and real-life pals like Fat Albert, Old Weird Harold, and Dumb Donald for his material:

"As I have discovered by examining my past, I started out as a child. Coincidentally, so did my brother. My mother did not put all her eggs in one basket, so to speak. She gave me a younger brother named Russell, who taught me what was meant by survival of the fittest."

Bill Cosby's truths were those of all familial units—truths like "Fatherhood is pretending the present you love most is soap-on-a-rope," or "My mother was an authority on pigsties. She would look at my room and say, 'This is the worst pigsty I've ever seen,'" or "Human beings are the only creatures that allow their children to come back home." These were observations that weren't just funny—the kernel of truth they contained gave them substance and depth.

When Cosby made the jump to television in 1965, he pioneered another area. Before he was teamed with Robert Culp in the hit series *I Spy*, no African-American had ever had a leading role in a weekly series. And when he launched *The Cosby Show* in 1984, he brought to television an Emmy winner that Coretta Scott King described as "the most positive portrayal of black family life that has ever been broadcast." But it was the series' cross-cultural appeal that made it an across-the-board smash. *Newsweek* said its genius was that it depicted "a tightly nuclear, upscale family coping with the same irritations and misunderstandings that afflict their white counterparts."

Even though he was a television superstar, Cosby never stopped doing stand-up—and he's the man a lot of critics and comedians call "America's best monologist." In the Jerry Seinfeld documentary *Comedian*, Chris Rock raves about Cosby, marveling at how he can do two and a half *hours* of killer material, when he and Seinfeld were sweating to put together a forty-five-minute set. Rock has said, "I have to give it up for Bill Cosby. He's one of the greatest comedians to have ever lived. He's one of the few guys who actually reinvents himself, the only comedian I ever saw grow up. He went from talking about being a kid to talking about having kids."

If Mr. and Mrs. Ben Klein had had their way, their kid, Robert, would now have "Dr." before his name. But at college the pre-med student took an elective class in drama and his parents' dreams of doctorhood went out the window. "I hung out with the actors," he recalls, "and I said, they didn't dress like my uncle, they didn't go to work like my father, nine to five. This is the way to be. There's got to be something about the bohemian actor life; making people laugh is a very high calling."

After spending a year in the Yale drama program, Klein auditioned for and landed a spot in the coveted improvisational comedy troupe Second City. Second City was one of the world's best comedy training grounds, whose graduates included Nichols and May and most of

the *Saturday Night Live* cast through the years. Klein says, "Getting hooked up with Second City was my single most important career event—because, first of all, I was a political person. I wasn't as radicalized as some comedy friends I had, but I cared. I loved the idea of getting ahead in show business, but it had to be on sort of acceptable terms to me, the ethical radicalist. I cared about not being just a song-and-dance man, and Second City was the perfect place, because they did the greatest political satire."

Robert Klein took what he had learned and quickly found work, landing gigs on Broadway, doing stand-up at the club Improvisation, and starring on television's *Comedy Tonight*, the summer replacement series for the *The Glen Campbell Goodtime Hour*. On July 7, 1970, he made the first of his fifty-plus appearances on *The Tonight Show*, doing a routine about substitute teachers. Klein made a big impression not only for the material in his act but also for what he was wearing. "I'd been a substitute teacher," he says. "I wore saddle shoes with sweaters—very multicolored sweaters. I never believed in gimmickry, but that was my outfit then. I wanted to be beyond what people thought of as a stand-up comedian. 'Hey, this guy is smart. He makes us think, and yet, he's not a snob.'"

Klein really broke through in 1973, with a Grammy-nominated album called "Child of the Fifties" and a subsequent sold-out show at Carnegie Hall. The album was filled with observations about growing up during the Cold War, like "Civil Defense" ("They taught us the siren means disaster, then they had the foresight to blow a siren every day at twelve o'clock"), "Foreigner" (I don't know much, but I'll tell you, if you're walking down the street and you see a man wearing sandals and socks, he's gonna have a foreign accent"), and "Childhood Myth" ("Do you really have to wait an hour after you eat before you go in swimming? I used to think the food would know—fifty-five minutes, fifty-six minutes . . .").

Though Robert Klein's comedy was influenced greatly by observational pioneers Lenny Bruce and Mort Sahl, it also included the viewpoint of a Bronx kid brought up with television. So, mixed in with Klein's reverence for Bruce was an appreciation for the Three Stooges, Laurel and Hardy, the Marx Brothers, and a hundred other comic legends he had watched on television. He was a hybrid who was to be the model for a generation of comedians to follow. Jerry Seinfeld considers Klein to be one of his great inspirations. "The older comedians—it was more of a simpler time. Phyllis Diller, Alan King—everybody had the hook, they had the tuxedo. And then you had a guy like Robert Klein and he was really thoughtful. And I felt like, 'Gee, this guy really reminds me of myself in some ways.'"

Klein himself sees it this way: "I think I definitely developed a trend in stand-up as an uncomedian comedian, talking reality. I wanted to be hip like Lenny Bruce, but not as shocking. I don't have to shock people, but I want to be truthful and hip. And my ideal—if I can be this New York–educated, somewhat erudite, urban Jewish man comedian and be myself, that'll be a great accomplishment."

Judging by the accolades of peers and his public, Klein has certainly reached his goals, as evidenced by a four-decade legacy that is sure to place him among the immortals in observational comedy.

Philadelphia's David Brenner is a born observer with show biz in his blood; his father was an entertainer in vaudeville. But before Brenner ever set foot on a comedy stage, he used those powers of observation to write, direct, and produce 115 documentary films. In 1970, he needed a break from documentaries and took a hiatus to reassess his career. To pass the time, he worked up a comedy act and began appearing at small clubs in New York City and was hooked. Just eighteen months later, on January 27, 1971, Brenner made the first of his 158 appearances on *The Tonight Show*—more than any other performer in the show's history. (*The Book of Lists #2* names Brenner as the Number-One Most Frequent Guest in Television History.)

Of all his appearances, that first night is Brenner's most cherished memory of the show. "If I were writing a movie about a stand-up comedian making a debut on national television," he says, "I couldn't have written a better scenario than what really happened. I received ten thousand dollars' worth of job offers within twenty-four hours after that."

Brenner's observational humor comes not just from Philly and his family, but also from endless hours of

research, reading "four to six newspapers a day, eighty to one hundred magazines a month. . . . I surf the Internet two hours in the morning, two hours at night before I go to bed. . . . I watch all television news on and off all day."

All that makes for an observer with a savant's knowledge of the news, presented with Brenner's average-guy-in-the-street viewpoint—someone trying to make sense of the senseless events that surround him:

"The only thing that bothered me about Clinton was his choice of women."

"Did you see where Philadelphia was elected the fattest city in America? Twenty-nine percent of the people living there are obese. The people of Philadelphia are really angry about that survey. In protest, they're going to form a million pound march on Washington."

And it all began with something Brenner says his father taught him when he was just four years old: "My father told me, when I was a little boy, that there's something funny in everything."

David Brenner has followed his father's advice ever since—finding the funny in the news events, big and small, that affect us all.

Most of the comedians in this generation have one thing in common—they believe that their big break came on *The Tonight Show Starring Johnny Carson*. Garry Shandling is no exception. He debuted on March 18, 1981, and the subjects of his self-effacing, observational humor were Laundromats, restaurants, visiting friends with babies, his dogs, going camping, his father eating dinner, and visiting Disneyland. His monologue was centered on the most common things in life, but seen through Shandling's off-kilter filter, they became new and funny.

"I once made love for an hour and fifteen minutes, but it was the night the clocks are set ahead."

After a long time paying his dues as a television comedy writer for shows like *Sanford and Son* and *Welcome Back, Kotter* and three years as a stand-up, Shandling's shot on Carson was incredibly moving. He recalls, "My first appearance was very emotional. I finished my last joke and as I walked behind the curtain I heard Johnny say, 'You're going to be hearing a lot about this guy.' My manager and I hugged each other and I actually started to cry."

If physical comedy is rooted in physical pain, Shandling's observational comedy is rooted in psychic pain—the pain of simply being Garry. It's something, he says, that was essential to his becoming a comedian. "I think absolutely that whatever generates that sense of humor is most likely some sort of defense mechanism against pain. I had a very good childhood growing up in Arizona, but I had an older brother who died when I was ten and I remember being traumatized by that. I became hypersensitive to life, being sixteen and wondering what I was going to be like when I was forty, and then I thought, 'I wonder if the other kids think about all this stuff?' So I had a pretty good inner dialogue going that led me to grab a microphone as soon as I was old enough."

"I once said to a woman in a bar, 'What's your name?' She said, 'Don't even bother.' I said, 'Is that an Indian name, because I'd like to meet Hot To Trot. Is she here?'"

Garry Shandling appeared on *The Tonight Show* fifty-five times, which helped land him his own series, *It's Garry Shandling's Show,* a groundbreaking television situation comedy that deconstructed TV sitcoms—all played out on a set that was a duplicate of Shandling's real apartment.

It's Garry Shandling's Show led, in 1992, to Shandling's biggest success, his HBO series, *The Larry Sanders Show.* The character, Larry Sanders, was a funhouse mirror version of Garry himself, a behind-the-scenes look at a super-neurotic, self-absorbed talk-show host surrounded by a staff of psychos, sycophants, and a simpleton sidekick, Hank Kingsley (Jeffrey Tambor).

In its seven years on HBO, *The Larry Sanders Show* and Shandling won a mantel-full of Cable Ace awards, and of its many Emmy nominations the show took home the award for Outstanding Writing for a Comedy Series in 1998.

Observational comedy, in what might have been its purest form, came to network television in 1989. That's the year Jerry Seinfeld debuted in his namesake series. From his humble beginnings in small clubs in New York City and gigs in the Catskills, Seinfeld has been the definition of an observational comedian someone who could shine his comic spotlight on life's most mundane events and make something funny out of practically nothing.

"Surveys show that the number-one fear of Americans is public speaking. Number two is death. That means that at a funeral the average American would rather be in the casket than doing the eulogy."

"Now they show you how detergents take out bloodstains—a pretty violent image there. I think if you've got a T-shirt with a bloodstain all over it, maybe laundry isn't your biggest problem. Maybe you should get rid of the body before you do the wash."

Seinfeld got his first break in 1976 when stand-up legend Rodney Dangerfield caught his act and invited him to guest on his HBO special. When he debuted on *The Tonight Show,* on May 6, 1981, he offered his observations on everything from weather reports, *Romper Room,* Switzerland, going through customs, making left turns, his car breaking down, and the fattest man in the world.

In the late 1980s, Jerry Seinfeld and fellow comedy writer Larry David developed a show called *The Seinfeld Chronicles,* a sitcom about a reasonably successful, amiably neurotic comedian (Jerry himself, just slightly twisted) and his equally offbeat friends, most of whom were amalgams of real people Seinfeld and David knew.

Something else Jerry Seinfeld knows about and appreciates is other comedians, especially observers like himself. At the top of his—and most everybody's—list is Chris Rock.

"You know the world is going crazy when the best rapper is a white guy, the best golfer is a black guy, the tallest guy in the NBA is Chinese, the Swiss hold the America's Cup, France is accusing the U.S. of arrogance, Germany doesn't want to go to war, and the three most powerful men in America are named 'Bush,' 'Dick,' and 'Colon.'"

Like the best in the business, Rock is serious about his comedy. When he's on the road he carries an iPod loaded with routines from comedy forebears like Buddy Hackett, Mel Brooks, Carl Reiner, Moms Mabley, Steve Martin, and Redd Foxx. When he's getting ready for a concert tour, he trains like an Olympian. "You need eight weeks before you do a gig—work out in New York, hit three clubs in a night seven nights a week for eight straight weeks."

Chris Rock has that drive because comedy has been very good to him and not just on a monetary level. "I've never done anything really good in my whole life," he says. "I suck at everything. I got on a comedy stage—at Catch a Rising Star—and it was more than just, 'Wow, I like doing comedy!' it was, 'Wow, I'm good at something!' And I don't ever want to lose the one thing I'm good at."

Eddie Murphy, who'd seen Rock live, recommended him for a spot on *Saturday Night Live*. But Chris Rock's real breakout in stand-up came in 1996, when *Bring the Pain*, his HBO concert filmed live in Washington, D.C., debuted. The special showcased not only Rock's innate talent, unedited language, and impeccable delivery but also a man who was clearly intelligent, had done his homework, and had some serious comments to make on race relations, culture in black America, and life in general. The show won a pair of Emmys, for Outstanding Variety, Music, or Comedy Special and for Outstanding Writing for a Variety or Music Program.

"If you've never wanted to kill your mate, you've never been in love. If you've never held a box of rat poison in your hand and stared at it for a good long while, you've NEVER been in love."

After *Bring the Pain*, Rock's career took off. He remembers that when it happened, Jerry Seinfeld called him and said facetiously, "Okay, now you're gonna get the Hot Comedian Kit: your own show, an album deal, a book deal, and you're gonna host awards shows—they're all in the kit.'"

In 2004, *Entertainment Weekly* ranked Chris Rock number one in their "Twenty-Five Funniest People in America" issue, beating out comedy heavyweights like Jon Stewart, Dave Chappelle, Bill Murray, Ellen DeGeneres, Larry David, and Jim Carrey.

When asked to define the essence of humor, legendary comedy writer Larry Gelbart said it is simply "looking at life through a different lens." Each of these superstars of observational comedy does exactly that, focusing in and letting us see things we've looked at every day from their completely different, and funny, point of view.

CHAPTER 14

TOO BIG FOR THE ROOM

It's rare for a comic to go beyond the relative minor-leagues of the comedy clubs to network television stardom. And it is rarer still for a comic to parlay success in stand-up and television into a full-blown movie career. These are the virtuoso stand-up comics, the superstars whose ranks are few but whose influence in comedy over the decades is indelible.

The first multimedia comedy superstar was the legendary Bob Hope. In his long career, Hope was a top star in all mediums: stage, film, radio, and television. The British-born Hope took his first steps toward his lifelong career in show business shortly after his family immigrated to Cleveland, Ohio. Hope later joked, "I left England at the age of four, when I found out I couldn't be king."

His first performance was imitating Charlie Chaplin in front of the Cleveland firehouse. By the late 1920s, Hope was learning to handle audiences at a small theater in New Castle, Pennsylvania, when he was hired to emcee a revue called *Whiz Bang*. In those early days, Hope was tireless. "I used to do four shows a day in vaudeville, then drop into a nightclub," he said. "I might do thirty or forty minutes off the cuff. I thought nothing of working from twelve noon to one o'clock the next morning." It was then that Hope developed his persona as a fast-talking wisecracker—his rapid-fire delivery leaving little room for

laughter (if there was any) before moving quickly to the next one-liner.

Vaudeville eventually led to Broadway and a role as the wisecracking Huckleberry Haines in the hit show *Roberta*. Hope received favorable notices and became a featured player in such entertainment extravaganzas as *Ziegfeld Follies of 1936* and *Red, Hot, and Blue*.

Hope made his Hollywood debut in *The Big Broadcast of 1938*, in which he introduced his lifelong theme song, "Thanks for the Memories." That same year, NBC gave him his own radio program, *Bob Hope's Pepsodent Show*, which ran for nearly twenty years. During World War II, his was the highest-rated show in America.

Bob Hope became a major movie star in 1940 when he teamed up with Bing Crosby and Dorothy Lamour for the first of their seven "road pictures," *Road to Singapore*. The movies were extremely popular. In fact, Woody Allen has said, "When my mother took me to see *Road to Morocco*, I knew exactly what I wanted to do with my life."

In all, Bob Hope appeared in close to eighty movies—and he hardly ever played anyone except a thinly disguised version of himself. Melville Shavelson, one of

Hope's longtime writers (and two-time director), said, "We took his own characteristics and exaggerated them. We just put them in. He thought he was playing a character. He was playing, really, the real Bob Hope."

Mort Lachman, who worked with Hope as a writer, director, and producer for nearly thirty years, says that being real was the key to Hope's popularity, "He was Everyman. He wasn't better than anybody else. He was the guy who never got the girl, who always said the wrong thing, who couldn't quite dance or sing."

Bob didn't move from television to movies; he did it the other way around. In the early 1950s, when his film career was on the wane, he signed a long-term contract with NBC and moved to the small screen. For the next forty years, Hope sprang eternal. Or as Bob himself put it, "Here's how long I've been on NBC: When I began, *TV Guide* had only one page."

In addition to his television shows, which almost always earned top ratings, Bob Hope's appearances as the host of the Academy Awards were a treasured annual event, and his overseas forays to entertain the troops made him one of the country's most beloved personalities and an American institution.

Like Bob Hope, Steve Martin was a born performer. After cutting his show-biz teeth as a concessionaire at Disneyland, Martin performed at parties, juggling, tap dancing,

performing sleight of hand, and balloon sculpting. In the mid-1960s he enrolled at UCLA, where he majored in theater and philosophy, and then, starting in 1967, he landed a string of staff-writer jobs for TV entertainers, beginning with the Smothers Brothers, Glen Campbell, John Denver, and Sonny and Cher. He was occasionally allowed to appear on the shows, but that wasn't enough for him. He needed to be out in front of an audience.

After a full decade of paying his stand-up dues, Martin started to connect with his audiences. In 1972 he made another breakthrough—the first of nearly forty appearances on *The Tonight Show Starring Johnny Carson*. By the mid-1970s he was on the road, opening for rock acts. Like most of his comedy contemporaries, he had a full beard and long hair and peppered his act with drug jokes. He was doing okay, but "okay" was not enough for an entertainer with Martin's drive. So in a moment of inspiration he shaved off

his beard, trimmed his hair, and put on a spotless white suit. It was a stroke of genius.

His act—a withering parody of traditional "establishment" comedians—was perfect for the times. Audiences fell out watching his fake enthusiasm over lame jokes, lame comedy props like his cheesy arrow-through-the-head, and his "It's impossible to play a sad song on the banjo" routine. Martin remembers it as a heady time: "It was like playing an instrument. The audience was an instrument. I can do this and they'll do this. There was a period of about a year and a half where I felt so good—my body, my fingers, everything was working."

Then, in 1976, Martin hosted *Saturday Night Live* for the first time and became internationally famous for such catchphrases as "Uh-oh, I've got happy feet!" "Ex-*cuse* me!" and "I am—one wild and crazy guy!" Martin's brilliance was that there was always something going on behind the act—and

Reiner describes Martin as "one of my favorite people in the world because he's a cool cat. He looks like an accountant, but he is one of the most tangential thinkers. He thinks in a way that nobody else thinks. He has a brilliant mind, putting things together that don't go together, and making you laugh. He's one of the great creative forces we have today."

Martin and the movie were a huge success. After *Pennies from Heaven* and another Carl Reiner film, *Dead Men Don't Wear Plaid*, he hit comedy pay dirt again, starring with Lily Tomlin in the 1984 movie *All of Me*. In the twenty years since, Steve Martin has appeared in another thirty films. Although some have been better received than others, Steve Martin is always compelling, always funny, always a star.

Robin Williams was also fated for a life of comedy. As the son of a rising Ford Motor Company executive who relocated often, Williams was an outsider who wasn't able to establish long-term friendships, a pudgy kid who was

we knew it. And he knew that we knew. "I always felt there was a deeper meaning to what I was doing than just being wild and crazy," he's said, "something more philosophical. I had a view that there was something funny about trying to be funny. I needed a theory behind it in order to justify it at the time, but now I don't. I see it for what it was. It was just fun, and it was stupid, and that's why it was successful."

By the late 1970s, Martin had conquered stand-up and television, so it was time to take on the movies—something, it seems, he'd been intending to do all along. Speaking to *Rolling Stone* magazine in 1982, Martin said: "Yeah, stand-up comedy was really just an accident. I was figuring out a way to get on stage. I made up a magic act and—"Hey, I'm in show business"—and that led to nightclubs. I felt like a comedian—that was my work. As I got into the movies, I was reminded, "Hey, this is really why I got into show business."

Martin had a couple of minor roles before his first real star vehicle, playing Navin R. Johnson, the lovable but dim-witted, bumbling title character in *The Jerk*, directed by Carl Reiner.

taunted and bullied by schoolmates. His defense was to fend them off with a lightning-quick sense of humor. His parents had busy lives, and he was often left alone for much of the day. He says, "I was an only child. There was no abuse or anything, but there was loneliness. I mean, I have a very happy life. But have I had a very lonely life at times? Yes."

Williams's favorite companion became his phonograph and his collection of Jonathan Winters comedy albums—LPs that Robin faithfully memorized. In his last year of high school, Robin's father retired and the family finally settled down in Marin County, California. Williams shaped up physically, and his humor earned him the popularity he craved. His graduating class prophetically voted him Funniest and Most Likely to Succeed.

Like Steve Martin, Williams entered college with determination, majoring in political science. Ultimately, neither was destined for the academic life. Both went into their college's theater departments—with Robin leaving

Claremont Men's College to study acting at Marin College, then finally going to Juilliard, where he studied under the tutelage of the legendary John Houseman (Robin helped pay his tuition by working as a mime). But Williams always came back to his first love, comedy, which he refers to as "the ultimate catharsis." He says: "Stand-up is the place where you can do things that you could never do in public. Once you step on stage, you're licensed to do that. It's an understood relationship. You walk on stage—it's your job."

After graduating, Williams moved back to California and started performing in clubs and studying his craft. The late John Ritter, who became one of Williams's best friends, was in his improv comedy class in Los Angeles. Ritter's first impression of Williams was a little misleading: "I saw the way this dude was dressed. In baggy pants, suspenders, a beaten-up tux over high-top sneakers, a straw hat with the brim falling off, and John Lennon

glasses with no glass in the frames. I thought, 'Well, this guy is definitely going for the sight gag.' I was almost a bit suspicious. So I watched carefully, and he turned out to be the funniest guy I've ever seen."

Robin was discovered doing his frenetic stand-up at L.A.'s famed Comedy Store. His act was a take-no-prisoners improvisational stream-of-consciousness rap that encompassed observational humor, political humor, impersonations, and imitations—all delivered at an impossible dizzying speed. It was hard to imagine a human mind working so quickly, so inventively, and so cleverly. Robin says there was a reason for his rapid-fire delivery: "I just kept moving—because in the clubs I was playing if you slowed down you'd get buried alive by hecklers. So I would just keep speaking really fast."

The unique talent of Robin Williams earned him gigs as a regular on Richard Pryor's short-lived variety show,

then guest shots as the manic alien "Mork (from Ork)" on the hit TV show *Happy Days*. Those electrifying appearances prompted *Happy Days* creator Gary Marshall to offer Robin his own series. *Mork and Mindy* ran for five seasons, from 1978 to 1982, and was a huge hit. Some of the most memorable episodes featured Robin's original comedy inspiration, Jonathan Winters, as Mearth, an overgrown alien baby. But the way the show ended still sticks in Robin's craw: "When they canceled *Mork and Mindy*, I read about it in the trades. I was doing this thing, *The Tale of the Frog Prince*, with Eric Idle, and—bingo! The trades basically said, '*Mork and Mindy* canceled.' I was so angry and hurt—and I was dressed as a frog!"

Robin Williams became one of the biggest live comedians of the late 1970s and early 1980s, and some consider him the best. The legendary Jerry Lewis ranks him at the top of the comedy heap: "Robin is numero one. I would say, from the last twenty-five years nobody can come near Robin Williams. Genius. He's got brains and adjacent material that I have no idea what it is and where it came from—he's so far ahead of anyone on the planet."

Williams's transition from television and stage star to movie star was anything but instantaneous. In 1980 he made his debut in the ill-fated Robert Altman film *Popeye*, then followed that with the critically acclaimed but box-office disappointment *World According to Garp*. Four stinkers and seven years later, Williams finally scored big. It was the Barry Levinson–directed movie *Good Morning, Vietnam*, in which Robin starred as real-life military disc jockey Adrian Cronauer. Levinson allowed Williams to ad-lib a substantial part of his dialogue, and the result was a big hit. He'd finally lived up to his billing.

It was in the box-office smash *Mrs. Doubtfire* that Williams's acting training at Juilliard really paid off. In *Mrs. Doubtfire* his job was to a play a man much like himself—a man in his thirties—and Mrs. Doubtfire, a Scottish woman in her fifties. And he had to play her so convincingly that it fools his estranged wife. Williams says that's when his training kicked in. One of his classes had been a "mask class," where students put on a mask and became a character. "It was like 'the costume of dreams'—if you wear it, she will come. Once I put the mask on—it wasn't really a mask, it was twelve separate body pieces that took four hours to fit—she started to emerge." The result was one of Williams's biggest hits—and one of his most beloved movie characters.

His own middle age hasn't slowed Williams either. His manic stand-up act proves he's still got the speed, the moves, and a razor-sharp intellect that focuses on the absurd, the obtuse, and the inane.

Unlike Robin Williams, Eddie Murphy was an instant movie star. The Brooklyn-raised comic's very first role was starring next to Nick Nolte in the 1982 comedy smash *48 Hrs.* Murphy, already a huge star on *Saturday Night Live*, was added to the cast at the last minute.

Eddie's street-smart attitude, his dazzling smile, and his infectious laugh—one of the most distinctive laughs in show business—helped propel him from class clown, to fifty-dollar-a-night comedy club gigs (at age fifteen), to a spot as a regular on one of the hottest shows on television, *Saturday Night Live*. Murphy was bold and impish and naturally funny—a direct descendant of his two comedy idols, Richard Pryor and Bill Cosby. And like the other comics in

this chapter, he had the will to make it. "I've always had confidence," he's said. "It came because I have lots of initiative. I wanted to make something of myself."

Murphy grew up in the middle-class Roosevelt neighborhood on Long Island, New York. His first and greatest love was television, and he absorbed the sitcoms, movies, and cartoons like a sponge. By the time he was in his teens, he was writing comedy bits and practicing his impersonations of Al Green, Elvis Presley, and Bruce Lee.

After his first public performance on July 9, 1976, hosting a local talent show, the fifteen-year old decided to pursue a show-business career. His stepfather, Vernon Lynch, recalls, "He would tell us both, 'I'm going to be a millionaire by the time I'm twenty-two.' He was."

Eddie earned the gig on *Saturday Night Live* when he was just nineteen. After six auditions, he joined the cast and originated unforgettable *Saturday Night Live* characters like a cigar-smoking Gumby, Buckwheat of *The Little Rascals*, Mr. Robinson (an urbanized parody of Mr. Rogers), prison poet Tyrone Green, and Silky the Pimp.

Eddie Murphy built on his *48 Hrs.* movie momentum with another smash, *Trading Places*, co-starring with fellow *Saturday Night Live* alumnus Dan Aykroyd. *Trading Places* proved that *48 Hrs.* was no fluke. His next project, 1984's *Beverly Hills Cop*, proved he could carry a movie himself, and it catapulted him to superstardom. After Clint Eastwood turned down the fish-out-of-water role of Detective Axel Foley, Murphy was chosen to star, and the movie became one of the most successful films of the 1980s. Now able to write his own ticket, he followed up with the smashes *Golden Child, Beverly Hills Cop II, Dr. Doolittle,* and his live stand-up films *Delirious* and *Raw.*

After experiencing a career ebb in the early 1990s, Murphy rebounded in the 1996 remake of Jerry Lewis's *Nutty Professor*, establishing him as a family favorite, one whose career now cast him repeatedly as the daddy rather than the delinquent. Eddie Murphy also used his personality to great effect in the blockbuster animated hit *Shrek*, in which he voiced a classic Murphy-like character named Donkey.

What's it like for someone who started out playing a smart-ass prison parolee in *48 Hrs.* to be sharing screen time with kindergartners? According to Eddie, it's rewarding: "The thing about kids is that they don't hold back. If they want to cry, they cry, and if they are in a good mood, they're in a good mood. I would do a scene with a little kid and they'd turn to me afterward and say, 'I love you, Eddie Murphy.' That's a new thing for me, to have my co-star in a scene turn to me and tell me they love me. In *48 Hrs.*, Nick Nolte never turned to me and went. 'I love you, Ed!'"

Like fellow *Saturday Night Live* alumnus Eddie Murphy, Adam Sandler is a comic who started his clowning in the classroom. It is perhaps surprising that one of his first comedy idols was the guy who gets no respect, Rodney Dangerfield. "I first saw Rodney perform in Florida when I was fourteen. I was sitting in the audience just saying the lines with him—every joke—because I'd memorized all his stuff."

Adam Sandler might never have considered a career in comedy if his brother hadn't convinced him to take the stage at an amateur comedy contest in Boston. That was the turning point. Sandler recalls: "I was seventeen, applying for college and stuff. I said, 'What am I gonna do?' And he said, 'You should be a stand-up.' So I went out and did some stand-up and I didn't do well. But it was the first time in my life where I said, 'All right, I think I can.' I became kind of obsessed with getting good at comedy."

Like Martin and Williams, Sandler entered college on an academic track, earning a degree in fine arts at New York University. In his spare time he honed his comedy chops playing local clubs. One holdover from those early days is Adam's stage fright. But he found out that, sometimes, fear leads to funny. "I still get scared when I step in front of a live audience," Sandler says. "When I was younger and did a stand-up gig, it'd take me two weeks to recover. Sometimes I'd get so panicked that I'd stutter. My brother said, 'You should sing more. Then you'd know exactly what words to use and you could relax more.' That's what got me started doing the funny songs."

Not as unrelentingly clever as Robin Williams or as earthy as Eddie Murphy, Sandler's humor straddles the line between childlike and grown-up. It's been called "affectionately offensive" and "an odd balance between tasteless vulgarity and innocent charm."

Sandler got his big break when *Saturday Night Live* cast member Dennis Miller caught his act at an L.A. comedy club and recommended him to *Saturday Night Live* producer Lorne Michaels. Michaels hired him as a writer, but frequent appearances as Opera Man and Canteen Boy

elevated him to featured player. Sandler was soon a star, and some have credited him with reinvigorating the show.

Movies and records soon followed. Adam Sandler's first album, *They're All Gonna Laugh at You,* was nominated for a Grammy, and he had parts in the film comedies *Shakes the Clown* and *Coneheads.* Then, in 1996, he made the leap to movie stardom with not one but two big hits: *Billy Madison* and *Happy Gilmore.* In both, Sandler played a lightly altered version of himself, a softhearted guy who's not afraid to look dumb, but one with a definite undercurrent of rage. It's a character Sandler really identifies with. "Everyone's been through a lot of humiliation in front of a lot of people—when you don't fight back and you feel stu-pid or you walk away. I went through that before in my life. I remember lying in my bed after getting some crap in school and feeling 'Why can't I fight that guy?' Your heart hurts the whole night."

After scoring again with 1998s *Waterboy,* Sandler expanded his audience exponentially with *The Wedding Singer,* a more mainstream romantic comedy. It featured him as a warm, personable character who appealed to a wider demographic than his established fan base of pre- and postadolescent boys. In 2002, Sandler stepped outside his usual screen persona to star in Paul Thomas Anderson's edgy romantic comedy *Punch-Drunk Love.* Though he received critical acclaim for his portrayal of Barry Egan, a

seemingly mild-mannered guy with an incredibly violent temper, the film earned mediocre box office and Adam retreated to his meat-and-potatoes roles with *Mr. Deeds* and *Anger Management*.

There's something in Sandler that speaks to the ten-year-old in every Gen Xer. Adam is a suburban bad-boy, not really dangerous, more like a prepubescent kid with a big firecracker and the will to use it. In fact, Sandler confesses, "I am one-eighth Happy Gilmore, two-eighths Sonny Koufax, two-eighths Bobby Boucher, one-eighth Billy Madison—and finally, two-eighths moron."

So, what is it these comedy superstars have in common—the X-factor that has allowed their style of comedy to translate to every medium? A style of comedy rooted in a tradition that extends all the way back to the court jesters of the Middle Ages. They are simply not afraid to make fools of themselves. Dignity be damned. Talent, charisma, funniness, self-deprecation, and ambition—in comedy, that's a formula for superstardom.

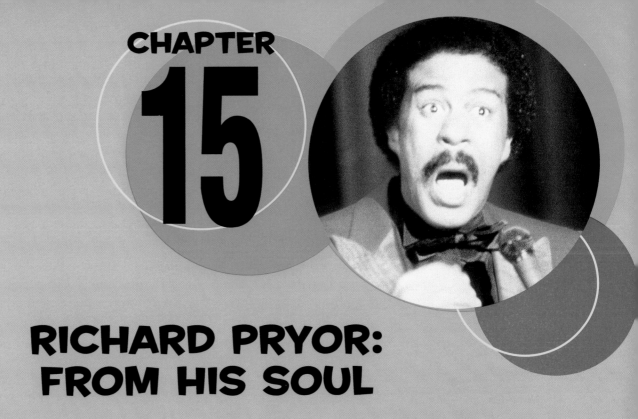

RICHARD PRYOR: FROM HIS SOUL

On October 20, 1998, Richard Pryor received the first annual Mark Twain Prize for Humor given by the Kennedy Center. There to honor him were peers Morgan Freeman, Danny Glover, Whoopi Goldberg, Chevy Chase, Damon Wayans, and Robin Williams. They all spoke, but Richard couldn't, silenced by multiple sclerosis.

Former Kennedy Center president Lawrence Wilker gave a fitting summation: "Richard Pryor was selected as the first recipient of the new Mark Twain Prize because as a stand-up comic, writer, and actor he struck a chord, and a nerve, with America, forcing it to look at large social questions of race and the more tragicomic aspects of the human condition. Though uncompromising in his wit, Pryor, like Twain, projects a generosity of spirit that unites us. They were both trenchant social critics who spoke the truth, however outrageous." And speaking "the truth" is what has made Richard Pryor the most influential comic force of our time.

One of four children born to Gertrude Thomas, a prostitute who married her madam's son, Richard Pryor is a man who climbed from the lowest rungs of society to the summit of the entertainment industry. As he was growing up, his escape from reality was the local movie theater in his hometown of Peoria, Illinois. Watching the outsized figures on the screen, the boy who'd been beaten up by gang members dreamed an impossible dream—he'd turn the tables on everyone by becoming a movie star.

His first tentative step toward that goal came at age twelve, when a supervisor at the local recreation center cast him in a neighborhood production of *Rumplestiltskin*. After a momentary indiscretion (he struck a teacher) got him ejected from school, the fourteen-year-old Richard went straight into the work world, getting a job as a janitor at a strip club. That low-level gig was followed by stints as a shoe-shiner, a drummer, a meat packer, a truck driver, and an attendant at a billiards hall. At the age of eighteen, Pryor joined the Army, but the hitch lasted only two years—an altercation (he stabbed a white soldier who was attacking a black soldier) with another soldier earned him a discharge. The one thing the military did for him was provide an outlet for his developing talents—while he was enlisted he performed at every Army amateur show he could.

Once out, Richard went to work back in Peoria, where he did a cabaret act, singing and playing piano. But it quickly became apparent that the audiences were much better entertained by his between-song joking than his vocalizing. So at age twenty the fledgling comedian hit the road, playing clubs throughout the Midwest.

In 1963, he landed in New York City, performing material that would have made his idol, Bill Cosby, proud. Actually, some say his act was based a little too closely on Cosby's. In any case, Richard Pryor was clean-cut and clean spoken, acceptable to integrated audiences and suitable for all ages.

Three years after that, in 1966, Richard Pryor made his network television debut, doing his act on mainstream variety shows like Rudy Vallee's *On Broadway Tonight* and *The Kraft Summer Music Hall*. In the 1960s he began acting as well, in the film *Busy Body* with Sid Caesar, the teen classic *Wild in the Streets*, and, inexplicably, the jingoistic military flick *Green Berets*. Plus, he landed guest spots in series television, on shows like *The Mod Squad*, *The Partridge Family* (an episode called "Soul Club"), and *The Wild Wild West*. Following great exposure on *The Ed Sullivan Show*, *The Tonight Show*, and *The Merv Griffin Show*, Pryor was booked into Las Vegas.

Richard Pryor had apparently made it. The kid with a pipe dream of becoming a star was making that dream come true—opening for Bobby Darin at the Flamingo. But outside the showrooms of Vegas, it was the turbulent 1960s, and there were wars raging—in Southeast Asia, on college campuses, and on inner-city streets. Pryor grew tired of constantly being compared to Bill Cosby, and more tired of fighting the restrictions imposed on him by his old-line Las Vegas bosses. The edgier, more hip material that began bubbling out of him had no place in that world.

So in 1970, feeling shackled by his job and disgusted by the irrelevance of his act, he burned his bridges, walking off the stage in the middle of a show at the Aladdin Hotel. It was a major turning point in his career—and one

that would transform a solid B-level comic into a superstar of comedy.

Pryor says that at that point it was the only decision he could make. "It was something I had to do to save my life. I was a joke, a bad joke, and a liar, doing all that phony material."

So Richard Pryor packed up and moved from America's gambling capital to the capital of American unrest: Berkeley, California. For the next two years he reacquainted himself with "the street," soaking up the vibes, hanging out with Huey Newton and the Black Panthers, reading Malcolm X's work, and collaborating with a group of African-American writers later tagged the "Black Pack." It brought him back to his roots, reconnecting him with the kid who'd grown up on the poor side of Peoria. When he started performing again, there was a new cast of characters in Pryor's repertoire—pimps, street hustlers, prostitutes, drug dealers, and drug buddies—and a whole new attitude: he was ready to say anything to convey his comedy. "After I lived in Berkeley for a while," Pryor says, "I found my real voice. Then I had no choice—I had to use it. Race had to be talked about openly and honestly after all that had happened to us in white America."

This was a career rebirth for Richard Pryor; the "Bill Cosby" in his act was history. "In his early days there was a lot of Bill Cosby in Richard's act," Cosby himself said in *People* magazine. "Then one evening I was in the audience when Richard took on a whole new persona—his own—in front of me and everyone else. Richard killed the Bill Cosby in his act, made people hate it. Then he worked on them, doing pure Richard Pryor, and it was the most astonishing metamorphosis I have ever seen. He was magnificent."

This was humor that was down and dirty, controversial, corrosive, and, most important, incredibly perceptive. It was humor that told the truth, transcending race, age, and economic status. Of course, it didn't hurt that Pryor was blessed with an elastic face and a loose-limbed physical presence that allowed him to transform himself instantly into an array of amalgamated characters, from a church sister to a wizened front-porch philosopher he named "Mudbone," to a pie-eyed "Willie the Drunk," to an LSD-soaked Caucasian tripper. Fellow comedian Damon Wayans describes his idol as a sextuple threat. "There are many different kinds of comedians," Wayans says. "The observational humorist, the impressionist, the character creator, the physical comedian, the self-deprecator, and the dirty-joke teller. What made Richard Pryor so brilliant is he was able to incorporate all these styles at once."

There are even those who would argue that in the 1970s Richard Pryor had as much to do with bringing the races closer together with his cross-cultural appeal as did the marches and the protests—and they wouldn't be far from the truth. "Black people got to look at themselves honestly," Pryor says, "the same as white people did. And the stuff I talked about helped them do that. They loved it. Probably some sort of relief to both races that they could finally be honest about their shit."

The reinvented Richard Pryor came through loud and clear on his second comedy album, *Live and Smokin'*, released in 1971. Though not as polished as his later work, the album, recorded at the New York Improvisation, was a clear indication of Pryor's new direction. It was here that he first talked publicly about his mother's being a prostitute and introduced his "Wino Preacher and Willie the Drunk," an alternately funny and sobering look at life on the streets of the ghetto.

In 1972 he scored the role of "Piano Man," a comic-tragic figure in the Diana Ross movie *Lady Sings the Blues*, and proved that he was more than just funny, that he really could act. If that wasn't enough, in the early 1970s Pryor began writing as well. He scripted episodes of *Sanford and Son* and *The Flip Wilson Show* and a 1973 Lily Tomlin special, for which he received an Emmy and a Writers Guild Award. His first attempt at screenwriting (collaborating with Mel Brooks and three others) was the 1974 comedy classic *Blazing Saddles*, which earned the quintet that year's Writers Guild Award for Best Comedy Written Directly for the Screen.

Mel Brooks recalls, "I knew how bright he was. I hired him because I was going to do a lot of black jokes. I said, 'I'm not gonna take the heat for these. I want somebody there to give me the okay, see if I cross the line, what's in good taste, what's in bad taste.'" But Brooks also remembers that things didn't exactly work out the way he planned them. "Strangely enough," he says, "Pryor wrote very little of the black stuff. I wound up doing that. Richie wanted to write Mongo [a villain played by Alex Karras]. He loved doing crazy lines like 'Mongo only pawn in game of life.'"

Throughout the 1970s, Pryor continued to add to his film résumé, appearing in such crowd pleasers as *Car Wash, Uptown Saturday Night*, and *The Bingo Long Traveling All-Stars and Motor Kings*. In 1976, Pryor was teamed up with Mel Brooks alumnus Gene Wilder in the hit *Silver Streak*, and one of the era's best-loved and funniest film duos was born. The next year, Pryor set the bar for Eddie Murphy (who portrayed several members of the Klump family in his *Nutty Professor* films) by playing three different characters in the comedy *Which Way Is Up?*

The surprise was that Richard Pryor was popular not only with African-Americans but also increasingly with whites. Much like early rock 'n' roll and rap music, it was black people who claimed Pryor first, and white fans who gave him the critical mass he needed to reach superstardom.

Joan Rivers, one of Pryor's early crossover fans, became a big booster. "He was brilliant," she says. "I remember taking a whole group of people from *Life* magazine down to see him in Greenwich Village, 'cause I had just been picked—1972—New Performer of the Year, and I said, "No, no, no, it shouldn't be—it should be this friend of mine." And I took them to see Richard and they all were totally offended. He was beyond brilliant."

Pryor appeared in film after film, and his live albums garnered gold and platinum status and brought home Grammys. He grabbed his first golden gramophone in 1974 for the genre-defining LP *That Nigger's Crazy*—an album with a title few would dare use even thirty years later. (In fact, after a revelatory visit to Africa in 1979, Richard himself swore off use of the "n" word.) The album showed the world a Richard Pryor now well on his way to becoming a

legend. His observations and his imitations were sharply drawn, his takes on man-woman, black-white relationships were deeply truthful and seriously funny, and his confidence in front of an audience was soaring.

Among the classic tracks are hilarious bits like "Nigger with a Seizure," "Wino Dealing with Dracula," "Black and White Lifestyles," "Have Your Ass Home by 11:00," "Black Man/White Woman," and "Exorcist."

It didn't matter that Pryor's material was grounded in the black experience; the universality of his material gave him the freedom to be as "dirty" as he wanted to be, and as controversial as he could be. A nation that a generation before would have listened to "blue" records like his only at stag parties now came to his concerts and listened to his albums in mixed company—male and female, black, white, brown, and yellow.

New York Times Magazine writer James McPherson speculated that Pryor actually created a whole new *style* of comedy, one that owed as much to theater as to traditional humor. Pryor's characters, McPherson wrote, "are winos, junkies, whores, street fighters, blue-collar drunks, pool hustlers. . . . He enters into his people and allows whatever is comic in them, whatever is human, to evolve out of what they say and how they look. . . . It is part of Richard Pryor's genius that, through the selective use of facial expressions, gestures, . . . speech, and movements, he can create a scene that is comic and at the same time recognizable as profoundly human."

Cable or satellite television would have been a perfect venue for Richard. As it was, *The Richard Pryor Show* was a brilliant bust. NBC signed Pryor for ten shows and unaccountably scheduled them at the "family hour," 8:00 to 9:00 P.M., opposite that season's number-one and number-two shows, *Happy Days* and *Laverne & Shirley*. Pryor had been assured that he would have creative control, but he was both astounded and dismayed by how short his leash was. Hounded by censors and network executives, he was forced to tone down both his language and his material. That didn't exactly sit well with him. In fact, the first skit of his first show addressed the censorship. It featured Richard—in a skintight flesh-colored body stocking—

vowing to the audience that he'd never, ever compromise his art. The camera gradually pulls back, revealing Pryor, "naked," minus his "manhood." NBC refused to air the bit—but that night all three network news shows did, giving Pryor many times more exposure than his own program would have.

Though *The Richard Pryor Show* drew critics' raves and featured some of the comedian's edgiest and most clever work, after just four shows Pryor and NBC mutually decided to call it quits. The remaining six shows were to be "specials," but they were never shot. Though he was involved with a short-lived children's show called *Pryor's Place* in the mid-1980s, he'd never star in series television again.

Pryor's prime-time failure did nothing to slow his career in movies, stand-up, and albums. He was doing two and three movies a year, and in 1979 he released *Richard Pryor Live in Concert*, which most critics consider his best live performance ever. In that movie—the sound track of which also was released as an album, and went Gold— Richard mined his own life for some of the funniest, most penetrating material of his career. The concert includes a classic Pryor routine about the time Deboragh McGuire, the third of his five wives, was gathering up her things and getting ready to leave him. Richard had been drinking vodka

and calmly watching her pack, the soul of propriety—that is, until it looked like she was actually going to leave in the Mercedes he'd bought her. Then something in him snapped, and Richard began firing a .44 Magnum at the car.

"It seemed fair to kill my car, right, because my wife was gonna leave my ass. 'If you leave it'll be in those Hush Puppies you got on.' I shot her tire, and the tire said, 'Awwwwwwwwwwwww.' . . . I shot another one— poom! And that vodka I was drinking said, 'Go ahead, shoot something else.'"

In another routine from *Richard Pryor Live in Concert*, Pryor talks about the time his own heart "attacked him." A great deal of the sketch's effectiveness comes from Richard "becoming" his own heart as it assaults him. As he walked across the stage, Richard recalls: "I was walking in the front yard. Something says, 'Don't breathe!'" (Richard stops and puts his fist to his chest and twists it, like someone has grabbed him by the heart.) "I said, 'Hmm?' Said, 'You heard me, muthafucka, don't breathe!'" (He twists his heart again, harder.) "'Okay, I won't breathe, I won't breathe, I won't breathe.' 'Then shut the fuck up, then!'" (Another vicious twist of the heart.) "'Okay, don't kill me,

After expressing his appreciation for all the love he received while he was recovering, Pryor said: "Also, ya'll did some nasty ass jokes on my ass. Oh yeah, ya'll didn't think I saw some of these. [He strikes a match] I remember this one: you strike the match like this. [He moves the lit match in front of himself.] What's this? Richard Pryor runnin' down the street."

Like a lot of Pryor's triumphs and tragedies, this horrifying episode became fodder for his art, and in 1986 it was immortalized in *Jo Jo Dancer, Your Life Is Calling*—the autobiographical film Richard wrote, directed, and starred in.

Back among the living, Pryor's popularity reached new heights. As an indicator, in 1983 he was paid four million dollars for his part in *Superman III* as an accomplice to the villain. Not only was this more than any black actor had earned on a movie before, it was also one million dollars more than the film's star, Christopher Reeve, received.

Then, in 1986, Richard Pryor was diagnosed with multiple sclerosis. Whether the degenerative nerve disease was brought on by all the stress of his drug use, or by the ordeal he suffered when he was burned, or was simply a medical time bomb, remains a matter of conjecture. But one thing is certain: the Richard Pryor of the 1970s and early 1980s would be no more.

As the years have gone by and the disease has progressed, he's become less and less mobile and less and less verbal. But he's no less combative, vowing, "The grim reaper—I'm gonna try to kick his ass again when he comes." Asked to sum up his life, Richard responded, "I tried to fill myself with all kinds of things that didn't work. Now I am full of M.S., and Jenny's back [Jennifer Lee, whom he remarried in 2001], and, believe it or not, I have some sense of peace. What a life."

Asked what he's learned from his travails, Richard says: "Complicated people have both sides, the light and the darkness. You just have to keep an eye on that darkness, so that it doesn't swallow you up. Just let it feed the art you wanna make and things you gotta say."

Though the voice has been silenced, the legacy of Richard Pryor speaks volumes, a huge body of work that establishes him as one of the true comedy legends of all time.

don't kill me, don't kill me.' 'Get on one knee and prove it!'" (Richard obeys, dropping to one knee on the stage.) "'Thinking about dying, now, ain't ya?'" (The heart attack is under control.) "'Didn't think about it when you was eating all that *pork!*'" (Pryor lies down on the stage, helpless, grimacing, begging his own heart not to kill him.)

Richard's heart attack didn't kill him, but something else came close—his drug use. In 1980, Pryor spilled alcohol on himself while freebasing cocaine, lit himself on fire, and found himself running down the street in his suburban neighborhood, burning to death. Finally rescued, Pryor wound up with third-degree burns over 50 percent of his body and spent six weeks in a burn clinic fighting for his life. Though at the time his manager convinced him to spin the incident and proclaim it an "accident," Pryor later confessed that he'd tried to take his own life.

The tragedy prompted a huge outpouring of sympathy and support, and Pryor got a new lease on life, fighting his way through agonizing pain and multiple skin grafts. By 1981 he was back to work—permanently scarred, chastened, and as funny as ever.

His concert return was immortalized in the 1982 film *Richard Pryor: Live on the Sunset Strip*, the album of which earned him another of his five Grammys. In one of the movie's most compelling sections he describes his near-death experience, managing to make it simultaneously frightening and incredibly funny.

PART 3

COMEDY IN THE
MOVIES

16

SILENT FILMS, LOUD LAUGHTER

• • •

A comedian does funny things; a good comedian does things funny.

—Buster Keaton

The Silent Era had long since receded into memory by the time two of its greatest stars teamed up on screen. Buster Keaton and Charlie Chaplin had spent their careers making millions laugh, and in the process had revolutionized film comedy. Now, in Chaplin's bittersweet *Limelight* (1952), they played a pair of forgotten vaudevillians trying one last time to recapture their former magic.

It had been more than a quarter-century since the two, along with comic actor Harold Lloyd, had dominated the silent screen as Hollywood's "holy trinity" of humor, and the ensuing years had taken their toll. Chaplin, hounded by federal authorities for his leftist politics, would soon leave America for good. Keaton was already displaying the ravages of alcoholism and a three-pack-a-day smoking habit that eventually killed him. But for a brief moment, the aging masters conjured the spirit of their bygone

days, romping through a madcap musical performance in the film's finale.

Comedy had changed. The joke had replaced the gag. Baggy pants and slap shoes had been tucked away in the trunk of cinematic history. But Chaplin and Keaton's short escapade in *Limelight* gave moviegoers a taste of what humor had been like in the heyday of silent film, when the great comic actors, relying solely on their physical presence and facial expressions, could captivate an audience without ever uttering a word.

"It all begins with Chaplin," proclaims film historian Leonard Maltin. "In my mind, he's the fount of everything that followed in comedy, certainly in screen comedy. And *The Gold Rush* is one of the peaks, one of the pinnacles."

When Chaplin's *Gold Rush* had opened in 1925, the thirty-six-year-old comedian and director was already a world-famous star who had appeared in nearly sixty films, primarily as the Little

Tramp, the wildly popular cane-wielding vagrant who waddled through the urban slums tweaking the nose of respectable society and getting himself into a whole lot of hot water.

Chaplin had modeled the character—and his recipe for humor—on the Dickensian figures of his London boyhood, those beaten-down men "with small black mustaches, tight-fighting clothes, and bamboo canes" who despite their shabby appearance made every effort to appear cultured and genteel. "All my pictures were built around the idea of getting me into trouble," Chaplin once said, "and so giving me the chance to be desperately serious in my attempt to appear as a normal little gentleman." *The Gold Rush* carried that comic formula from the Bowery to the boondocks, dumping the earnest Little Tramp into the frozen wilds of Canada to contend with a horde of bigger, stronger fortune-seekers.

Inspired by the Klondike gold rush of 1898, *The Gold Rush* featured Chaplin as a lone prospector—preposterously underclad in his trademark sagging trousers, ragged waistcoat, and bowler—who hobbles through a succession of perilous misadventures, high-tailing it from bears and homicidal claim-jumpers, rumbling with violent toughs, outwitting cannibals, and falling hopelessly in love with a haughty dance-hall girl who mocks him behind his back.

"*The Gold Rush* is a wonderful amalgam of broad slapstick comedy and pathos," says Maltin, "which was Chaplin's other specialty. And few people have ever woven the two together as well as he did. He set it in a realistic backdrop, the Chilkoot Pass. So there's a realistic setting, behind all the comedy and behind the character that he introduces there."

Chaplin, who had grown up in dire poverty, had always had a knack for wresting comedy from bleak situations, and the crushing adversity of the Yukon would yield some of the film's funniest bits, including one in which the freezing Tramp seeks refuge at the cabin of the starving brute Big Jim (Mack Swain) by offering to cook his own shoe.

Bringing his brilliance as a pantomimist to bear, Chaplin sets about stewing the tattered boot with the all ostentation of a five-star chef—sniffing, tasting, throwing in dashes of seasoning, and tenderly ladling the cooked juices over his culinary atrocity. As the incredulous Big Jim looks on, the Tramp delicately carves the shoe, arranges the laces spaghetti-style, and, after setting the

table, gives a firm maitre-d' tug on his vest before presenting the leathery mess as if it were an exquisite delicacy.

The "boiled boot" episode made use of an essential Chaplinesque ruse, one that hinged on the Tramp's unflappable seriousness in the midst of an absurd situation, and it got major laughs. But that did not come without a price. After three days of filming the routine—the perfectionist Chaplin was notorious for shooting scenes hundreds of times until he got the nuances just right—Swain had gnawed through enough licorice footwear to fill a socialite's closet and collapsed from severe intestinal distress.

Although Chaplin had long moved beyond the heavy-handed, pie-heaving slapstick popularized in the silents' early days, *The Gold Rush* wouldn't have been a proper Tramp vehicle without a few old-time big man–small man gags thrown in for good measure. The bantam Chaplin loved playing against giant oafs ("I get the sympathy of the audience"), and when the deranged Big Jim attempts to dismember his diminutive guest with an axe, thinking he is a giant chicken, Chaplin does comic double-time—as

the frightened Tramp scurrying circles around the lumpish butcher, and as Big Jim's hallucination, herking and jerking hysterically in a feathered suit.

But the comedian also found room to display his physical talents with a lighter touch, particularly in the "Dance of the Bread Rolls" dream sequence, during which he entertains his love interest by performing a graceful tabletop jig using two forks stuck into dinner rolls as legs. In Berlin, the convulsed opening-night audience demanded that the projectionist rewind the film and present the scene a second time before continuing. BBC radio in London broadcast several minutes of solid laughter said to have been recorded after the gag was shown.

The Gold Rush may have proven that there were big laughs in hunger and hypothermia, but it also cemented Chaplin's reputation as a director and visual storyteller of consummate skill. His fairy-tale saga, in which the pitiable Tramp strikes it rich despite himself, and gets the girl to boot, landed him on the cover of *Time* and was hailed by *Variety* as "the greatest and most elaborate comedy ever

filmed." Years later, his colleague and competitor Buster Keaton would marvel at Chaplin's "skill in the use of detail, at the clockwork way his films unfold. [This is] the essence of his genius, more important than his ability to come up with gags."

It was heady praise from a comedian who, by most accounts, considered Chaplin a pretentious snob, and Keaton was always quick to point out their dissimilarities. "There was, to me, a basic difference from the start," he said. "Charlie's Tramp was a bum with a bum's philosophy. Lovable as he was, he would steal if he got the chance. My little fellow was a working man, and honest."

It is interesting that his honest little fellow was also utterly devoid of expression, a trait Keaton had honed to great comic effect since his early childhood in vaudeville, when, as "The Little Boy Who Can't Be Damaged,'" he was kicked, slapped, and catapulted around theaters by his comedian father, who expected Buster to endure it all with dispassionate humor. Whereas an audience could always expect a display of emotion from Chaplin—a tender smile, a conspiratorially cocked eyebrow—Keaton's "Great Stoneface" gave them nothing, retaining a sphinxlike and impassive mask that by contrast highlighted the craziness of a universe that always seemed to be whirling out of control around him.

Sherlock Jr. (1924) would incorporate the twenty-eight-year-old Keaton's greatest traits as an actor and director—deadpan comedy, audacious stunts, and amazing innovations in cinematography—to create a film that was at once a knee-slapping farce and a deeply insightful commentary on the ability of cinema to affect our lives. And he would literally break his neck doing it.

Sherlock's action revolves around the exploits of a pipe-dreaming movie projectionist and aspiring detective who discovers that he can insinuate himself into films by leaping on screen. "This was the reason for making that whole picture," Keaton later said. "Just that one situation."

That one situation made for some of Keaton's most impressive and original comedy, as his projectionist is initially booted back into the audience by the film's characters but tenaciously dives in again, only to find himself caught in a maelstrom of lightning-quick edits. Ping-ponging from a tranquil garden to a bustling thoroughfare to a tiger-filled jungle, the poker-faced interloper finally ends up stranded on a rock in the middle of a raging sea, and when he dives off he lands—after a final scene change—headfirst in a snowbank.

"It's a small wonder surrealists love Buster Keaton," asserts Leonard Maltin, "especially this film, in particular, where he plays with reality and illusion and does it so well. And this was long before computers, of course, long before the special effects of today were even a glint in someone's eye. But Keaton had kind of an engineer's mind and he also

had the physical dexterity to carry out some of these wild gags that no one else could possibly do. He had a great cameraman too, Elgin Leslie, who understood the workings of this stuff. So, every gag, every moment, is perfectly set up and perfectly timed. There's not a wasted moment in that film. But everything fits into place just perfectly."

The *New York Times* called the sequence "one of the best tricks ever incorporated in a comedy," and eighty years later it is still mind-boggling in its seamlessness and fluidity. Keaton's fascination with experimental photography and editing—something Chaplin loathed, preferring simple pantomime—had become a cornerstone of his comedy ever since he had delighted audiences by cloning himself several dozen times for a single shot in 1921's *The Playhouse*.

But Buster's love of things mechanical extended far beyond the cutting room to include trucks, trains, and other large contraptions, which often figured prominently in his acrobatic stunts. As the Machine Age's laugh-a-minute booster, he couldn't resist the thrill and spectacle of motorized mayhem. And *Sherlock Jr.* provided it in spades.

Following his rude welcome to the film-within-a-film, Keaton enters the next scene not as a lowly projectionist but as "the crime-crushing criminologist Sherlock Jr." come to recover a set of missing pearls and rescue a kidnapped heroine. Gone are the work clothes, the porkpie hat, and the slouching demeanor, replaced by a natty tuxedo and a cocksure attitude. It was a wonderfully funny exercise in silver-screen wish fulfillment.

And so the intrepid Sherlock Jr. careens from one hair-raising incident to the next in classic Keaton style, forever a half-step ahead of catastrophe. Perched on the handlebars of a motorcycle, he zips across a damaged bridge whose gap is momentarily filled by the tops of two trucks passing below; his car veers into a lake and miraculously turns into a boat; and stuck atop a moving train, he leaps from the last boxcar, grabbing the spout of a nearby water tank, which lowers him to the ground amid a torrential gush. The last feat knocked Keaton unconscious, and a chance X-ray ten years later revealed that he'd cracked a vertebra in the fall.

Sherlock closes with a poetic tableau in which Keaton, having solved the movie crime as Sherlock Jr. and reassumed his everyday identity, embraces his girl in the projection booth, the entire time peering unblinkingly at an on-screen love scene for pointers on the proper technique.

With *Sherlock Jr.*, Keaton not only confirmed his stand-ing as a groundbreaking comic director who would push the medium to its limits in search of laughs, but also left audiences agape with the arrant bravado of his high-risk gymnastics. When asked by a journalist years later why, with all the perils, he insisted on performing his own stunts, Keaton replied deadpan, "Stuntmen don't get laughs."

As one of the Silent Era's most celebrated daredevils, Harold Lloyd would likely have agreed—that is, until he blew his right hand to ribbons with an accidentally loaded prop bomb during a 1919 photo shoot. From that point on, he performed wearing a rubber prosthesis, and stuntmen would incur the worst of the bumps and bruises for him.

It is surprising that today Lloyd is the least celebrated member of the "holy trinity" of humor, though during the Silent Era he outgrossed both Chaplin and Keaton and starred in more comedies than the two of them combined. The explanation may lie in the abiding "normalcy" of his screen persona. While Chaplin's down-at-the-heels Tramp and Keaton's stoic observer were more or less eccentric outsiders, Lloyd's bespectacled Everyman, sometimes called "The Kid" or simply "Glasses," was as representative of his times as the bob-cut and the Charleston—boyish, innocent, charming, exuberant, and boundlessly optimistic.

Lloyd had arrived at the character after years trying to emulate Chaplin's Tramp with minor success, eventually coming to the conclusion that a hero who looked and behaved like a regular middle-class joe would be more believable and sympathetic—and therefore funnier in true-to-life circumstances—than a costumed clown. "I would need no eccentric makeup or funny clothes," he said of the Kid. "I would be an average, recognizable American youth and let the situations take care of the comedy."

"Lloyd's films, I think are the most audience-proof of them all," lauds Maltin. "I've seen Keaton play well and not so well. I've seen Chaplin play well and not so well. Harold Lloyd's films never fail, because he was the most determined of the three. Harold Lloyd was a really driven man in the best way. And he was driven to perfection. When he decided to take up bowling, he bowled a 300 game. Anything he did was going to be perfect. And that was how it was going to be with his films. So even though other people are credited with directing most of his movies, he was the brains of the outfit. And he really pulled the strings."

In *The Kid Brother* (1927), the thirty-three-year-old Lloyd's average youth was Harold Hickory, the lily-livered youngest son of a tough country sheriff, who is forced to take down a gang of thieves and restore his family's good name. A Cinderella tale, and Lloyd's personal favorite, the film took the comedian's high-energy physical gags and wrapped them in an elegantly constructed and suspenseful story.

Lloyd sets up the action immediately with a flawlessly acted pantomime in which the nerdy Harold dons his father's sheriff's outfit while the elder Hickory and Harold's two abusive brothers are away. When he turns and catches sight of the badge-bedecked figure in the mirror, he recoils in fear, failing to recognize himself, then slowly warms to the image, sampling a number of very funny tough-guy grimaces and ultra-masculine poses.

Lloyd believed that in the age of the feature-length comedy (he, Chaplin, and Keaton had all moved from twenty-minute two-reelers to features in the early 1920s) gags for gags sake were passé, and humor should be used only to advance character development and plot. "It's got to move, but for a reason," he would say. The "Badge'" scene did just that, demonstrating Harold's intense desire to be considered manly while subsequently getting him into a snafu of mistaken identity on which the entire story turned.

"The more trouble you get a man into, the more comedy you get out of him," had become Lloyd's motto, and Harold Hickory paid off in the comedian's trademark madcap style, tumbling out of windows; being beaten, handcuffed, and strung up a pole by his trousers; and generally making a flailing mess as he scampered from enraged brothers, bullying neighbors, and a gang of vindictive community elders.

In an inventive scene that managed to highlight both Lloyd's penchant for acrobatics and the Kid's youthful romanticism, Harold clambers up a tree to catch sight of a pretty girl in the distance. As she continuously disappears over a hill, Lloyd is forced to climb higher and higher for a glimpse before crashing to the ground in a flurry of leaves and broken branches. Landing in a field of daisies, he wistfully begins a childlike game of She Loves Me, She Loves Me Not.

But the Kid, for all his harmlessness and naiveté, was never a harebrain, and with an ingenuity Lloyd carefully foreshadowed earlier in the film—having dispatched his house chores with chuckle-inducing creativity—Harold manages to outwit his criminal nemesis (who has snatched a sack of county funds from the Hickory home) using a trained monkey in work boots and an old broom.

Returning to town with the booty, the former black sheep is feted as a hero and a man worthy of the Hickory name.

Lloyd would make just one more soundless feature, 1928's *Speedy*, before moving to "talkies," but he would never match the success he'd had as a silent comedian. Keaton, likewise, made his first sound appearance in 1929, just two years after creating his silent masterpiece *The General*. Forever the rebel, Chaplin would hold out until 1940 on the grounds that synchronized sound was destroying the art of film comedy, replacing the universality of silent pantomime with a babel of low-grade productions and bad acting. When he finally did succumb, his high-flown manner of speaking baffled many who could not square the new aristocratic voice with the lovable, beggarly Tramp he'd created. But for future generations of comedic actors, directors, screenwriters, and fans it was enough that these three men had taken a fledgling form and, through their dazzling innovations and sheer comic exuberance, literally defined what was possible.

SILENT CLOWN COLLEGE: MACK SENNETT AND HAL ROACH

ONE HOLLYWOOD TALE HAS IT that when aspiring comedian Roscoe "Fatty" Arbuckle arrived at the recently formed Keystone Film Company in the spring of 1913 looking for work, the studio chief took one look at him, lobbed a mouthful of tobacco juice onto the young man's white pants, and told him, "Big boy, be here tomorrow morning at eight," before slamming the door in his face. Within three years, Arbuckle had become a comic sensation, and the chaw-spewing Mack Sennett was quarterbacking the world's most productive laugh factory.

No great comedian steps on stage fully formed, and during the pioneer days of the silent era, nearly every top-line comic cut his or her teeth at Sennett's bustling slapstick college, or at that of his crosstown rival, Hal Roach.

A boilermaker by trade, Sennett had founded Keystone in 1912 after an unremarkable stint as a silent actor, and his brand of knockabout, caper-fueled high jinks was quickly enshrined as the company's blueprint. "You will find [comedy] either in sex or in crime," Sennett said. "Those two fields are the great feeding grounds of funny ideas."

Known as a hands-on producer who regularly oversaw dozens of productions, Sennett fielded a broad stable of actors that at one time or another included Arbuckle ("the rare combination of fat and perfect athlete"); Charlie Chaplin, who cut thirty-five films during his year-long tenure in 1914; the cross-eyed Ben Turpin, a gifted mimic payable by Lloyd's of London if his defective peepers ever realigned; Mabel Normand, the multitalented comedienne who scripted, directed, and starred in a number of Chaplin's Keystone vehicles and was sometimes referred to as "the female Chaplin"; and the popular baby-faced foundling Harry Langdon.

But Sennett was perhaps best known for his constabulary pranksters, the Keystone Kops, a gang of uniformed buffoons who took great pleasure in straining the public's faith in law and order. Between 1912 and 1917, Sennett produced a slew of Kops comedies packed with the rough-and-tumble, pie-throwing pratfalls that would make the bumbling police force a household name.

Less than ten miles away, Hal Roach—who had earned his bread as a mule-skinner, a truck driver, and a film extra before throwing his hat into the production ring in 1914—was churning out short and feature-length comedies with his own team of talented jokers. Actors like Harold Lloyd, Charlie Chase, the wisecracking bombshell Thelma Todd, and Will Rogers thrived in the chummy, relaxed atmosphere of Roach's studios, lovingly dubbed "The Lot of Fun" by its comic denizens, and Roach's laid-back approach to producing (he'd offer a gag on occasion, but otherwise kept his hands out of the fire) allowed writers and directors to experiment with new comic formulas and techniques.

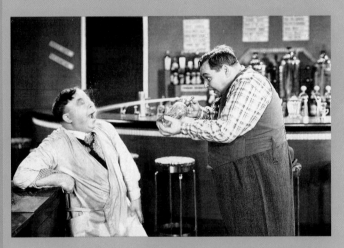

Like dozens of Sennett prodigies, many of Roach's brightest stars spent a few years honing their comic chops at the studio before decamping for greener pastures and bigger bucks. But Roach always managed to keep the hits coming with a fresh pool of cutups. After Lloyd's departure in 1923, the producer achieved his greatest success with Laurel and Hardy and the *Our Gang* shorts (later immortalized on television as *The Little Rascals*), both of which survived, and thrived, well into the sound era.

CHAPTER 17

LET'S GET PHYSICAL

A pratfall, a pie to the face, or a wild car chase—there's something intrinsically funny about physical comedy. The Germans define it with the word *schadenfreude*, which literally means "harming joy." The fundamental reason that physical comedy works—pain, *other people' pain*—can inspire our own pleasure.

In the days of vaudeville, physical comedy became known as "slapstick," a term derived from the noise produced by a simple device operated by a stagehand. When a performer got smacked, the "slapstick," two flat pieces of wood fastened together at one end, was clapped together and produced the loud "slapping" noise.

Slapstick in movies has existed almost as long as the movies themselves. One early comedy duo who bridged the silent to sound revolution was Stan Laurel and Oliver Hardy. Their comedy was slapstick at slow speed. The two former vaudevillians had been teamed up in 1926 by studio owner Hal Roach, and the pair were a perfect team. Stan was the skinny one—a silly but sensitive birdbrain who was prone to scratching his head when confused, and crying when trouble loomed. Oliver wasn't any smarter—he just thought he was. Where Stan was always very slow to act, Oliver rushed in, usually with disastrous results. His famous and often-imitated reaction was to twiddle his

necktie. In actuality, Laurel and Hardy were far from dimwitted. Stan Laurel wrote the majority of the duo's material and was most responsible for creating their indelibly unique characters.

Jerry Lewis says of his friend Stan Laurel, "His magic was, he loved the regular man. He loved plain people. And he loved being one of them. He enjoyed participating in the art of going out into the world and getting in trouble."

The film that may represent Laurel and Hardy's comic genius best is the twenty-nine-minute short *The Music Box*, which won the first ever Academy Award for Best Live-

Action Short. The premise is simplicity itself: Laurel and Hardy are movers who have to deliver an unwieldy crated player piano up a towering flight of concrete stairs. It's a surprise gift for the cranky Professor Von Schwarzenhoffen. The boys fight not only gravity but also their own short-sightedness, "helpful" tenants of the building, and the cantankerous professor himself. At one point, they finally get the piano all the way to the top of the stairs, find out it's the wrong way around, and have to take it back down again and start over. *The Music Box* is a masterpiece of physical comedy, with perfect timing, spontaneous action, and classic "business."

"What sets Laurel and Hardy apart from so many other comedians and certainly so many other teams is that you could fall in love with them," explains film historian and critic Leonard Maltin. "They were lovable characters because you believed them. You never had a sense that it was Stan Laurel playing a character or Oliver Hardy playing a character. You just believed they were those two guys. And, of course, in those days, before the era of talk shows, there was never any revealing the illusion. Yes, there were fan magazine articles and there was the radio show that might interview someone. But they were very canny about that. They never wanted to be seen and heard by the public, out of character. That was very smart."

Like Laurel and Hardy, the Three Stooges evolved from vaudeville—in fact, the term "stooge" is an early show-business term meaning someone who's a "second banana" or a foil to a comedian, the butt of his jokes. That's how the famous trio came to be. Starting in 1925, they were stooges for an early star of stage, vaudeville, and movies named Ted Healy.

Their first incarnation consisted of Healy's lifelong friend, Moe Howard (real last name Horwitz), Howard's brother Shemp, and the violin-playing vaudevillian Larry Fine. To set them apart, Healy gave each a distinctive haircut: Moe had an eyebrow-skimming bowl cut, Larry had a frizzy Einstein-like "do," and Shemp had a long, greasy, parted-down-the-middle look. In 1932, Shemp had a falling

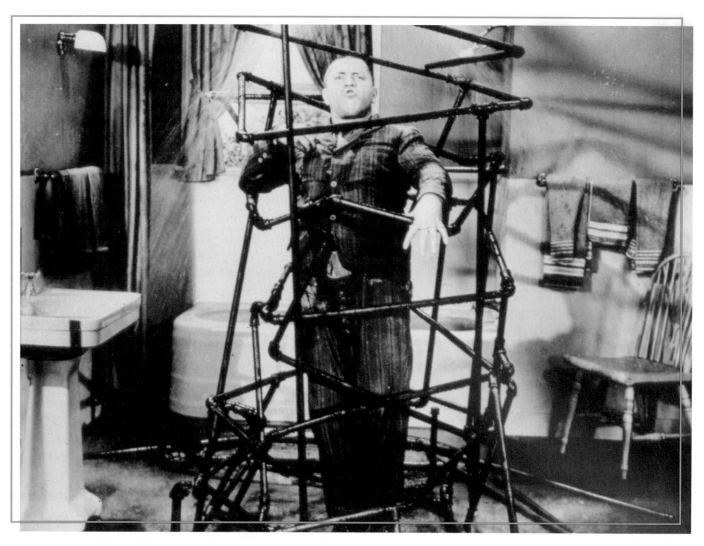

out with Healy and left the act, so Moe suggested replacing him with the youngest Horwitz brother, Jerome. But first they had to come up with a Stooge hairstyle for the impeccably coiffed kid. Jerome recalled, "I had beautiful wavy hair and a waxed mustache. When I went to see Ted Healy about a job as one of the Stooges, he said, 'What can you do?' I said, 'I don't know.' He said, 'I know what you can do. You can shave off your hair to start with.' Then later I had to shave off my poor mustache." Thus Jerome became "Curly."

As physical comedians who dealt out and received pain, the Three Stooges are the gold standard. Moe believed that the key to all comedy is the "upsetting of dignity," and the Stooges certainly did that. Moe was the intolerant "boss," handing out brutal punishment to his two accomplices for the slightest infraction. Middleman Larry suffered a ton of mistreatment as the perpetually apologetic foil whose line was most often "I'm sorry, Moe, it was an accident." Curly (or Shemp) took the most physical abuse: fin-

gers to the eyes, a pipe wrench to the noggin, a blowtorch to the backside. But with his irreverent, antiestablishment attitude and his defiant silliness, Curly became the most imitated of the Stooges with trademark catchphrases like "Nyuk, nyuk, nyuk," "Woo woo," and "Soitainly!"

The trio stuck with Healy until 1934, when they struck out on their own. They landed a deal with the short-subject unit of Columbia Pictures and stayed there twenty-three years, during which time they made 190 "two-reelers" or short comedies. A reel of film is about nine minutes long, and two-reelers were fifteen to eighteen minutes long—the Stooges' contract called for eight of them annually. Though the Columbia contract paid the trio a paltry sixty thousand dollars a year, they more than doubled their earnings by taking their slapstick show on the road for personal appearances.

A Plumbing We Will Go is quintessential Stooges, one of their highest-rated films and reportedly Curly Howard's all-time favorite. The scene where Curly, posing as a plumber, encases himself in his own pipework is classic, as is the gag where the trio switch the water and electricity in a fancy mansion they've systematically destroyed, turning a television broadcast of a picture of Niagara Falls into an actual gusher.

"You look at Curly in *A Plumbing We Will Go,* which is arguably his greatest scene ever," Leonard Maltin points out, "it's his reactions that really sell it and make it a wonderful comedy scene." *A Plumbing We Will Go* was so inventive and well loved that the Stooges remade it twice (with Shemp), as *Vagabond Loafers* and *Scheming Schemers.*

The Stooges enjoyed a long successful run, but by the late 1940s Curly suffered a series of strokes. He died in 1952, and his replacement, big brother Shemp, died three years later. Their popularity was at its lowest point. They were on the brink of extinction when Columbia's television arm, Screen Gems, released the two-reelers to television. Introduced to the baby boomers, a generation who'd never seen them in theaters, the Three Stooges suddenly became one of television's hottest properties. Taking advantage of their renewed popularity, Moe, Larry, and Curly look-alike "Curly Joe" DeRita made two movies in the Sixties, crossed the country doing personal appearances, and provided voices and live-action vignettes for the *Three Stooges* cartoon series.

As the Stooges were embarking on their riotous two-decade run with Columbia in 1934, a gangly eight-year-old kid from Newark, New Jersey, was already staking his claim as the next generation's premier slapstick gagman. The son of vaudevillians, Jerry Lewis literally grew up on stage, watching from the wings and periodically playing bit parts in his parents' Borscht Belt act.

At the age of five the budding comic had a revelation. "I was taking my bow at the end of the show," he remembered, "and my foot slipped, and I hit one of the footlights and it exploded. The audience went hysterical. They laughed. And I *heard* that laugh."

There was, it seems, currency in clumsiness, and over the next seven decades Lewis would flop and stumble all the way to the bank, becoming one of the world's highest paid performers and biggest stars.

In many respects, Lewis was a throwback to the great pantomimists of the Silent Era—a physical comedian with a maestro's sense of rhythm and timing who could bring a crowd to their knees with a wobbly-legged lurch or a

goofy smile. And like Chaplin's Tramp or Keaton's Stoneface, Lewis's comic persona—a grown man with the soul of an unconstrained nine-year-old boy—would over time become synonymous with the performer himself.

In 1946 the twenty-year-old joker found the perfect foil for his rambunctious buffoonery in debonair nightclub crooner Dean Martin. With Martin playing straight man, Lewis rollicked across the stage, endlessly thwarting his partner's song-and-dance routines with inane interjections, rubber-faced mugging, and plenty of exuberant pratfalls.

"Don't ask me to remember what they do," one Las Vegas critic remarked, "for much of their nonsense doesn't make sense—but you'll laugh your ribs sore."

Writer and comedian Carl Reiner was one of the duo's casualties. "I saw the single funniest evening in comedy I'd ever seen," he recalled of their act. "I don't think I've ever seen anybody get that many laughs, and make us laugh so hard, as those two guys just tearing up a stage."

When the pair split after ten years, they were the hottest ticket in show business, stars of stage, radio, and

television who had also shattered box-office records with their sixteen feature films.

And it was in cinema that Lewis, now on his own, became a legend. The majority of his early screen efforts traded on his inveterate childlike bungling by throwing him into high-pressure situations—as a cop, a military man, a babysitter, a private detective—and allowing him to wreak slapstick havoc on his surroundings. Films like *The Delicate Delinquent*, *The Sad Sack*, *Cinderfella*, *The Bellboy*, *The Ladies' Man*, and *The Errand Boy* were masterworks of physical comedy, some with a hard edge of social satire. But it was 1963's *Nutty Professor*, generally considered Lewis's masterpiece, that cemented his reputation as a writer, director, and comedic actor of consummate skill.

A modern take on the Jekyll-and-Hyde legend, the film featured Lewis as both the bumbling Dr. Julius Kelp— a buck-toothed, nearsighted college chemistry professor who has as much trouble fanning the flames of romance with campus cutie Stella Purdy (Stella Stevens) as he does keeping his laboratory from exploding—and as Kelp's alter ego, the smooth-talking Buddy Love, a suave but soulless chick-magnet, a warped version of Hugh Hefner's Playboy ethos come to life through the magic of the hapless chemist's secret elixir.

As an exercise in comic pantomime, *The Nutty Professor* was a testament not only to Lewis's range but also to his supreme control of his body. Transforming himself from the slump-shouldered, flailing nebish into the confident, strutting ladies' man required much more than a gob of Brylcreem and a dash of makeup—in fact, most of Lewis's morphing occurred on screen with a minimum of editing, requiring him to straddle the divide between the two characters by insinuating traits from one into the other as the potion took effect or wore off.

But for all its shape-shifting hilarity, *The Nutty Professor* was at its core a film about the human condition, a comic meditation on the fine line between self-love and self-loathing, and Kelp's heartfelt speech in the final scene about accepting oneself warts and all left no doubt about the picture's intent.

With its uncanny mix of physical high jinks and moral poignancy, Lewis's work as an actor and a director has invariably drawn comparisons to the greats. "I believe Jerry Lewis is the funniest visual comedian since Charlie Chaplin," comedian Steve Allen declared. And the cognoscenti in Europe, who have always been ebullient in their praise of the loose-limbed comic, agreed, rating him "better than Chaplin and Keaton" and "the foremost comic artist of [our] time." To this day, Lewis is widely considered as not only one of the cinema's best clowns but also one of the greatest comic *auteurs* in movie history.

Peter Sellers is another comedian who was a born showman. His parents were vaudevillians in England, and he made his debut even earlier than Jerry Lewis did. At a mere two days old, his proud papa carried Peter on stage during an encore. Sellers moved up the show-biz ladder with the pioneering British comedy troupe *The Goon Show* and landed his first solo film role in the original version of *The Ladykillers*.

Then, in 1964, Sellers's career exploded. That year he had starring roles in four big films: the Stanley Kubrick masterpiece *Dr. Strangelove, or How I Learned to Stop Worry-*

ing and Love the Bomb, The World of Henry Orient, The Pink Panther, and its sequel, *A Shot in the Dark.*

Though Peter Sellers forte was his ability to totally disappear into a comic character, he was a gifted physical comedian as well. In the *Pink Panther* series, he got to show the full range of his talents as the bumbling French detective, Inspector Jacques Clouseau. Clouseau was a danger not only to himself but also to everyone around him, especially his long-suffering boss, Chief Inspector Charles Drey-fus (Herbert Lom), whom he turns into a homicidal maniac. This also applies to his dedicated houseboy, Cato (Burt Kwouk). A running gag in the *Panther* films is Cato's "surprise judo attacks" (like once jumping out of his boss's refrigerator), meant to sharpen Clouseau's martial skills but inevitably causing Cato grievous bodily harm and usually resulting in major property damage.

There was a large body count in the *Pink Panther* movies, but it wasn't the bad guys who took the punishment; it was usually Clouseau, Chief Inspector Dreyfus, or any poor citizen within range. Sellers would fall into ponds, pocket a cigarette lighter while it was still lit, open doors into people's faces, and explode bombs in the worst locations. He even fell through the floor in his own apartment during one of Cato's "sneak attacks." Inspector Clouseau always catches the criminal—not by stealth but by stupidity.

The movies were directed and co-written by comedy master Blake Edwards, who once defined Sellers as a "mercurial clown" who was able to turn comedy into drama and back again, all in the blink of an eye. A true chameleon, Sellers most famously said: "There is no me. I do not exist. There used to be a me, but I had it surgically removed."

A comedian to the end, Peter Sellers specified in his will that the Glenn Miller tune "In the Mood" be played for his funeral; it was a song he truly despised.

In the lineage of Laurel and Hardy, Lewis, and Sellers is Canadian-born actor Jim Carrey. Nobody has been better or more successful in the realm of physical comedy in the last decade than Carrey.

Like slapstick itself, Jim Carrey's comedy is rooted in pain: the pain of his family's poverty, the pain of his mother's early death from kidney disease, the pain of being ostracized at school. He's said, "My focus is to forget the pain, mock the pain, reduce it."

"The minute any of us saw Jim Carrey, particularly when he burst onto the screen in *Ace Ventura Pet Detective*," declares Leonard Maltin, "we all had to think of Jerry Lewis. Few others have really exploited their physicality so thoroughly. Not just in body language, but in a rubber-faced way. And Jim Carrey is willing to go farther than anybody else of his generation. He just takes it one giant step more. And sometimes that's a little too far for some people's tastes. And sometimes it's just far enough that it's outlandish and outrageous and funny."

Carrey's earliest inspirations were the two legends Jerry Lewis and Peter Sellers. "Anybody who came to my house was entertained first by a ten-year-old child flailing, throwing himself down a long flight of stairs," admits Carrey. "That was how it began, and then it just deteriorated from there."

He would spend countless hours in front of the mirror, rehearsing their routines as well as those of Dick Van Dyke. And then he'd use them (and bits like his dolphin impersonation) to ease the pain of his bedridden mother.

Jim Carrey made an inauspicious club debut at the age of sixteen but soon was providing major financial support for his family. By the age of twenty-two, he was in Los Angeles, doing stand-up and working in a short-lived television series called *The Duck Factory*. Supporting roles in movies like *Peggy Sue Got Married* and *Earth Girls Are Easy* got him his first screen acting experience, but it was the four seasons he spent on the sketch-comedy television series *In Living Color* that really showcased his incredible talent for creating imaginatively original characters. Carrey is probably remembered most for his infamous "Fire Marshall Bill," a pyromaniac who handed out fire-safety tips.

In 1994, Carrey became a major star, headlining three top-grossing movies, *Ace Ventura: Pet Detective*, *The Mask*, and *Dumb and Dumber*—not that he was getting any respect from the critics. Carrey's memorable "Can I ass you a few questions?" routine from *Ace Ventura* (where he lets his backside do the talking) had critics Gene Siskel and Roger Ebert questioning whether the movie signaled the end of Western civilization.

According to Carrey friend and the movie's director Tom Shadyac, the "ass talking" was Jim's invention. At an early point in Jim's career, he "had read a script that really wasn't what he had hoped it would be. So at a table read, when all the actors read their lines in front of big network and studio execs, Jim stood on his chair and he talked out his ass." It was Jim's twisted way of "voicing" his disapproval. Jim defended his inspired move saying, "I am a serious actor. I was a serious actor when I was talking through my arse, because that's what the movie needed."

Since then, Jim Carrey has demonstrated just how versatile an actor he can be—truly going from the ridiculous to the sublime, carrying on the comic tradition of the loveable loser, the schlemiel who triumphs over adversity. Very much like Jerry Lewis's performance in *The Nutty Professor*, Jim's dual role of Charlie/Hank from *Me, Myself, and Irene* is another take on the Jekyll and Hyde legend—except in this case the monster is Charlie's alter ego, an out-of-control "control freak" named Hank. Where Lewis downed a potion to bring on the monster, Carrey takes medicine to keep him at bay.

One great example of Jim's "getting physical" is the scene in which he's knocked backward over a fence and down a hill. After he goes over the fence, he disappears

from sight for a beat, then pops up again down the hill. Normally, a stuntman would handle the fall, but Carrey decided that it might look fake to the audience, so he did it himself—eagerly. "I love getting into physical comedy," he says. "Nobody else would know halfway down the hill how to push themselves back up again to get back into the camera. It doesn't work, it doesn't look like me. It's the Buster Keaton thing—part of you wants to know it's him in there."

Liar, Liar was a breakthrough vehicle for Carrey because it allowed him to be a human being as well as a comedian.

There's a generous helping of physical comedy in *Liar Liar*, especially the scene where Carrey, as lawyer Fletcher Reede, literally beats himself to a pulp in a courthouse bathroom. Director Tom Shadyac says that what started as a simple bit really evolved once Carrey applied his particular genius to it. Shadyac says practically all he had to do was give Carrey the premise and stand back. "This is on a set. We built a bathroom and I walked Jim in and I said, 'Jim, what do you want to do here?' And he looked around, looked at the toilet, the sink, the radiator, and he goes, 'Pad that,' and he's pointing over toward the radiator 'Um, get me a toilet pad so I can do that, and, um, I'm gonna go from here to there to here. Jim's the one who came up with punching himself, with taking the toilet seat and slamming it on his head. Jim needs to have room for that genius to come out."

Shadyac thinks Jim Carrey's appeal, like Lewis's, has a lot to do with his remaining in touch with the kid in him, the kid in all of us. "I look at [him] as being childlike," he says, "because children, as you know, can go from zero to hero in a second. Jim has that, embodies that child. And so I think it's cathartic for us to go see Jim, to watch his movies, because it gets us back in touch with our own sense of youth. I think future generations will look back on him, and maybe he's sort of the pinnacle of those physically gifted comics."

However you analyze it, Jim Carrey is an amalgam of the comedy legends who have gone before him. He's a supreme physical comedian who's taken the very best comic qualities of his heroes and forged them into a vibrant new presence all his own.

Whether it's embarrassment, mishap and indignity, pratfalls, practical jokes, accidents, acrobatic death-defying stunts, water soakings, getting pied, or wild chase-scenes with trains and cars—physical comedy is still one of the most potent forms of entertainment.

CHAPTER 18

THROW US A SCREWBALL

What better way to endure the depths of the Great Depression than to laugh, and laugh hard, at the antics of the rich and foolish. With an infusion of fast-talking New York playwrights lured to Hollywood as writers by the advent of talkies, the 1930s saw the birth of a modern, less sentimental genre of romantic comedy: the screwball, in which women gave as good as they got, the foibles of high society were laid bare even as its glamour and glory presented a glimmer of hope for everyone else, and plots were twisted so far that they bent in on themselves and everyone had a snappy comeback—or two or three.

While the first of the screwball genre was the 1931 adaptation of the Broadway play *The Front Page*, the genre really took off in 1934 with *Twentieth Century*, *The Thin Man*, and, most significant, Frank Capra's *It Happened One Night*.

Like its characters, *It Happened One Night* traveled a long, bumpy road to success. Capra and writer Robert Riskin adapted a short story called "Night Bus," about a runaway heiress and a chemist, changing the former from a purely spoiled brat to someone aching for freedom, and the latter character to a tough-talking reporter. In the movie, rich girl Ellie Andrews runs away from her domineering father, who was trying to prevent her eloping with her ne'er-do-well fiancé. On her own and desperate to get to New York, she encounters the "real" America, embodied by newsman Peter Warne, who is cynical and candid but later proves to be brave, loyal, and adventurous. He at first sees in her only an opportunity, a sensationalistic story, before ultimately falling for her.

Robert Montgomery, having just appeared in a bus-related movie called *Fugitive Lovers*, turned down the part of Peter, to Capra's great good fortune. MGM studio chief Louis Mayer was angry at Clark Gable's salary demands and, out of spite, lent the actor—typecast until then as a sexy villain—to the low-budget Columbia movie. Myrna Loy rejected the role of the heiress, Ellie, saying the early script she saw was awful. Several other actresses said no as well, before Claudette Colbert said she'd do it for fifty thousand dollars (double her regular salary) and only during the four weeks before her vacation began. (Colbert hated the whole experience and told friends afterward, "I just finished the worst picture in the world.")

Just getting the film off the ground exhausted Capra, who later wrote, "I was like the overtrained fighter who left his fight in the gym," but the result was that he worked in a loose style "fast and unworried"—that fit the film's flavor. Even Colbert's apathy worked in their favor, Capra wrote. "All her little tantrums . . . were rehearsals

for the picture. All she had to do was bug Gable on camera as she had bugged me off camera."

Shot on a low budget with minimal sets (the on-the-run protagonists wore the same outfits for virtually the entire movie), the movie relied on crackling writing and clever chemistry to entertain and amuse while scoring a few points about gender roles and social class. Along the way, Capra, Riskin, Gable, and Colbert created several classic comedy scenes.

Forced to spend a stormy night in a motel, Peter nabs them a room (pretending to be husband and wife)—Ellie is shocked and refuses to stay with him, even though there are two single beds. He explains he's interested only in her story and threatens to turn her over to her father otherwise. Then he demonstrates his chastity in the famous "Walls of Jericho" scene, draping a blanket over a clothesline between the beds.

"Well, I like privacy when I retire," he says with mock sincerity. "Behold the walls of Jericho! Uh, maybe not as

thick as the ones that Joshua blew down with his trumpet, but a lot safer."

When she refuses to go along, he says that if she prefers she can just stay and watch him undress. "Perhaps you're interested in how a man undresses—quite a study in psychology. No two men do it alike. If you notice, the coat came first, then the tie, then the shirt. [When Gable revealed his bare chest, T-shirt sales in America plummeted.] Now, uh, according to Hoyle, after that, the, uh, pants should be next."

Finally Peter reaches for his belt buckle, slyly warning Ellie, "After that, it's every man for himself," prompting her hasty retreat to her side of the "wall."

Later, however, Ellie teaches Peter a thing or two about sexuality. He is expounding on his hitchhiking skills, lecturing long-windedly about the "ol' thumb," demonstrating three different styles—the "short, jerky movement, you don't care whether they stop or not"; a wider motion, "a smile goes with this one, like this, that means you've got a brand-new story about the farmer's daughter"; and the long, sweeping movement for when "you're broke and hungry and everything looks black." But when he fails again and again in an increasingly fran-

tic (and funny) thumbing effort, Ellie takes over, raising her skirt above her knee, bringing the very next driver to a screeching halt. She then boasts to Peter that she had proved "the limb is mightier than the thumb." (Colbert initially refused to show skin until Capra brought in a leggy body double to take her place.)

The movie received lackluster reviews and had poor initial ticket sales, but word-of-mouth at the few remaining movie theaters propelled it to popularity, convincing the producers to redistribute it.

The film soon took off, playing to sellout crowds, winning Oscars for Best Picture, Director, Actor, Actress, and Screenplay Adaptation—a feat since matched only twice—and establishing a rich woman–ordinary man formula that would be copied in numerous screwball comedies.

One of most creative twists on that formula came two years later in *My Man Godfrey,* which told the story of a ditzy but well-meaning rich girl (Carole Lombard) who brings a homeless man (William Powell) to a society scavenger hunt in order to win a prize. Feeling guilty, she then hires Godfrey as her butler and soon falls in love with him. Then, halfway through the movie, audiences learn that

Godfrey is actually a wealthy Boston scion who, suicidal over a broken love affair, had "wandered down to the East River one night thinking I'd just slide in and get it over with. But I met some fellas living there on a city dump. Here were people who were fighting it out and not complaining." Impressed, he decided to live with them for a while. Thus begins a whole other level of wacky plot twists.

The movie is filled with delectable dialogue, and much of it was improvised or worked out on the set by director Gregory La Cava, screenwriter Morrie Ryskind (a Pulitzer Prize–winning playwright who helped Eric Hatch adapt his short novel *1011 Fifth Avenue*), and Powell and Lombard, who had actually been married from 1931 to 1933.

Film historian Ted Sennett has written that the movie "had the audacity to juxtapose the glittering fashionable environment of the Park Avenue swells with the harsh Depression world of the hobo colonies. . . . Few comedies of the period addressed the gap between the haves and have-nots with such a biting edge."

Many of the quips comment on the plight of the poor. When we first meet Godfrey, he's reassuring a fellow hobo, saying, "Prosperity's just around the corner." To which Mike (Pat Flaherty) responds, "Yeah. It's been there a long time. I wish I knew which corner." And when Irene asks this "forgotten man" why he'd live in such a dump, Godfrey deadpans, "Because my real-estate agent felt the altitude would be very good for my asthma."

At the society scavenger hunt in a hotel ballroom, Irene's father, Alexander Bullock (Eugene Pallette), watches as the city's elite scurry about with their cast-off collectibles. When his friend Blake (Selmer Jackson), says, "This place slightly resembles an insane asylum," he replies dryly, "Well, all you need to start an asylum is an empty room and the right kind of people."

The film's screwball elements were firmly in place as well—the morning after the scavenger hunt, a carriage driver shows up at the Bullock mansion, demanding a fifty-dollar fee—and his horse back. It seems Irene insisted on driving the beast up the front steps and into the library, where she left it overnight.

Later, during a party, Godfrey's old Harvard pal Tommy is a guest and recognizes him, letting out that they knew each other at Harvard. Godfrey tells the Bullocks he was Tommy's valet and forces Tommy to improvise a wild story about Godfrey's Indian wife and five children to keep his cover intact. Later, when Godfrey tries explaining his situation and his complicated future plans to Tommy, he quips, "There's a very peculiar mental process called thinking—you wouldn't know much about it."

In the end, Godfrey saves the family's fortune, teaches them humility, starts a fancy new restaurant that employs and provides housing for his hobo pals—and of course gets the girl.

By contrast, Leo McCarey's 1937 film *The Awful Truth* is relatively simple; there are no societal points to be scored in this relatively skimpy plot. All the plot twists revolve around a husband (Cary Grant) and wife (Irene Dunne); after a fight about trust and faith in marriage, Jerry and Lucy decide to divorce and date other people, then realize they're still in love with each other and instead work to undermine the other's new relationships and win their soon-to-be-ex back.

McCarey, who built plots about trivial incidents leading to enormous consequences, used his screenplays as a

basic guideline, adding one-liners or even comic set-pieces during the course of filming. "He came in every morning with a small piece of brown wrapping paper on which he'd written his ideas," co-star Ralph Bellamy once recalled. "We were all mad as could be." Grant, in his first romantic comedy lead, at first disliked this improvisatory approach so much that he offered studio head Harry Cohn five thousand dollars to be let out of the movie. Cohn said no. "After a few days, we realized McCarey was a comedy genius," Bellamy said. And indeed, this was the movie that created that famous cheeky Cary Grant persona.

The screwiest and funniest scenes come when the couple tries breaking up each other's relationships. Once, during a court-appointed visit to their shared dog, Mr. Smith, Jerry plays piano while Mr. Smith "sings" along, making it impossible for Lucy to chat with new beau Dan (Ralph Bellamy), a goofy, naive Oklahoma oilman dominated by his mother. (The terrier, by the way, had quite a screwball résumé as well, co-starring in *The Thin Man* and *Bringing Up Baby*.)

Later, the exes met in a nightclub, where Jerry taunts Lucy, "Ah, so you're gonna live in Ok-la-ho-ma, eh Lucy? How I envy you."

When Daniel boasts they'll live "right in Oklahoma City!" Jerry has a field day:

"Not Oklahoma City *itself*? Lucy, you lucky girl! No more running around to nightspots. No more prowling around in New York shops—and if it should get dull, you can always go over to *Tul-sa* for the weekend. I think a big change like that does one good, don't you?"

Then he encourages the couple to dance and watches with glee as Daniel embarrasses Lucy with his absurdly goofy country style. Jerry even bribes the orchestra to "play the same number again for an encore."

Grant pulls off typically absurd screwball plot maneuvers perfectly—hiding behind a door at Lucy's apartment so Daniel won't know he's been visiting. He tickles Lucy while Daniel reads his sappy but heartfelt poem—"To you, my little prairie flower, I'm thinkin' of you every hour"—forcing her to laugh in poor Daniel's face.

The chaos culminates in a bit of well-timed silliness when Lucy's music teacher, Armand—whom Jerry had erroneously accused of having an affair with Lucy—comes to Lucy offering to straighten things out for Jerry. But when Jerry suddenly bursts in, Armand ducks into the bedroom, leaving his derby by the door. Lucy hides the derby, but while Jerry apologizes for his recent behavior, Mr. Smith, thinking Lucy is playing hide-and-seek, keeps retrieving the hat no matter how desperately she tries to get rid of it. Finally, Jerry, thinking it's his new derby, takes it—only to find it's comically large. Before Jerry can deduce how his hat grew, Daniel and his beloved "Maw" suddenly arrive for a "talk," and it's Jerry's turn to duck into the bedroom—where he finds Armand. While Daniel and Lucy talk, they hear an increasingly loud, messy brawl between Armand and Jerry coming from behind closed doors, which ends with Dan and "Maw" watching the two men chase each other out of Lucy's bedroom.

Lucy has her revenge, however. She answers Jerry's ringing phone, and his new fiancée, Barbara Vance, on the other end wonders who this woman is. Jerry covers up and says it's his sister visiting him. That night she pays the high society Vance family a visit, pretending to be the drunk, low-class, outrageous sister, Lola. "Well, I don't want to be rude, but may I have a drink? I had three or four before I got here, but they're beginning to wear off, and you know how that is," she says, adding that Jerry is secretly a heavy drinker himself. "I've seen him go along a whole evening and apparently not have a thing to drink and all of a sudden fall flat on his puss."

Lucy caps it all off with a demonstration of the vulgar song she allegedly performed in a nightclub, gyrating and buckling her knees, to Jerry's amusement and the stuffy Vances' dismay. It is proof that these two lovebirds love only each other, and soon they're heading off together for a happy ending.

But Grant's screwball masterpiece—combining his trademark mix of slapstick, devilish delivery, and a debonair air—came in 1940 in Howard Hawks's *His Girl Friday*, where he is matched step for step by Rosalind Russell in the role of a lifetime reportedly turned down by Hepburn, Colbert, and Lombard, among others.

Hawks had already directed screwball gems *Twentieth Century* and *Bringing Up Baby* when he decided to remake the Broadway hit *The Front Page*, which had already been a talkie in 1931. But Hawks had two tricks up his sleeve for this movie about a sleazy, hard-charging editor and reluctant reporter. First, when he had his secretary help read the script aloud with him one day, he realized that changing the reporter to a woman—and ex-wife of the editor—would add an entirely new layer to the comic conflict. Second, he transformed it into the fastest-paced film on record, with the actors directed to take their cues from the third word from the end of the other actor's line. He didn't want them to wait until the one actor finished speaking to pick up the dialogue, spewing overlapping dialogue averaging 240 words a minute—nearly twice the normal speaking pace.

In just ninety-two minutes, Hawks jammed in jail-breaks and false arrests along with sideswipes at political corruption and jaded journalists, while telling the story of Walter Burns (Grant) wooing his ex-wife, Hildy Johnson (Russell), away from a quiet life with new beau Bruce Baldwin (Ralph Bellamy) and back to a life of journalism.

The movie was also surprisingly modern in its pop-culture inside jokes. At one point, Walter describes Baldwin as resembling "that fellow in the movies—you know, Ralph Bellamy"—which is funny not only because it really is Bellamy but also because Bellamy had already become typecast as the second lead who never gets the girl, which happened against Grant in *The Awful Truth* and would soon happen again here. (Bellamy has said that Grant improvised that line himself.) Then, at another point, the mayor is threatening to arrest Walter and says, "You're through," to which the editor sneers, "The last man who said that to me was Archie Leach just a week before he cut his throat." Archie Leach was Grant's real name.

The bustling plot hinges on Walter's end-justifies-the-means efforts to get a big headline out of saving the life of a murderer about to be executed. When Hildy walks in to say she's getting married, he uses her to land the story, and the story to win her back—even if it means lying to her, setting her future husband up to be arrested numerous times on false charges to keep him out of the way, and hiding the prisoner (after an escape attempt) inside a rolltop desk.

In their first scene together, Walter begins seducing Hildy saying, "There's been a lamp burning in the window for you," which she cuts down by saying, "I jumped out of that window a long time ago, Walter," before teasing him: "A big fat lummox like you, hiring an airplane to write 'Hildy, don't be hasty, remember my dimple—Walter.' It delayed our divorce twenty minutes while the judge went

out to watch it." To which the shameless Walter responds, "I've still got the dimple, and in the same place."

One of the funniest scenes comes when Walter takes Hildy and Bruce out to lunch, hoping to plant seeds of dissension and lure Hildy into covering the story. He learns they'll be living with Bruce's mother in Albany, which Bruce declares "a mighty good insurance town—most people there take it out pretty early in life," to which Walter deadpans, "Yeah, well, I can see why they would," prompting a shin-kick beneath the table from Hildy. But Bruce can't see Walter for what he is, saying to Hildy, "I sort of like him. He's got a lot of charm," setting up Hildy for a perfect zinger: "Well, he comes by it naturally. His grandfather was a snake."

Walter hooks Hildy in, but once she realizes Walter has deceived her and Bruce (whom he had pickpocketed and arrested), she lights into him, yelling into the phone: "I wouldn't cover the burning of Rome for you if they were just lighting it up. And if I ever lay my two eyes on you again, I'm gonna walk right up to you and hammer on that monkey skull of yours till it rings like a Chinese gong!"

But the story is too big, and newspapering is in her blood, so Hildy is stuck, especially once she and Walter trap the prisoner in the desk. In one frantically funny scene, she is writing her story while Bruce is asking about his mother (whom Walter has sent off into peril) and Walter is on the phone shouting over them, ordering the front page rearranged: "No, no, never mind the Chinese earthquake for

heaven's sake. . . . Look, I don't care if there's a million dead. . . . No, no, junk the Polish Corridor. . . . Take Hitler and stick him on the funny page. . . . No, no, leave the rooster story alone—that's human interest."

In the end, of course, Walter and Hildy save the man, get the story, and find each other—but the modern twist meant that Hildy would relinquish a "woman's" life of making babies for her "newspaperman" life of hard-boiled journalism. This prompted a spate of screwball and romantic comedies that raised the issue of women facing conflicts between marriage and work.

Although the screwball comedy of our imagination is a 1930s Depression-era classic like *It Happened One Night, My Man Godfrey, The Awful Truth*, or *His Girl Friday*, the genre would actually adapt and achieve its zenith in the next few years, covering a wide array of topics with only one thing in common: the masterful director Preston Sturges. After Sturges's career faded, the screwball fell out of favor, although when it has briefly arisen again over the last fifty years, it has always packed in plenty of laughs.

PRESTON STURGES: MASTER OF THE SCREWBALL COMEDY

PRESTON STURGES was one of Hollywood's earliest writer-directors. He relentlessly skewered hypocrites and the narrow-minded, in politics, high society, or small-town America, and even poked fun at himself. He was the master of witty dialogue and perfectly timed pratfalls, balanced by his over-the-top plotting with grounded, endearing protagonists. Sturges's career was cut short by his losing battle with studios over control, but with such gems as "If it weren't for graft, you'd get a very low type of people in politics," offered in self-rationalization by a corrupt politician in *The Great McGinty*, he packed enough classics into a few years to last a lifetime.

The Lady Eve (1941)

In *The Lady Eve*, the romantic equivalent of three-card monte, Jean (Barbara Stanwyck, in a rare comic role created just for her by Sturges) sets out to con millionaire Charles "Hopsie" Pike (Henry Fonda), only to fall in love with him, only to have her criminal past exposed, only to feel betrayed by the hurt "Hopsie," only to seduce him once again as a look-alike Lady Eve, only to betray him again, only to regain his love again as Jean.

Their first meeting on board a ship encompasses three of moviedom's greatest comic-romantic scenes. In the dining area, Jean watches through her compact makeup mirror and provides a scathing but hysterical narration as every debutante vainly tries to get Charles's attention. "Every Jane in the room is giving him the thermometer, and he feels they're just a waste of time. . . . Oh, now how about this one. . . . Holy smoke, the dropped kerchief! That hasn't been used since Lily Langtry."

As Hopsie leaves the room, Jean trips him up, literally. Then, using her broken shoe as an excuse, she lures him back to her cabin, where he continually explains that he's overwhelmed by her perfume and black exposed-midriff outfit because he has "been up the Amazon for a year." Jean gets Hopsie down on his knees putting on her new shoes, but then rejects his pass—for now.

Soon after, however, Jean finds herself back in her cabin on a chaise with Hopsie on the floor next to her. She nuzzles and caresses his head while they talk about love. She starts out teasing him but ends up falling for him, but it is indelibly funny because of Hopsie's barely repressed lust—he has trouble even speaking in his normal voice.

And that's all in just the first twenty-five minutes of the movie.

Sullivan's Travels (1942)

In *Sullivan's Travels*, a satire of Hollywood and of Sturges himself, Sullivan (Joel McCrea) is a director of fluffy comedies who wants to make a serious, socially conscious film called *O, Brother, Where Art Thou?* ("with a little sex," as the studio heads keep pleading). So he decides to become a hobo to research the plight of the homeless.

But Sullivan is hilariously clueless, trying on tramp outfits assisted by his valet and butler, only to find that the studio is providing a protective cocoon and transforming his journey into a publicity stunt with a fully loaded "land yacht" to trail him and "an advance man in front, and a follow-upper behind."

Eventually he's allowed to go off by himself for a while, but then finds himself toiling for two unattractive yet overly amorous sisters. He sneaks out, tearing his pants, falling into a rain barrel, and hitching a ride that, unfortunately, lands him right back in Hollywood, where he meets a down-on-her-luck blonde (Veronica Lake), called only "The Girl," who is going to hitchhike back east. He offers to "borrow" a car, saying he's a friend of this director Sullivan (whom she has never heard of). They're soon arrested for driving a stolen car, and Sullivan has to be sprung from jail by his valet and butler, setting up one of Sturges's classic lines. The police sergeant asks Sullivan, "How does the girl fit in this picture?" and Sullivan, who has been desperately trying to break free of Hollywood's clichés, retorts, "There's *always* a girl in the picture. Haven't you ever been to the movies?"

The Palm Beach Story (1942)

Written and directed by Preston Sturges, *The Palm Beach Story* was one of his frothier flicks. It features Tom (Joel McCrea), a loving husband but failed entrepreneur, ditched by wife Gerry (Claudette Colbert), who loves him but loves the "good life" more—or so she thinks. She inadvertently seduces the world's wealthiest man, J. D. Hackensacker III, then ropes Tom into pretending he's her brother. She ultimately realizes she loves hubby best, but she still gets money from Hackensacker.

Among the slapstick highlights is a wild scene on a moving train in which the drunken millionaires of the Ale and Quail Club start skeet-shooting (with real bullets) at crackers and end up leading their dogs on a wild goose—or, rather, girl—chase through the dining and sleeping cars.

But there's also plenty of classic Sturges dialogue. Gerry expresses surprisingly frank and modern ideas, with witticisms like "You have no idea what a long-legged gal can do without doing anything" and "Don't you know that the greatest men in the world have told lies and let things be misunderstood if it was useful to them? Didn't you ever hear of a campaign promise?"

The Miracle of Morgan's Creek (1944)

In *The Miracle of Morgan's Creek*, Sturges turned to satirize small-town social mores in the saga of Trudy Knockenlocker (Betty Hutton), who goes out drinking with some soldiers and gets married and knocked up by—well, she's not quite sure who, although she thinks it might be Ratzkiwatzki, a twisted variation on one of the Hollywood censor's names. (It is not surprising that censors delayed this film's release for more than a year. Of course, it then became Sturges's biggest box-office hit.)

When she seeks help from a lawyer, Sturges manages to mock both lecturing lawyers and society's double standards in one scene as the attorney decrees, "No man is going to jeopardize his present or poison his future with a lot of little brats running around unless he's forced to. It's up to a woman to knock him down, hog-tie him, and drag him in front of witnesses immediately, if not sooner."

Meanwhile, overly nervous Norval (Eddie Bracken), who has always loved Trudy, tries to rescue her—by claiming to be the father and marrying her under an assumed name—but gets himself into an increasingly disastrous mess. He ultimately ends up in jail, where the town constable, Papa Knockenlocker (Sturges regular William Demarest) tries to encourage Norval to escape to go help save Trudy. The naive Norval misunderstands in a hilarious slapstick scene in which Papa practically ties himself up and knocks himself out trying to convince the too-honest lad to escape.

But there's a happy ending, Sturges-style. When this wartime bride gives birth to sextuplets, she and Norval become heroes, thanks only to craven politicians looking to gain attention for themselves from Trudy's mini-squadron. In a classic Sturges touch, the governor in question is none other than Dan McGinty, the protagonist from *The Great McGinty* (with Brian Donlevy reprising his role and Akim Tamiroff joining him for a cameo as the political boss.)

19

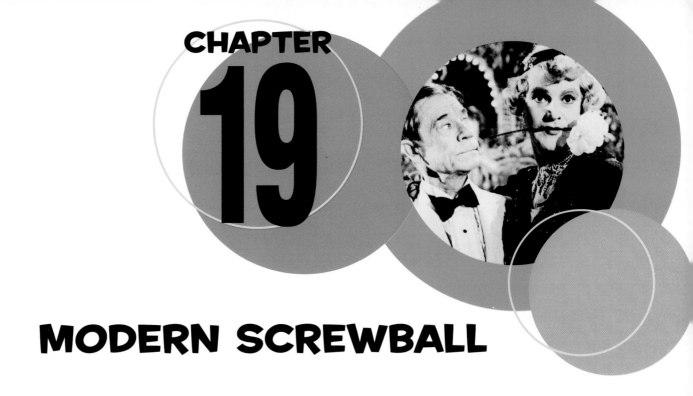

MODERN SCREWBALL

Since the screwball heyday of the 1930s and 1940s, the screwball comedic style has popped up only occasionally. But the few films that have adapted the atmosphere and attitudes of screwball comedies to fit modern morals and moviemaking have produced some true classics.

It's difficult to top Billy Wilder's *Some Like It Hot* on just about any level. This legendary film—which became the highest-grossing comedy at that time and was declared by the American Film Institute as the number-one comedy film of all time—featured great directing, sizzling dialogue, and near-perfect casting in Jack Lemmon, Tony Curtis, and Marilyn Monroe. Curtis and Lemmon play "Joe" and "Jerry," down-on-their-luck Chicago musicians who inadvertently witness the Saint Valentine's Day Massacre. To escape, they disguise themselves as women ("Josephine" and "Daphne") and join an all-girl orchestra on a train ride to Florida. (Curtis's "female" voice is dubbed because his impersonations kept cracking.)

While the story lines may seem tame today, they were quite risqué in 1959, adding an element of bawdiness and even naughtiness to the humor. Set during Prohibition, the film's endless sexual allusions of all types—bisexuality, transvestism, androgyny, homosexuality, transexuality, lesbianism, and impotence—helped push the weakened Production Code censorship system further into decline.

Curtis and Lemmon made the film's central joke work by taking it seriously. They were coached by female impersonators, watched Mae West films for tips on hip-shaking, and had the costume department custom-make their dresses. Monroe, who plays the sultry "Sugar Kane," by contrast, was just Marilyn—unprepared and often unable to perform. Her inability on countless takes to remember the simple line "Where's the bourbon?" while looking in a dresser drawer prompted Wilder to paste the line inside the drawer. On the next take, Monroe opened the wrong drawer. So he had the line pasted inside every drawer. Yet her performance of that line, and every scene in the film, plays flawlessly.

The film is packed with memorable lines, such as Jerry's response to seeing Sugar Kane for the first time: "Look how she moves. That's just like Jell-O on springs. She must have some sort of built-in motors. I tell you, it's a whole different sex!"

But the film hinged on the script's meticulously crafted screwball plot twists, which Wilder spun out with a polish occasionally lacking in the original screwballs.

In this film, nothing plays out the way the characters or audience would expect. Both men fall for Sugar, the boozy singer who dreams of marrying a millionaire but "always gets the fuzzy end of the lollipop," but their masquerading as women makes seducing her tricky. When she crawls into Daphne's train berth to say thanks for getting her out of a jam, Daphne/Jerry can barely control her/himself, but the innocent Sugar soon invites all the girls in, and he finds himself surrounded by frolicking women, unable to enjoy it at all.

The screwball nature of the film spins even faster when the girls arrive in Florida. (The film was actually shot on location at the Hotel Del Coronado in San Diego, California.) Curtis comes up with a scheme to win Sugar over: when not in his drag outfit, he disguises himself as a millionaire. (Curtis himself came up with the notion of parodying the voice of the original king of the screwballs, Cary Grant.) Meanwhile, Lemmon's Daphne is pretending to be successfully wooed by a real millionaire, Osgood Fielding (Joe E. Brown).

The absurdity of the situations makes every clever quip that much funnier. Joe seduces Sugar out to Osgood's yacht, pretending it's his own. Then he proceeds to tell her about his life of skeet shoot and water polo, prompting Sugar to ask, "Water polo? Isn't that terribly dangerous?" setting Joe up to exclaim in faux excitement, "I'll say! I had two ponies drown under me."

Then Joe gets down to business, pretending that a heartbreaking tragedy has rendered him impotent, tricking Sugar into trying to kiss him back to health. In this classic scene, Joe feigns frigidity until finally she "rescues" him with her passionate kisses, his response symbolized with phallic imagery by his leg lifting up straight off the couch (again Curtis's idea).

Meanwhile, the oft-divorced Osgood learns that "Daphne" plays the bow fiddle, prompting him to ask mischievously, "Do you use a bow or do you just pluck it?" to which Daphne quips, "Most of the time, I slap it!" Osgood comes back with, "You must be quite a girl," and Daphne retorts sharply, "Wanna bet?"

But when Osgood and Jerry go tangoing and Osgood proposes, Jerry actually gets caught up in his role, much to Joe's shock and dismay. "I'm engaged," Jerry jubilantly announces, but when Joe asks who the lucky girl is and Jerry responds "I am," gleefully snapping his castanets, Joe howls in protest. "You're not a girl! You're a guy! Why would a guy want to marry a guy?" To which Jerry, caught up in the momentum of it all, responds earnestly, "Security!"

Wilder heightened the sexual silliness by cutting back and forth between these two stories, then throwing in one final crazy confrontation with the Chicago gangsters before the two couples ride off happily ever after—sort of. The night before shooting the last scene, Wilder's writing partner, I. A. L. "Iz" Diamond, came up with a possible last line, which the director tossed in just to see how it worked. In the scene, "Daphne" tries desperately to explain to Osgood all the reasons they can't marry, citing his smoking, inability to have children, and everything else, before finally tearing off his wig and confessing in his real voice, "I'm a man," to which Osgood responds, cheerfully and without missing a beat, "Well, nobody's perfect." It was a *perfect* screwball ending, leaving a whole uncertain future to the imagination.

While *Some Like It Hot* twisted the traditional screwball formula by playing with gender roles and sexual identity, *The In-Laws* subverted it by ignoring the story's romantic framework almost entirely. This madcap classic was born not out of inspiration but out of Alan Arkin's simple desire to make a movie with Peter Falk.

Arkin asked Falk if he'd appear in a *Freebie and the Bean* sequel, and when Falk said no, he'd rather do something less violent, Arkin asked screenwriter Andrew Bergman to concoct something where the two characters didn't previously know each other. Bergman spent two months trying to think of a concept where the two men would conceivably be "stuck together," so audiences could enjoy watching Falk "eating into Alan," before hitting on the idea of making them in-laws-to-be. After that, it was relatively easy, writing for these two well-established personas: the tightly wound Arkin as dentist Sheldon Kornpett, who seems always to be stunned by the turns his life has taken, enduring a slow burn or exploding in full neurotic outrage, and the raffishly charming Falk as Vince Ricardo, a possibly deranged CIA agent leading his new friend on a wildly dangerous goose chase, making small talk about split-pea soup and espresso while undertaking an increasingly perilous mission.

The relationship is established in their first meeting, a dinner just days before their children's wedding. Vince, presenting himself as an international businessman, tells—with humble sincerity—increasingly preposterous tall tales about living in the bush where "tse-tse flies the size of eagles pick children off the ground and carry them away" and can't be stopped because these flies with beaks are protected by "The Guacamole Act of 1917." Everyone is charmed except Sheldon, who grows agitated at everyone else's blithe acceptance of such nonsense.

But that's just the beginning. Soon the affable Vince shows up at Sheldon's office, interrupting his practice to ask "a small favor"—to borrow Sheldon for five minutes on his lunch hour. "It's nine o'clock in the morning," Sheldon points out, to which Vince responds, seemingly unaware how odd his behavior is, "You never take an early lunch?"

Sheldon is suspicious and reluctant but has promised his daughter that he will make nice with his new family members. So he goes along and soon finds himself breaking into Vince's office for him, being chased down fire escapes, and being shot at, before Vince finally reveals his true job—CIA agent—and explains to him over split-pea soup that Sheldon is now an accomplice to Vince's unauthorized robbery of the U.S. Treasury to foil a Latin American attempt to destabilize the economy. (What really sets Sheldon off is learning that Vince is doing this after his bosses deemed it too risky and that Vince was not just once involved in the ill-fated Bay of Pigs incident—"It was my idea.")

The plot is absurd, of course, serving as little more than a device to throw Arkin and Falk together in increasingly over-the-top situations. Vince convinces Sheldon to go with him to Scranton, Pennsylvania—but really takes him to an island banana republic aboard a private plane with Chinese co-pilots (who deliver a safety drill in Chinese but act it out with hilarious body language for Sheldon's benefit).

Their arrival at the airport is one of the most beloved comedy scenes (although before filming, Falk actually told Arkin he didn't think it was particularly funny). When snipers shoot the crooked politician they're coming to meet, Vince and Sheldon hit the ground. But to escape alive they must make it to the man's car. And to get there safely, they must use Vince's tactic: "Serpentine, Shelly, serpentine!" he shouts as they weave and wind in a breathtakingly silly way that keeps them exposed to gunfire for five times longer than necessary. When they reach the car, the keys aren't there, and Sheldon—afraid to have Vince killed and be left alone—volunteers to go back to the dead man to find them, "serpentining" all the way there and all the way back. This Keystone Cop–like scene is undeniably goofy but inarguably a classic.

The movie keeps getting zanier, climaxing finally at a meeting with the utterly insane General Garcia (Richard Libertini)—who has a Señor Wences–type companion tattooed on his hand (and pours water all over himself when his hand, as Señor Pepe, "says" he's thirsty), spends thousands collecting garish black-velvet paintings, and has his troops serenade Vince and Sheldon before giving the two men medals and then putting them in front of a firing squad.

Vince and Sheldon are saved by the CIA, pocket five million dollars apiece in ill-gotten booty and make it to the wedding in the nick of time—and they all live happily ever after, of course. In its lightheartedness, *The In-Laws* is perhaps the most old-school of the modern screwballs, while *Tootsie*, which came along three years later, is far more ambitious. This Dustin Hoffman gem shares a crossdressing theme with *Some Like It Hot* but explores gender differences and stereotypes more seriously than its predecessor. That's largely a tribute to Hoffman, who helped originate the idea for the script and had it written into his contract that—if after two months of screen-test preparations he felt he wasn't convincing as a woman—the movie would be shelved.

"We shaved his legs, his arms, and the backs of his fingers," director and co-star Sydney Pollack once explained. "We designed a wardrobe full of high necklines and scarves at the throat, because he's got a size sixteen and a half neck and a big Adam's apple. . . . We went up to Columbia University and put an oscilloscope of a woman's voice on his throat, so that he could try to get his voice up to match the lines."

All that perfectionism was typical of Hoffman, whose character, Michael Dorsey, was imbued with many of Hoffman's traits, creating an odd screwball, which-is-life-and-which-is-art effect. At one point, Michael argues with his agent George Fields, who says no one will work with him because he's too difficult and demanding, pointing out that he couldn't even play a tomato in a commercial without delaying production because he found it illogical for a tomato to sit down.

"*You were a tomato*," George roars. "A tomato doesn't have logic. A tomato can't move." To which Dorsey responds in total seriousness, "That's what I said. So if he can't move, how's he gonna sit down, George? I was a stand-up tomato: a juicy, sexy, beefsteak tomato."

Making this connection even stronger, and stranger, is that Fields is played by Pollack because Hoffman reportedly said the director was the only person he'd believe could make him do things he didn't want to—and yet during filming there were points at which the Pollack-Hoffman relationship was strained. The pair had strong differing opinions.

In the movie, Michael is desperate for money to produce and star in a play written by his cynical roommate, Jeff (Bill Murray, who improvised almost all his lines). To earn some cash and get some work, Michael transforms himself into "Dorothy Michaels" in order to audition for and ultimately earn a role as a hospital administrator on a daytime soap.

While the movie veers between light social drama, romantic comedy, and Hollywood satire, it never loses sight of its screwball soul. Dorothy becomes a huge star and role model for her female audience, but she runs into serious trouble by standing up to the chauvinist director Ron (Dabney Coleman), falling in love with co-star Julie (Jessica Lange), and attracting the attention of Julie's widowed dad Les (Charles Durning), while avoiding his friend Sandy (Teri Garr), who had originally auditioned for the role "Dorothy" won.

One of the funniest scenes came soon after Michael's

transformation when Dorothy confronts George Fields outside the Russian Tea Room. Dorothy asks where the Russian Tea Room is, then follows George inside and sits down with him without invitation before finally startling the agent by revealing her true self. When some of George's acquaintances come over, Dorothy puts him on the spot, pretending to be a paramour.

This scene was inspired by Hoffman's real-life experience. When Hoffman had been practicing as Dorothy, he ran into Jon Voight at the Russian Tea Room and chatted him up—even complimenting the actor on his work in *Midnight Cowboy* (in which Hoffman had co-starred)—without Voight's realizing that the woman was actually Hoffman.

Pollack, who shot the scene at his own regular booth

at the Russian Tea Room, later said people would subsequently do a double take when they'd see him sitting there in real life.

The quintessential screwball moment comes when Dorothy emerges as a media darling, posing for photo shoot after photo shoot, appearing on the covers of *Cosmopolitan, Ms., TV Guide* (with Gene Shalit), *People* (with Andy Warhol), and in an iconic *New York* magazine shot with the American flag behind her.

Then the movie hurtles toward its frantic climax as Michael tries to undo the mess he has made—Sandy thinks he's gay, Julie thinks Dorothy is a lesbian, and Les thinks she's going to accept his marriage proposal—by revealing Dorothy's "true" self, "Edwin Kimberly" (Dorothy's brother), to the stunned crew, cast, and television audience.

"Dustin Hoffman puts 100 percent into that performance," asserts film historian Leonard Maltin. "If you don't believe he's a guy that desperate, and you do, and if you don't believe that he's a guy who gets so taken in by his own masquerade, which he does, then the movie falls flat, it's not going to work. But you do believe it. He's so extreme as that failed actor, and then he's so good as Dorothy that he even convinces himself," observes Maltin.

As fantastical as these (and the original) screwball comedies were in their twists and turns, they were all ultimately grounded in reality. *Groundhog Day* broke the rules and created a new variation—the existential screwball untethered by the normal boundaries of time and space.

Groundhog Day takes a simple premise—what would you do if you were literally trapped in the same day over and over again—and plays it out with great comic inventiveness. Jaded Pittsburgh weatherman Phil Connors (Bill Murray) is being sent out, yet again, to cover the ultra-cutesy Groundhog Day festivities in Punxsutawney, Pennsylvania, accompanied by smart-aleck cameraman Larry (Chris Elliot) and his beautiful but standoffish news producer Rita (Andie MacDowell).

The entire day, beginning with Sonny and Cher's "I Got You Babe" blaring on the clock-radio precisely at 6:00 A.M. is an utter annoyance, but everything gets a whole lot worse—and funnier—when Phil wakes up to find out it's Groundhog Day again. And again. And again. Just as he feels trapped in his day-to-day life, he's now a prisoner of time and place, trapped in this alternate universe. To escape, Phil tries everything, from killing himself to learning enough about Rita to win her love. He almost gets the

girl: at one point Rita says, sighing, "You couldn't *plan* a day like this," to which Phil responds, "Well, you can. It just takes an awful lot of work." But his insincere romancing leaves him stuck in Groundhog Day. Finally, however, he realizes that he has to actually change himself, for his own sake, and he sets out to become a better human being, showing curiosity and compassion, striving to make other people happy—he masters the piano and ice sculpting, catches a young boy falling from a tree (every day), and cares for a freezing homeless man. In the end, his newfound attitude wins Rita over and sets him free.

Writer Danny Rubin's original script took the concept too far, beginning with Phil already stuck, leaving him trapped for thousands of years and ending with the dispiriting discovery that Rita was stuck in her own Groundhog Day. Director Harold Ramis rewrote the script to make it more hopeful and humorous (clashing with his star, who was interested in the philosophical dilemmas as much as the comedy). To give the twists and turns their full comedic impact, Ramis added character-setting scenes in Pittsburgh at the beginning of the film, showing Phil developing an understanding of his plight and deepening the love story with Rita.

Murray was the natural choice for the ornery Phil, screenwriter Danny Rubin once said, because "he's not afraid to be cruel and self-centered." One of the funniest bits in the movie is Phil's repeated encounters with his old high school classmate, the obnoxiously friendly Ned "Needlenose" Ryerson (Stephen Tobolowsky), who goes to great lengths to remind Phil of their linked past. ("Got the shingles real bad senior year. Almost didn't graduate. . . . I dated your sister Mary Pat till you told me not to anymore.") Ned is a life-insurance salesman desperate to pitch Phil, who is increasingly desperate to get away. Finally, realizing that he can act out his true feelings without consequence, Phil greets Ned the next "day" by recognizing him first—"Ned? Ned Ryerson?"—then by hauling off and socking Ned in the nose. Later, Phil learns to kill him with kindness, hugging him too long and saying, "I don't know where you're needed, but couldn't you call in sick?"—which sends Ned running in fright.

Knowing that tomorrow will again be today with his mishaps erased, Phil indulges in an orgy of pastries, deceives and seduces a local woman, even steals money from an armored truck (he knows exactly when the guards will be distracted, having watched the event for "days" on end). But as he learns that a lack of consequences is not a dream come true, he becomes suicidal, even drives head-on into

a train, and then kidnaps the groundhog and drives off a cliff. But the self-destructive phase of the film is played for screwball laughs. When Phil takes the drunks Ralph and Gus for a drive and then plows through a mailbox, Gus (Rick Ducommun) says, "Hey, Phil, if we wanted to hit mailboxes we could let Ralph drive."

The movie was more than just a typical screwball romance, the metaphor for being stuck in ruts and routines and learning to live and love fully. It struck a chord with moviegoers and all who loved the movie's spiritual side, and with filmmakers, whose works like *50 First Dates* and *Being John Malkovich* bore its influence. Of course, any modern screwball comedy will in some way be a descendant not so much of the original screwballs, like *It Happened One Night*, but of these modern classics—the crackling dialogue of *Some Like It Hot*, the affable zaniness of *The In-Laws*, the sophistication and thoughtfulness of *Tootsie*, or the blend of the silly and the spiritual in *Groundhog Day*.

BILL MURRAY: A SCREWBALL COMEDY UNTO HIMSELF

BILL MURRAY can take the most predictable story, scene, or line and twist it into something totally surprising, thanks to his smirks and smiles and his deadpan sarcasm and his charming insouciance. Murray, who perfected the misunderstood, misfit antihero, is perhaps the greatest improvisational comedic actor of the past quarter-century. But what makes him so funny on screen is his naturalism—his ability to make even scripted lines seem as if they just popped into his head.

Meatballs (1979)

Murray plays Tripper Harrison, the head counselor at a wacky summer camp populated with social outcasts. Murray sets the tone for his film persona when Tripper tells the campers, "These are the camp rules," then tears them up and tosses them in the trash. "They'll be in here if you want to check them out later."

He also gets big laughs with absurd statements delivered with Murray's trademark mock gravitas: "Here's an update on tonight's dinner. It was veal. I repeat, veal. The winner of tonight's mystery meat contest is Jeffrey Corbin, who guessed "some kind of beef.""

The quintessential Murray speech comes the night before the Summer Olympics against the rival camp filled with rich, athletic kids. In it, he articulates ideas that would return in some form in movies ranging from *Stripes* to *Rushmore*: "Even if we play so far above our heads that our noses bleed for a week to ten days; even if God in heaven above points his hand at our side of the field—it just wouldn't matter, because all the really good-looking girls would still go out with the guys from Mohawk because they've got all the money! *It just doesn't matter!*" He then revs the campers up (and removes any sense of pressure) with the oddly inspiring cheer *"It just doesn't matter."*

Stripes (1981)

Bill Murray in an Army uniform is the ultimate incongruity, and Murray plays off that conflict to perfection. He rallies his ramshackle unit, which is about to fail basic training, with another spirited underdog speech, positioning himself as the un-Patton. "We're Americans with a capital A. Do you know what that means? Our forefathers were kicked out of every country in the world."

He then compares the men to mutts, luring them all into confessing that they not only had seen *Old Yeller* but also cried when Old Yeller died. This inspirational speech leads into a dizzying parade performance, with his half-dressed troops barking out distinctly untraditional calls like "He stepped out of rank, got hit by a tank, he ain't a chicken no more" and "The quick brown fox jumped over the lazy dog, sir."

Ghostbusters (1984)

Murray's nonchalance and his smirk are more than just seen-it-all smugness. They're a reminder that no matter how absurd the situation might be, he's still the one who can remain untouched and amused by the insanity of it all.

When Dana (Sigourney Weaver) tells of her spooked refrigerator, Murray's Dr. Venkman skeptically replies, "Generally you don't see that kind of behavior in a major appliance." And when he visits her place, he plays a few tinkling notes at the high end of the piano, saying, with faux seriousness, "They hate this. I like to torture them. That's right boys, it's Dr. Venkman," and seems more intent on seducing Dana than finding paranormal behavior.

Even after Dana becomes possessed, he remains seemingly unfazed, telling the sexily dressed seductress, "I make it a rule never to get involved with possessed people," only to admit, after a passionate kiss, "Actually, that's more of a guideline than a rule."

Quick Change (1990)

What's more perfect than the first glimpse of a disgruntled Murray with his face painted and dressed in full clown regalia sitting glumly in a crowded subway car? Perhaps the moment we realize the clown outfit is a disguise for a bank robbery that kicks off this screwball crime caper. When the bank guard disdainfully tells the clown, "We're closed, Bozo," Grimm (Murray) pulls a gun and corrects him saying, "That's *Mr.* Bozo." Grimm then shows the explosives attached to his body, and the guard asks in surprise, "What kind of clown are you?" setting Grimm up for the perfect comeback delivered with that signature Murray deadpan: "The crying on the inside kind, I guess."

The Man Who Knew Too Little (1997)

This minor Murray film is a charming but silly screwball comedy in which Murray plays a bumbling innocent who believes he's participating in "Theater of Life," an experimental theater performance, when he has really stumbled into a murderous web of international intrigue. With not much of consequence to work with, Murray pulls out all the stops, whether he's pretending to be an undercover agent, claiming that performing torture is the downside of having license to kill, or joining in a costumed dance of the Cossacks. And, of course, this is the movie that proves Bill Murray can even make a struggle with postnasal drip funny.

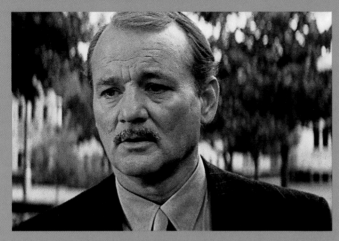

Rushmore (1998)

As Herman Blume, a jaded wealthy prep school parent, Murray is no longer an underdog, but he retains his persona and sets the tone for the entire movie with this assembly speech: "I never had it like this where I grew up. . . . Now for some of you it doesn't matter. You were born rich and you're going to stay rich. My advice to the rest of you is take dead aim at the rich boys. Get them in crosshairs and bring them down. . . . They can buy anything but they can't buy backbone. Don't let them forget it. Thank you."

CHAPTER
20

LAUGHING IN THE FACE OF LOVE

Free love. Women's liberation. Open homosexuality. Skyrocketing divorce rates. Love and romance have certainly become more complicated since the earliest days of romantic comedies. The best of the early genre typically elicited knowing smiles or warm chuckles, but the more recent variations, even though—or perhaps because—they are reflections of all the tension and complications, are generating deeper, heartier laughs.

Annie Hall dealt with many of the same topics as director, co-author, and star Woody Allen's earlier films—anti-Semitism, pessimism, intellectualism, failed love, sex, death, and New York—but the bittersweet, realistic tone marked Allen's transformation from the king of philosophical slapstick into a cinematic auteur and heralded a new era of mature romantic comedies. This, after all, ends with the boy losing the girl for good, but perhaps understanding himself a bit better.

Annie Hall, which had working titles that included "Woody Allen's Anxiety," "It Had to Be Jew," and "Anhedonia," was autobiographical in many ways, large and small: Alvy Singer, like Allen, is a neurotic, soul-searching Jewish comedian from Brooklyn; Allen had previously lived with Diane Keaton, as lover and intellectual mentor; Keaton's real name was Diane Hall, her nickname was Annie, and the trend-setting mix-and-match man's clothes

Annie wore were actually Keaton's. But for all the connections, the helplessly introspective Alvy and la-di-da Annie are also fully fleshed-out characters. "Here there weren't nearly as many laughs to go by. I had to trust the relationships to carry the film," Allen once said.

For all its angst, *Annie Hall* is still flat-out funny, thanks in part to Allen's unconventional moviemaking—characters talk to the camera, travel back to childhood and interact with their younger selves, and even break with reality in search of truth, understanding, and a good laugh.

Many of the more famous scenes meld a realistic relationship with Allen's witty dialogue and comic imagination. In one scene Annie forces Alvy to try cocaine at a party, saying, "You never want to try anything new, Alvy." Alvy retorts, "How can you say that? I said that you, I, and that girl from your acting class should sleep together in a threesome," and when Annie says "That's just sick" he answers, "But it's new. You didn't say it couldn't be sick." Finally, he's pressured into snorting the cocaine, but instead he accidentally sneezes an entire pile of it into oblivion. It was an actual unscripted sneeze, but the scene got such laughs during previews that Allen left it in.

And when Alvy is jealous of Annie's college professor, he derides her class as "mental masturbation." "Oh, well, now we're finally getting to a subject you know something

about," she sneers back." But Alvy isn't ashamed, saying, "Hey, don't knock masturbation. It's sex with someone I love."

This was not the sort of pillow talk you'd find in a Doris Day comedy, and Allen was rewarded with his biggest box-office hit and Oscars for Best Picture, Best Director, and Best Screenplay, rare for a comedy. (He was also nominated for Best Actor, a feat only Orson Welles had previously achieved. Keaton also won for Best Actress.)

Not every new romantic comedy follows such an idiosyncratic vision, of course. One of the funniest films of the 1980s was *Arthur*, which thrived on the fairy-tale atmosphere of the old screwball romantic comedies—down to the glamorous Manhattan location shots of the Plaza Hotel and St. Bartholomew's Church. Dudley Moore plays Arthur Bach, a spoiled drunken playboy heir to a fortune who doesn't want to marry Susan Johnson (Jill Eikenberry), a spoiled prim-and-proper heir to another fortune. By happenstance, Arthur discovers true love with

Linda, "a nobody from Queens" (Liza Minnelli), after he rescues her from being arrested when she's caught shoplifting a tie for her father's birthday. And finally, after he watches his beloved valet, Hobson (Sir John Gielgud), die, Arthur is forced to finally grow up and face life.

Writer-director Steve Gordon once said the film could have flopped had Arthur not been so lovable, and he praised Dudley Moore for finding the character's innocence. After all, his vices never hurt anyone else directly.

Indeed, Arthur is filled with a childlike joy and will say (clearly oblivious to the realities of money and responsibility), "Aren't waiters great. You ask for things and they bring them to you. Same principle as Santa Claus."

Many of the film's most memorable lines belong to the mordant but protective Hobson and are delivered with pitch-perfect sarcasm by the aristocratic Gielgud. After Arthur spends a night out drinking and cavorting with a prostitute, Hobson arrives with "orange juice, coffee, and aspirins. Or, do you need to throw up?"

When the prostitute Gloria (Anne De Salvo) is too awed by the opulence to manage more than a feeble "Hi," Hobson responds, "You obviously have a wonderful economy with words." After Hobson gets rid of her, Arthur puts on his tophat and announces, "I'm going to take a bath," to which Hobson, without looking up from his newspaper, dryly responds, "I'll alert the media." When Arthur asks if Hobson wants to run his bath, he mutters, "It's what I live for." Their relationship gives the movie emotional ballast. When Hobson gets sick, Arthur sobers up and takes care of him, at first in an immature, jokey way but finally in a truly comforting way that prompts Hobson to say, "You're a good son."

But much of the rest of the film is irrepressibly silly. When Arthur goes to Susan's house to meet with her overprotective father, Burt (Stephen Elliott), he's left alone in a room beneath a stuffed moose. "This must be awfully embarrassing for you," Arthur says to the dead animal. When Burt arrives, Arthur infuriates him by ignoring Burt's attempts to steer the conversation, instead asking, "Where is the rest of this moose?" and later adding, "You

must have really hated this moose." (The scene had to be reshot, because Moore's sly looks at the moose were so funny that the crew's lighting man laughed so hard he fell off his ladder.)

At the movie's climax, when Arthur shows up drunk and late for his marriage to Susan, then breaks it off, confessing his love for Linda, Burt flies into a murderous rage. He throws Arthur to the ground and then grabs a knife from a wedge of cheese on the table. Even then, Arthur keeps the jokes coming, saying, "Either he wants some cheese . . ."

This throwback, however, requires a Hollywood ending, so Arthur gets the girl and the money, but among the classic romantic comedies of the last twenty-five years, *Arthur* is more an exception than the rule. Most, including *When Harry Met Sally, Four Weddings and a Funeral,* and *High Fidelity,* have happy endings, but they also deal honestly and realistically with the complexity of modern life: there's divorce, a gay couple more stable than any straight couple, and a continuing search, Alvy Singer–style, to find one's true self while learning how to grow up and commit to a real-world relationship.

When Harry Met Sally was born out of director Rob Reiner's and writer Nora Ephron's own real-world relationships. Reiner was newly divorced and just beginning to date again when he and producer Andrew Scheinman started discussing with Ephron men, women, and relationships. Much of their conversations made it into Ephron's screenplay about Harry and Sally, who meet and remeet over the years, first seemingly as adversaries, then as friends, before finally realizing that they are truly meant for each other.

"The best comedy is always based on truth," observes film historian Leonard Maltin. "We may laugh at a cheap joke, but we're not gonna take it with us or remember it or talk about it the next day. It won't get any kind of memory association." Maltin offers, "The reason that so many romantic comedies fail is that they're contrivances. And they don't really have that eye and ear for the truth that *When Harry Met Sally* does."

The late-night intimate phone chat between insomniac Harry Burns (Billy Crystal) and Sally Albright (Meg Ryan) when they were just friends, in which Harry says he's suffering from a "twenty-four-hour tumor" and that after they hang up he'll just "stay up and moan," were actually based on Reiner and his best friend, Billy Crystal. Like Sally, Ephron was a control freak who ordered food with a million modifiers and Reiner was so struck by the habit that he had her incorporate it into the script.

The movie's most famously funny and forthright scenes about the differences between the sexes also came from the creators' life experience. The men's confession led to the scene in which Harry explains that men and women can't be friends because "the sex part always gets in the way. . . . Because no man can be friends with a woman that he finds attractive. He always wants to have sex with her." When Sally asks if that means a man can be friends with an unattractive woman, Harry matter-of-factly confesses to man's animalistic nature: "No. You pretty much want to nail 'em too."

Later, Harry reveals another area of conflict—"How long do you like to be held after sex? All night, right? See, that's your problem. Somewhere between thirty seconds and all night is your problem."

But Ephron had her revenge when she told a disbelieving Reiner that all women fake orgasms at some point. Reiner did a survey in his office and was shocked by the results, which led to the famous "faking it" scene in New York City's Katz's Delicatessen.

Reiner thought Ryan's first take was "tepid"; after several more inhibited takes, Reiner sat at the table and demonstrated it himself, pounding the table, sweating and shouting, "Yes! Yes!"—at which point Crystal improvised the memorable "I'll have what she's having" line delivered by the older woman at the next table (played by Estelle Reiner, the director's mother).

Four Weddings and a Funeral brought a similar mix of frothy fun and realism to romance, including some sardonic commentary on the institution of marriage. At one point, the ebullient Gareth (Simon Callow) explains his new theory to the protagonist, Charles (Hugh Grant): "Two people are in love, they live together, and then suddenly one day they run out of conversation. Totally. . . . That's it. Panic! Then suddenly it occurs to the chap that there is a way out of the deadlock—he'll ask her to marry him. Suddenly they've got something to talk about for the rest of their lives."

Charles, slightly stunned, says, "Basically you're saying marriage is just a way of getting out of an embarrassing pause in conversation," and Gareth confidently affirms that: "The definitive icebreaker."

While the movie often feels lighthearted and predictable, it's notable that among the film's group of friends the only stable couple—the role models—at the start, are gay. When Gareth dies near the movie's end, his brokenhearted Matthew (John Hannah) gives a eulogy that is both funny and moving. "In order to prepare this speech, I rang a few people to get a general picture of how Gareth was regarded by those who met him. "Fat" seems to have been a word people most connected with him. On the other hand . . . you loved him. You remember his . . . his strange experimental cooking. The recipe for Duck à la Banana fortunately goes with him to his grave." Matthew then reads W. H. Auden's poem "Funeral Blues," which gives added weight to the comic antics that precede and follow.

And comic it is—this movie, for all its charming fluff, is outright funny. The bumbling, passive Charles meets a beautiful American stranger, Carrie (Andie MacDowell), but when he fails to truly pursue a relationship, she gets engaged to someone else—and humiliates him by making him help her select a wedding gown and then endure a recitation of her past lovers, including number nine, "against fence—very uncomfortable, don't try it"; number twenty-two, who kept falling asleep; twenty-three and twenty-four, who happened together, a man named Spencer at number twenty-eight; and his father at number twenty-nine. He responds later that day with one of the most hilariously inept professions of love in movie history: "I really feel, ehh, in short, to recap it slightly in a clearer version, eh, the words of David Cassidy, in fact, eh, while he was still with the Partridge family, eh, 'I think I love you,' and, eh, I—I—just wondered by any chance you wouldn't like to—eh—eh—No, no, no, of course not—I'm an idiot, he's not—sorry to disturb—Better get on—"

Charles has plenty of other humiliating experiences along the way, most notably at the wedding, where he hides in a dark room, only to have the newlyweds sneak in for a quickie, at which point Charles tries to sneak out but chooses the wrong door and ends up in a closet, where he must listen to the entire act. That scene, like many in the movie, was loosely based on screenwriter Richard Curtis's life—he went to sixty-seven weddings over ten years. Audiences could relate too, making the low-budget film (extras had to bring their own suits for the wedding) the highest-grossing British film ever.

High Fidelity brought romantic comedy into the twenty-first century with record-store owner Rob Gordon (John Cusack), who had a blend of Alvy's neuroses,

Arthur's refusal to grow up, Harry's guy's-eye view on love and lust, and Charles's inability to commit to a woman.

Much of the film's wry humor elicits the dry laughter of self-recognition, coming from the character's pain and from his emotional connection to music, a touchstone for anyone who survived adolescence. *High Fidelity* is a very modern romantic comedy. It begins with Rob getting dumped by Laura (Iben Hjejle) because she "has been growing while he has stagnated." Rob is "a guy who oughta know better—he's slovenly, lazy, self-deluded, vain," John Cusack has said, adding that the film reveals "men's shadows and imperfections" while showing them overcoming their weaknesses.

The opening breakup creates an instant emotional resonance, as does Rob's subsequent listing of his Top 5 Most Memorable Breakups, which date back to junior high school and Allison. That relationship with Allison lasted only six hours, "two hours after school and before *The Rockford Files* for three days in a row," until Allison was spotted kissing another boy.

The movie follows Rob as he tracks down his exes in a self-indulgent, self-pitying attempt to understand why he's "doomed to be left, doomed to be rejected."

Based on Nick Hornby's hit British novel, the movie lifts many of the best lines straight from the page. But despite its British director—Stephen Frears—it is quintessentially American, thanks to Cusack's decision to transport the story from London to his hometown of Chicago,

filling it with local details. Cusack co-wrote the script with childhood friends (D. V. DeVincentis, Steve Pink, and Scott Rosenberg). Frears was worried because Hornby saw the book as being about England's pessimism as a nation—he once said that America's natural optimism robbed the story of some of its stoicism yet made it more romantic.

Ultimately Rob realizes that while life with Laura "wasn't spectacular, it was just—good, very good," and he gets his act together, offering up one of cinema's most unromantic but honest and heartfelt proposals, in which he confesses that he is through being distracted by his fantasy of the next new girl with her "cute problems" and closet of lingerie. When Laura points out that she too has lingerie, he explains: "You have great lingerie, but you also have cotton underwear that's been washed a thousand times."

He explains that he's tired of the fantasy but not of her, but this is the new Hollywood, so Laura doesn't rush into his arms, and the movie ends on an unresolved but hopeful note, with Rob making a tape of songs for Laura.

High Fidelity, like these other romantic classics, balances the romance with silliness and a sophisticated and modern wit, yet it always stays true to the lives of its characters. In these films, both love and laughter is truly earned.

CLASSIC ROMANTIC COMEDY REPARTEE: LOVE AND LUST, WIT AND WISDOM

NO MATTER WHAT the role or the plot, Mae West was always herself and was always quick with a quip, usually one with layered meanings.

Night After Night (1932)

HATCHECK GIRL: Goodness, what beautiful diamonds!

MAUDIE TRIPLETT (Mae West): Goodness had nothing to do with it, dearie.

She Done Him Wrong (1933)

SALLY (Rochelle Hudson): Who'd want me after what I've done?

LADY LOU (West): Listen, when women go wrong, men go right after them.

LADY LOU (*being handcuffed for jail*): Those absolutely necessary? You know I wasn't born with them.

CAPTAIN CUMMINGS (Cary Grant): No. A lot of men would have been safer if you had.

LADY LOU: Oh, I don't know. Hands ain't everything.

I'm No Angel (1933)

JACK (Cary Grant): Tonight, you were especially good.

TIRA (West): When I'm good, I'm very good. But when I'm bad, I'm better.

When asked by a reporter why she had admitted knowing so many men in her life, Tira responds: Well, it's not the men in your life that counts, it's the life in your men.

Dinner at Eight (1933)

Marie Dressler plays aging actress Carlotta Vance while Jean Harlow wows as Kitty Packard, a brazen, sensual gold-digging former hatcheck girl.

KITTY: I was reading a book the other day.

CARLOTTA: Reading a book!

KITTY: Yes. It's all about civilization or something, a nutty kind of a book. Do you know that the guy said that machinery is going to take the place of every profession?

CARLOTTA (*eyeing Kitty's sexy figure and outfit*): Oh, my dear, that's something you need never worry about.

The Thin Man (1934)

William Powell and Myrna Loy starred as Nick and Nora Charles, heavy-drinking, fast-thinking, wisecracking newlyweds who spar verbally throughout this murder-mystery comedy. Nora noisily enters a restaurant, lugging packages and being dragged by her dog, Asta; a waiter tells her the dog must go, but Nick, a regular there, steps in.

NICK: Oh, it's all right, Joe. It's all right. It's my dog. And, uh, my wife.

NORA: Well, you might have mentioned me first on the billing.

Later on, a man attempts to shoot Nick, which they subsequently read about in the newspapers.

NICK: I know as much about the murder as they do. Oh, I'm a hero. I was shot twice in the *Tribune*.

NORA: I read you were shot five times in the tabloids.

NICK: It's not true. He didn't come anywhere near my tabloids.

Pillow Talk (1959)

Lothario Brad Allen (Rock Hudson) and prim Jan Morrow (Doris Day) battle over a party line, until she finally reports him to the phone company—which sends out an attractive young agent.

MS. DICKENSON (Karen Norris): I'm Miss Dickenson. I'm an inspector.

BRAD: What would you like to inspect?

MS. DICKENSON (*instinctively*): You— (*flustered*) I mean—

Brad then pointed out to Jan how impolite her action was.

BRAD: You don't see me going to complain about your affairs.

JAN: I have none to complain about.

BRAD: It figures.

Later on, however, she returns with a snappy one-liner of her own.

JAN: Mr. Allen, this may come as a shock, but there are some men who don't end every sentence with a proposition.

When Brad's thrice-married buddy Jonathan Forbes (Tony Randall) tries to get him to settle down, the smart aleck Brad parries every thrust with a single, amused response that sums up the attitude of all single guys.

JONATHAN: You ought to quit all this chasing around and get married.

BRAD: Why?

JONATHAN: There comes a time when a man wants to give up that kind of life.

BRAD: Why?

JONATHAN: There's nothing in this world so wonderful, so fulfilling as coming home to the same woman every night.

BRAD: Why?

JONATHAN: Because that's what it means to be an adult. A mature man wants those responsibilities.

BRAD: Why?

CHAPTER 21

PULL MY FINGER

Tasteless. Crude. Gross. Disgusting. Superlatives one would hardly expect filmmakers to strive for. But these are the adjectives that best describe what in recent years has fast become a mainstay of filmed entertainment: gross-out or bathroom humor comedies.

Writer-director Tom Shadyac, the man responsible for coaxing Jim Carrey to speak through his rear end in *Ace Ventura: Pet Detective,* has a theory: "I think it's instinctive. If you watch any kid, they crack up when somebody burps. There's a childlike joy there, and it takes the culture to suck that out of you. You'll hear, 'That's not very refined of you.' It's still funny. Is it the highest level of humor? No. Is it base? Yes. But is there anything wrong with that? No."

Back in the 1930s and 1940s the Marx Brothers were as irreverent as could be. They were famous for mercilessly deflating the rich and the pompous, but they never did a joke about expelling bodily gases. As physically outrageous as the Three Stooges were, they only threw pies, they never got intimate with one. While those pioneers certainly helped paved the way for gross-out and bathroom humor comedies, the movie most credited with—or blamed for—obliterating the line of good taste in cinema is *Blazing Saddles,* a comedy classic directed and co-written by Mel Brooks.

In 1974, Brooks set out to create a western spoof, soliciting then nightclub comic Richard Pryor to help write the movie. The result was a new bar for comic crudity, originally titled *Tex X,* then *Black Bart.* Brooks loved working with Pryor and wanted to cast him in the lead as Bart, the sheriff of Black Rock (the town's name was later renamed Rock Ridge). Unfortunately, studio executives at the time were put off by Pryor's edginess, so Brooks ended up casting off-Broadway actor Cleavon Little in the role.

Memorable *Blazing Saddles* comic inventions include Alex Karras punching out a horse; Cleavon Little's gasp-inducing line "Pardon me while I whip this out," while reaching beneath his belt line; Mel Brooks's turn as the cross-eyed Governor Le Petomane (which is French for "fart master") and the Yiddish-speaking Jewish-Sioux Indian chief; Madeline Kahn's portrayal of the oversexed, Marlena Dietrich–inspired character with a speech impediment named "Lili Von Shtupp." That year, Kahn was Oscar-nominated for Best Supporting Actress, and the quintet of scripters won the Writers Guild Award for Best Comedy Written Directly for the Screen.

But it is the campfire scene that remains one of the best-known and best-remembered gross-outs in movie comedy history. It consists simply of a group of trail-hardened cowboys sitting around a campfire, eating baked beans, belching, and passing gas. But according to Brooks, no actual gas was ever passed: "I said, 'Do the normal gestures

ADMINISTRATIVE
PERSONNEL
ONLY
KNOCK ON BARBED WIRE
BEFORE ENTERING

you would do to let a fart escape.' Then the sound editors got their friends together and they put wet soap under their armpits. And they made air pockets and did the noises that way. I came in to do some with my voice—a few high ones that they couldn't do from under their arms. But nobody put an actual fart on the sound track."

Regardless, it's a scene that even Brooks had trepidation about. "There was no such thing as politically correct. We knew that a lot of farts have never been done in a movie. I'll never forget—I went up to John Calley's [then head of Warner Brothers] office, and I said, 'John, you've said nothing about this, but we're a little worried about this farting scene, about the audience, turning them off.' He said, 'Mel, if you're gonna go up to the bell, ring it!'"

Well, ring it they did. The scene was simultaneously silly, mischievous, juvenile, disgusting, and unexpectedly funny. "We have watched thousands of cowboys sitting around a thousand campfires eating beans, and nobody

farted until *Blazing Saddles* . . . finally somebody told the truth," notes critic Joel Siegel.

Observes film historian Leonard Maltin, "That's why it's not a cheap joke. That's why it's a great scene and a hysterically funny scene. Now, does that mean that every other person ever since who's made those jokes is walking in the shoes of Mel Brooks? I don't think so."

Blazing Saddles, with nearly fifty million dollars in box-office receipts, became the second highest grossing film of 1974, and the campfire scene became the shot heard 'round Hollywood, signaling a new level of permissibility on the part of the studios with respect to content.

That same year, England's legendary comedy troupe Monty Python came out with their second movie. The group was formed in 1969 by John Cleese, Eric Idle, Terry Gilliam, Terry Jones, Michael Palin, and Graham Chapman. All had been writing and performing on British television in the mid to late 1960s, and their paths had often crossed.

In 1969, Cleese was offered his own show, but he preferred working as part of a troupe and he pulled Python together.

The show was a big hit on British television, and in 1971 the group graduated to film, producing a big-screen version of their best television sketches, *And Now for Something Completely Different*. After three seasons on British television, the extraordinarily clever, irreverent, and silly troupe went their separate ways, as much from their inability to be in the same room without arguing as from anything else. Then, in 1974, after PBS reran the shows and made them a huge hit in America, they came back together for *Monty Python and the Holy Grail*.

Holy Grail was a spoof on the ever-popular Crusades / King Arthur / Knights of the Round Table movies. The film had a minuscule budget of money obtained from a variety of investors, including British rock bands Led Zeppelin and Pink Floyd. The group itself agreed to work for a paltry two thousand British pounds and a percentage of the gross.

Unable to afford the luxury of real horses, the group came up with the idea of *pretending* to ride horses—an invention that was both funnier, and much cheaper, than actual equines. The only cost was the coconut, which, cut in half and banged together by one of the actors in the scene, supplied the sound of clopping hooves.

Each of the Pythons played multiple roles, both male and female, and though much of the movie seemed improvised, the script was tightly adhered to. John Cleese explains, "People always ask if we improvised on set, but the thing is, there was no improvisation at all in *Python*. We had five weeks to shoot the film, and we couldn't afford to shoot another word."

Many innovative Python creations in *Holy Grail* have become comedy classics, such as the three-headed knights who say "Ni!," the Ferocious French Taunter who stands atop a castle wall and hurls withering insults at the Crusaders ("Your mother was a hamster, and your father smelt of elderberries!"), the "Holy Hand Grenade," and the famous Trojan horse reimagined as a giant wooden Killer Rabbit.

However, the scene that puts *Holy Grail* in the Gross-Out Hall of Fame is the encounter in the woods between King Arthur (Graham Chapman) and the Black Knight (John Cleese). Inspired by the Black Knight of Arthurian legend, the Python's Black Knight is the ferocious protector

members are at distinct odds with a crass new member, the nouveau riche and unbearably tacky Al Czervik (Rodney Dangerfield). They're also at odds with the staff, who are poor, irreverent, and not a little subversive. Bill Murray, as weirdo groundskeeper "Carl Spackler," is at odds with a very pesky, obviously animatronic gopher (created and operated by special-effects wizard John Dykstra, of *Stars Wars* fame) who is tearing up the golf course with his tunnels. Murray's mostly improvised role, which was originally intended as a cameo, grew exponentially as the movie progressed.

Though more silly than crude, the movie does have one instance of extreme grossitude—known universally as "the Baby Ruth in the pool." To set the scene, Bushwood's one concession to its young staff is to allow them into the pool for a parsimonious fifteen minutes, once. After a very funny Esther Williams synchronized swimming parody by the caddies, an unwrapped Baby Ruth candy bar is accidentally flipped into the pool, where, underscored by the ominous shark's theme from "Jaws," it's naturally mistaken for human waste. A warning cry of "Doodeeeee!" is followed by horrified panic and a mad dash evacuation of the pool. Later, Bill Murray, clad in a hazardous-material outfit, drains the pool, locates the suspicious brown substance, and to the disgust and horror of everyone watching, picks it up, sniffs it, and then takes a bite.

of a tiny bridge in the forest. King Arthur is challenged by the Black Knight—he will not let Arthur pass without a fight to the death.

In the ensuing battle, Arthur hacks off first one arm, then another, with quick cuts disguising the low-tech dismemberment as the Black Knight's fake appendages drop to the ground and buckets of fake blood stream from tubing hidden in his armor. The knight is left with nothing but bloody stumps (actually raw meat) but still denies his injury, claiming it's but a flesh wound. Finally, Arthur reduces the Black Knight to nothing more than a torso—actually Cleese simply buried up to his belt line. As Arthur and his servant Patsy "ride" by, the Black Knight mocks him one last time: "Oh, I see. Running away, eh? You yellow bastard! Come back here and take what's coming to you—I'll bite your legs off!" The scene is at once bloody, disgusting—and bloody funny.

It didn't take bloodshed to turn the movie *Caddyshack* into a gross-out classic—all it took was a sugary snack. In 1980, Brian Doyle Murray co-wrote a script that turned his and his brother's real-life adventures as adolescent golf caddies into a hit film. The movie stars Brian's brother, Bill Murray, along with Chevy Chase, Michael O'Keefe, Rodney Dangerfield, and Ted Knight. In "Cinderella Story: My Life in Golf," longtime links-o-holic Bill Murray explains, "The film is the gripping tale of the Murray brothers' first experiments with employment. . . . [Brian] wrote the events of his and my brother Ed's caddie life in a way that showed he'd paid attention."

Caddyshack takes place at the exclusive Bushwood Country Club, an institution whose wealthy and eccentric

Though the movie's 1988 sequel, *Caddyshack II*, earned only a quarter of the original's forty-one-million-dollar gross, the legend of Carl Spackler lives on. In 2001 the brothers Murray began opening "Murray Brothers' Caddyshack" theme restaurants in the southeastern United States. One of the less tempting items on the menu was— Baby Ruth Cheesecake!

As gross-out comedies were nearing their apex at the end of the 1990s, *There's Something About Mary* featured, among other crude yet hilarious moments, a scene in which Cameron Diaz unwittingly gels her hair with semen from co-star Ben Stiller's character, who has been "clearing his pipes" before their date. The film brought in more than $175 million and the race was on. Movie studios are always eager to copy success, so there followed a parade of gross-out movies, each one eager to top the other in toppling taboos.

Universal Studios was hoping to duplicate the success of the 1963 film *The Nutty Professor,* and director Tom Shadyac wanted to pay homage to the film by pushing his 1996 remake to the next level.

While Shadyac stuck closely to the original story line of the Jerry Lewis masterpiece, this rendition of the Dr. Jekyll and Mr. Hyde plot cast the hero as the grotesquely overweight Professor Sherman Klump, played with amazing dexterity by Eddie Murphy, with the help of some state-of-the-art makeup and computer graphics. To win the love of luminous graduate student Carla Purty (Jada Pinkett Smith), Klump has to somehow overcome his bulging obesity as well as his unrelenting ineptness. And, as in the classic version, this nutty professor resorts to guzzling a magic elixir that transforms him into a slim and dapper Buddy Love, even more testosterone driven and repulsive than the original.

Combining classic elements of slapstick with a healthy dose of bathroom humor, the film tells its "love yourself for who you are" story, by way of a raucous and often raunchy vehicle that showcased Eddie Murphy's uncanny ability to assimilate different personas. "It was genius," says Tom Shadyac. "It's as if he studied a character profile. He knows where Sherman Klump studied, where he was first embarrassed. He knows where Papa Klump took Mama Klump on a haystack out behind the barn."

Jerry Lewis displayed his prowess as a physical comedian in portraying the vulnerable side of his Professor Kelp, but Murphy and Shadyac tapped into the universal appeal of good old "pull my finger" humor to make us appreciate Sherman Klump's humanity. Indeed, the enduring legacy of the "fart joke" has never been more celebrated than by the cavalcade of flatulence at the infamous dinner table scene, where Eddie Murphy stars as virtually every member of the Klump family, as they debate health and diet.

"The only thing you need to study is your ass!" exclaims Papa Klump. "I got a big ass, yo mama got a big ass . . . so you gotta get used to that."

Mama Klump offers a meek protest and then mentions having recently heard about the health benefits of colon cleansing. "I'm thinking about getting me an appointment and getting my colon cleansed thoroughly."

"You want your colon cleansed?" asks Papa Klump. "Fine, I'm gonna clean mine right now!" And he cuts loose with a loud *Farrummmppph!* Over the family's pleas and objections, Papa Klump continues to break wind like an explosive tuba horn until it becomes so contagious that even little Ernie Klump Jr. lets loose with a nice resonant rip.

Giving credit where credit is due, Tom Shadyac concedes, "The dinner table scene in *The Nutty Professor* was kind of like the next level of *Blazing Saddles* humor."

But executives at Universal Studios initially balked at shooting the scene and wanted it scrapped. Shadyac threatened to walk off the picture. Given the spate of mid-'90s gross-out comedies that had scored big at the box office, Shadyac was incredulous that the studio would find the gaseous vignette to be offensive. "The studio didn't find that it was important to the movie," he reflects, "and I said 'It is the movie.'" But Shadyac also realized the risk that the scene could backfire. "We knew that the movie was either going to be really funny to some people, or a huge stink bomb."

Was it crude? No question. Did it make us laugh? It brought down the house! And Tom Shadyac says that scene has stood the test of time because of Eddie Murphy's powerful, innate ability to get us to laugh like children. "If you're in touch with the child inside you," says Shadyac, "you can't help but laugh."

The age of the gross-out comedy may have peaked in the late 1990s, but as long as there are teenagers who buy movie tickets—and adults who laugh in the dark with them—Hollywood will continue to produce movies that are comic, and crude.

THE SPOOF IS IN THE PUDDING

Parody has long been a part of literature—the fourteenth-century poet Geoffrey Chaucer used parody in *The Canterbury Tales*. But never have parodies been funnier than in the last thirty years, with moviemakers making movies mocking movies. Nearly every topic has been spoofed, and those irreverent lampoons have provided us some of the biggest laughs in movie history.

In the 1970s there were two masters of the madcap movie. One was Woody Allen, who even at his silliest in *Sleeper* and *Bananas* tickled the brain as well as the funny bone; the other, Mel Brooks, preferred going for the big belly-laugh no matter how lowbrow he had to go. Brooks rode to stardom on spoofs like *Blazing Saddles, Young Frankenstein,* and *High Anxiety*.

Young Frankenstein is more than just funny; it's a beautifully filmed, impeccably acted, and carefully scripted movie. Much of the humor derives from the plotting, watching everything go awry for Gene Wilder's descendant of Dr. Frankenstein— "that's Frahnk-en-shteen!"—as he tries denying, then extolling, his heritage.

This monster flick was born in Gene Wilder's head when he was suddenly struck with the notion of a tale of "Young Frankenstein." He fleshed out a story and, after his agent suggested that Wilder work with fellow clients Marty

Feldman and Peter Boyle, penned a script spoofing the whole old horror genre, but especially *Bride of Frankenstein*.

Wilder then handed the script off to Brooks, his director in *Blazing Saddles* and *The Producers*. Brooks reworked the screenplay, but even while directing he maintained a constant give-and-take with Wilder, who once said: "My job was to make Mel more subtle. His job was to make me more broad. I would say, 'I don't want this to be "Blazing Frankenstein,"' and he'd answer, 'I don't want an art film that only fourteen people see.'"

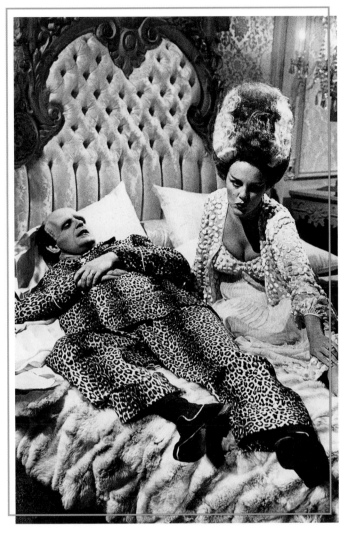

way" and then turns the old vaudeville bit on its head by handing the doctor his cane and expecting him to copy his crippled walk.

The movie is in full form after Frankenstein's creature comes to life, with the wrong brain. Igor is sent to steal a great brain, one of a "saint and scientist." When he accidentally drops the jar spilling the prized gray matter all over the floor, he grabs the next one on the shelf. After the creature is brought to life, grunting and moaning like an animal, the doctor realizes something has gone terribly wrong and asks his servant just whose brain is in the hulking giant.

"Abby someone," Igor replies, feigning nonchalance.

"Abby who?" Frankenstein asks, momentarily repressing an explosion that will be unleashed when he hears Igor's answer:

"Abby normal. Yes, that's it. Abby normal."

The meticulous Brooks also nailed dead-on spoofs, like his take on the blind-man scene from *Bride of Frankenstein*." Wilder's friend Gene Hackman had asked for a quick walk-on role, but Brooks spent four days getting the slapstick scene just perfect—as Hackman's gentle blind hermit unknowingly pours burning soup into the hungry but docile monster's lap, then shatters his wineglass and lights his thumb on fire.

But the true highlight comes from a scene that, oddly enough, Brooks wanted to remove for being too silly: when Dr. Frankenstein presents his monster to his fellow scientists as a cultured creature in a tux and tails, tap dancing and braying out lyrics in a duet of "Puttin' on the Ritz," Brooks worried that the scene veered too far off course and would lose the audience, but Wilder convinced him otherwise, proving that anything could work as long as it was funny.

Brooks gently mocked beloved movie institutions, but a new approach to parody soon crashed the scene. Jerry and David Zucker and Jim Abrahams (known together as ZAZ), who, while growing up, were influenced by *Mad* magazine, chose to ridicule the tired formulaic Hollywood disaster movies of the 1970s, and in the process were willing to blow up the traditional notions of filmmaking and spoofs.

They found the ideal balance. To make it look old-fashioned, Brooks fought the studio to be allowed to make a black-and-white film and to use old-style optical devices, including the 1:85 ratio for height and width of the picture's frame in the castle; he even used lab equipment from the original Frankenstein movie. But when the set design and visual style looked too faithful, Brooks pushed his crew for outsized satire.

The casting was impeccable, especially the wild-eyed Feldman and restrained Boyle. Feldman hammed it up as Igor, a hunchback who doesn't acknowledge his hump—even when it switches sides—but when asked how he knew some vital information says knowingly, "Call it a hunch." (The hump was a "pregnancy" pad.) Even with his frozen features, Boyle imbued his monster with surprising range of emotion.

Brooks filled the film with silly gags, like when Igor (pronounced Eye-gor) tells Frankenstein to "walk this

When the ZAZ team asked *Mission Impossible*'s Peter Graves to star alongside other dramatic actor heavyweights, like Robert Stack, Lloyd Bridges, and Leslie Nielsen, in their new disaster comedy spoof *Airplane!* Graves replied, "Why don't you get some funny people?"

The reason was simple. The ZAZ boys were throwing out all the rules and reinventing the parody genre, creating the joke-a-minute, anything-for-a-laugh approach that has been copied but never again equaled. The first-time directors preferred these straight men to the smirks of a Marty Feldman or a Madeline Kahn because it made the spoofing seem serious—you could believe for a moment you were watching a real disaster movie—and therefore they felt it was much funnier. David Zucker once said, "We would say to the actors, 'Play it absolutely like you don't know you're in a comedy.'" That's what makes it so funny when Nielsen's Dr. Rumack, in the midst of a crisis responding gravely to the flight attendant's skeptical query "Surely, you can't be serious," answers, "I am serious. And don't call me Shirley."

The writer-director's original inspiration came not from a 1970s disaster movie but from a late-night television viewing of *Zero Hour*, a comically bad 1957 film that featured food poisoning and a traumatized veteran landing the plane. The ZAZ guys lifted so much plot and dialogue directly from that film that Paramount had to buy the rights to *Zero Hour* to protect against a plagiarism lawsuit. (Lines from *Airplane!* like "We have to find somebody who not only can fly this plane but also didn't have fish for dinner" are verbatim from *Zero Hour*, where they were meant to be taken seriously.)

The spoofing began almost from the first frame of the film with the opening *Jaws* knockoff (the plane's fin poking through clouds), through side trips to parody *Saturday Night Fever* and *From Here to Eternity* and poke fun at Kareem Abdul-Jabbar's image (a part originally written for Pete Rose), jive talk, addictions (Bridges's air-control chief Steve McCroskey deciding he picked "the wrong week to give up smoking—and drinking—and sniffing glue"), and even pederasty (Graves's pilot, Clarence Oveur, asking a young boy, "Have you ever seen a grown man naked?"). *Airplane!* proved that nothing was off-limits and that everything was funny.

There were other stupendously silly gags from out of nowhere—like Otto, the inflatable autopilot who requires belt-high "blowing" up in mid-flight, and a scene in a veterans' hospital where a shell-shocked soldier believes he's Ethel Merman, and then the real Ethel Merman is revealed playing the part of the soldier.

But still, the heart of the movie remained its deadpan delivery.

When reluctant hero Ted Striker (Robert Hays) looks scared before takeoff, a woman kindly asks, "Nervous?"

"Yes," he replies.

"First time?" referring to flying, as anyone would realize.

"No, I've been nervous lots of times," he responds.

And when food poisoning strikes, Dr. Rumack declares, "This woman has to be gotten to a hospital."

"A hospital—What is it?" a stewardess asks, worrying about the illness.

"A big building with patients, but that's not important right now," Rumack intones.

As Captain Rex Kramer, the man in charge of coaching Striker to a safe landing, Robert Stack adds impressive gravitas to absurdities like "Flying a plane is no different than riding a bicycle. It's just a lot harder to put baseball cards in the spokes."

Or even the silliest premise of all, that the pilots are named Clarence Oveur, Roger, and Victor, leading to stoically acted confusion about "Clearance, Clarence," "Roger, Roger," "Over, Oveur," and "What's our vector, Victor?"

Airplane! used straight men to re-create the feel of disaster films, but *This Is Spinal Tap* went one step further in its efforts to create a reality-based spoof. You might even say it went to eleven.

Spinal Tap simultaneously satirized both rock 'n' roll documentaries and the lifestyles they chronicled. The film was an improvised "mockumentary" telling the tale of a 1960s rock group called "Spinal Tap" that was proudly billed as England's loudest band. By the 1980s, however, the group was being torn apart by a diminishing career and growing tension among lead singer David St. Hubbins (Michael McKean), guitarist Nigel Tufnel (Christopher Guest), and bassist Derek Smalls (Harry Shearer). This was all captured by overeager documentarian Marty DiBergi (real-life director Rob Reiner satirizing director Martin Scorsese's making of the Band's documentary, *The Last Waltz*).

The idea developed when the four friends were working on a television show together in 1978 called *The TV Show*. "It was a satire of different things on television," explains Reiner, "and one of the things we did was a take-off of *The Midnight Special,* which was a rock show back in the seventies. I played Wolfman Jack who introduced them, and it was the first we saw Spinal Tap. And I thought, boy, you know, we gotta find some way to do something more than just this little vignette on television. So, we started talking about it."

Guest and his buddies had long been tinkering with the characters of Spinal Tap, performing improvised sets mostly at friends' parties. Once the concept for the documentary-style film was in place, they found that most studios wanted nothing to do with it—a satire with an untested director and unknown actors in wigs doing British accents was already a tough sell, but saying that it would be entirely improvised really scared the studios off.

But the actors and Reiner soon proved that although the dialogue was improvised the movie was not entirely off-the-cuff. (They shot fifty hours of film in only five weeks, then the four creators worked together in the editing room.)

All three bandmates were experienced musicians—Guest and McKean had met in 1967 while playing together in a band—and they actually wrote the songs for the film, from "Give Me Some Money" to "Big Bottoms," rehearsed, and even played live gigs in character in order to get a feel for their parts.

The foursome also wrote out the entire seventeen-year history of the group. At first calling themselves "The Originals," they found that another group had the same name, so they changed to "The New Originals"—including back stories for each character, every record Spinal Tap had "recorded," and every person who ever played in the band. It was a tall task, considering how many drummers they'd burned through: one died of "spontaneous combustion," another choked on "vomit—someone else's," and a third died in "a bizarre gardening accident."

Many of the absurdities were taken from real life—both Bob Dylan and Tom Petty had been seen wandering lost backstage in real "rockumentaries," and Van Halen reportedly insisted that their backstage bowls of M&Ms had all brown ones removed.

Each scene was structured to present certain information, but no lines were written out, and the actors never knew what questions documentarian DiBergi (Reiner) intended to ask. It was that combination of preparedness and spontaneity that makes the interview scenes sound so natural and perfectly in character but also brilliantly funny.

As DiBergi, Reiner constantly kept the actors guessing by throwing out unusual topics. But the actors were equal to the task. McKean as David claims that his name, St. Hubbins, derives from the little-known "patron saint of quality footwear."

DiBergi also confronts the band with a review of their *Intravenous de Milo* album that slams them for "treading water in a sea of retarded sexuality and bad poetry," but Nigel is unfazed. His calm and oblivious response: "That's just nit-picking, isn't it?"

Of course, Nigel lives in his own world. At one point he plays a quiet, pretty piano piece and explains to DiBergi, "I'm really influenced by Mozart and Bach, and it's sort of in between those, really. It's like a Mach piece, really—" The mournful tune's name: "Well, this piece is called 'Lick My Love Pump.'"

But Nigel's pièce de résistance is, of course, his amp. Spinal Tap is a volume-oriented band, and as Nigel explains, his amp goes "to eleven."

"Is that any louder?" DiBergi asks skeptically.

"Well, it's one louder, isn't it? It's not ten," Nigel explains confidently. "You see, most blokes will be playing at ten. You're on ten on your guitar. Where can you go

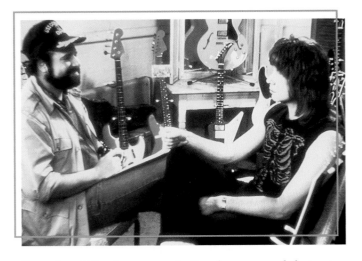

The spy spoof began in style, with Myers listening to Burt Bacharach's "The Look of Love" and yearning for a comedy that captured the song and its era's swinging exuberance. He immediately began talking in Austin's accent and soon was performing this kooky character with a rock band in Los Angeles. Finally, he sold a movie script that knocked off Bond but also 1960s Bond knockoffs like *In Like Flint, Agent for H.A.R.M.*, and *Funeral in Berlin*, featuring Michael Caine as the first movie spy to wear bad glasses.

Myers plays both Austin Powers and his arch-nemesis, Dr. Evil, whom he modeled on Donald Pleasance's *You Only Live Twice* villain. Dr. Evil returned from cryogenic suspended animation after thirty years, so Austin, frozen for the same period of time, is quickly defrosted. But thawed into the 1990s, Austin was an "eight-track tape in a CD world," as Myers once said.

The movie parodies much of the 1960s, from its clever opening "Hard Day's Night" homage, to the resemblance between Austin's leather-attired lover Vanessa, played by Elizabeth Hurley (and even her mother, Mimi Rogers), to

from there? Nowhere, exactly. So when we need that extra push over the cliff, you know what we do?"

"Put it to eleven," responds DiBergi.

"Exactly," says Nigel. "One louder."

"Why don't you just make ten louder and make ten be the top number and make that a little louder?" queries DiBergi.

Nigel pauses, then responds as if his answer explains all: "These go to eleven."

Life, of course, imitates art, and when the movie became a hit, every rock band claimed it had influenced or been ripped off by the movie. But they also all copied it. Eddie Van Halen even reportedly requested an amp with dials going to eleven. (Guest says Marshall, the amp company, had made him one that went to eleven but that when so many rockers mimicked that, Marshall made him a panel that goes to infinity.)

The gems also include manager Ian Faith (Tony Hendra) rationalizing the band's plunging popularity, "Their appeal is becoming more selective," and David, when asked how he could so blithely dismiss Nigel after their breakup, replies, "I'd feel much worse if I weren't under such heavy sedation."

Although David worries in the film that "it's such a fine line between stupid, and clever," Spinal Tap the band is always on one side and *Spinal Tap* the movie is always on the other.

Austin Powers: International Man of Mystery continually crossed the line between crude and clever, always resulting in great laughs. *Powers* creator Mike Myers is credited for reviving spoofs by throwing James Bond and his paler imitators into a blender with Hollywood time-travel movies and coming up with something that is—shagadelic.

The Avengers' Emma Peel, to Austin's seduction scene with Alotta Fagina, which plays off the shot through Anne Bancroft's sexy leg in *The Graduate*.

The movie's highlights are many, particularly the brilliantly botched Bondian moments: when Powers sits at a casino table and, instead of a suave "Bond, James Bond" type introduction, trips through "Allow myself to, ah, introduce myself"; when U.N. officials are baffled by Dr. Evil, also gloriously behind the times, threatening to hold the world hostage for a mere "one million dollars" ransom; when Austin and Vanessa make a frantic getaway in a slow-moving steamroller; and when Austin gets caught by Vanessa dallying with the Fembots (sexy, murderous robots) when he should be saving the world.

The Fembots double-barreled bra gun was actually lifted from a 1960s Ursula Andress film, *10th Victim*. Andress, of course, was the original Bond girl, and Bacharach once told Myers that "The Look of Love" was inspired by Andress. But Myers did more than go full circle with his parody; his Austin Powers movie franchise takes spoofs to a whole new level.

There are inside jokes about spy spoofs—in *The Spy Who Shagged Me*, Powers catches the 1960s spy film *In Like Flint* on television and shouts, "It's my favorite movie!" At one point in the second movie, Powers tries figuring out the fuzzy logic of the script (written, of course, by Myers, who plays Powers) as he uses time travel to save a past version of himself. It doesn't add up, but his boss, played by Michael York, nonchalantly advises him just to enjoy himself and not worry about it. Then York looks at the camera and addresses the audience: "That goes for you too."

But Myers was also aiming for something bigger. The Powers series is so aware of its own clichés that in the third installment, *Goldmember*, it parodied itself, brilliantly blurring the line between movies and reality.

Goldmember opens with an action-packed chase scene that ends with the revelation that Tom Cruise is "playing" Austin Powers, Gwyneth Paltrow is love interest "Dixie Normous," Kevin Spacey is Dr. Evil, and Danny DeVito is Mini Me. Then the movie pulls back to show us that Steven Spielberg is directing a movie of Austin Powers's life called "Austinpussy" (another Bond parody, of *Octo-*

pussy). When the "real" Austin Powers (Myers) finds the movie too Hollywood and tries to make a suggestion, Spielberg holds up an Oscar and says, "My friend here thinks it's fine the way it is." Then the movie ends with the revelation that "Goldmember" is John Travolta—until the camera pulls back and we see that Travolta really plays Goldmember only in *Austinpussy*. After all, Myers plays Goldmember. Then we see that Austin Powers, Dr. Evil, and the gang are all watching *Austinpussy* at a glamorous Hollywood-premiere screening.

The era of *Young Frankenstein, Airplane!* and *Spinal Tap* may have been the apex of the spoof. However, in the past decade, tightly made films like *Austin Powers* and films like *I'm Gonna Get You, Sucka* and *Not Another Scary Teen Movie* have kept parodies pushing new boundaries. With every topic—from our pop-culture society to the parodies themselves—fair game for lampooning, the laughs have grown large and audiences have learned not to take their eyes off the screen even for a second. These days, it seems, the spoofing doesn't stop until the credits are done.

CHRISTOPHER GUEST followed *Spinal Tap* by directing three witty and silly "mockumentaries" that rely on the improvisational skills of Guest, Harry Shearer, Michael McKean, and compatriots like Eugene Levy, Fred Willard, and Catherine O'Hara. The results are nuanced, character-based comedies that spoof not a film genre but mankind's delusions and foibles.

Waiting for Guffman (1996)

In *Waiting for Guffman*, a small town with big dreams produces the cheesiest of original musicals.

Highlights:

Corky St. Clair (Guest), a Broadway reject who leads the town of Blaine's theatrical pretensions, saying of his musical version of the Kurt Russell action film *Backdraft*, "The obtuseness of the production was what fascinated me."

Ron and Sheila Albertson (Willard and O'Hara), local travel agents ("the glamour profession") and wanna-be sophisticates, confessing that they have never left the town of Blaine except to have one embarrassing surgical procedure.

Best in Show (2000)

Guest's sharpest film, *Best in Show*, punctures the punctilious, the pompous, and the obsessed at a snooty dog show.

Highlights:

Buck Laughlin (Willard), the hilariously boorish broadcaster who knows nothing about dogs or dog shows, asking if contestants could dress bloodhounds in Sherlock Holmes regalia, pondering how and why miniature schnauzers are shrunk down and absurdly commenting on a dog that gets kicked out: "He's still a champion, even though he is sent off in disgrace."

When a hotel employee notes, "We have you down for a queen" (as in bed size), the flamboyantly gay Scott (John Michael Higgins) flirts back, "What are you suggesting, my dear man?"

Mighty Wind (2003)

There is plenty of charm in *Mighty Wind*, an almost too affectionate look at washed-up folksingers who briefly return to the spotlight.

Highlights:

Terry Bohner's (Higgins) explanation for how he became a folkie: "There had been abuse in my family, but of a musical nature."

Mark Shubb's (Shearer) realization that he is a "blonde female folksinger trapped in the body of a bald male folksinger."

CHAPTER

23

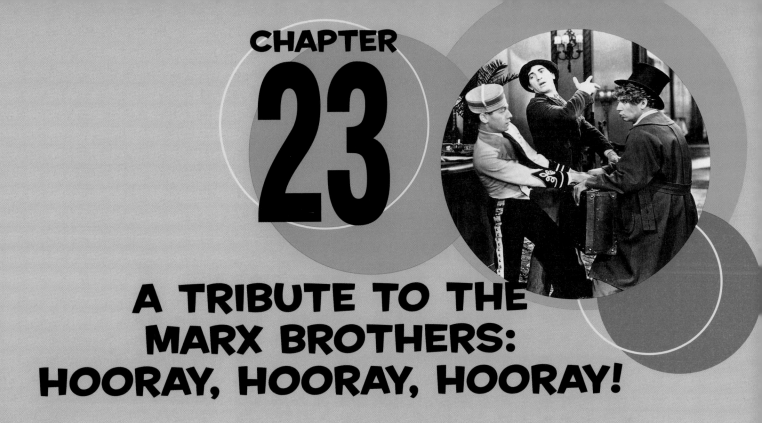

A TRIBUTE TO THE MARX BROTHERS: HOORAY, HOORAY, HOORAY!

No other comedy team in film history has left a more indelible legacy in comedy than the Marx Brothers. "The magic of the Marx Brothers is that they are the embodiment of our wish fulfillment," notes film historian Leonard Maltin. "Groucho is the guy we'd all like to be—the one who has the moxie to make fun of authority to its face and poke pins in the balloon of pomposity. Harpo is the unbridled child we would all like to be—he has no inhibitions at all. Chico is the con-guy who can even be conned himself but who is able to put one over on Groucho, the guy who thinks he's the smartest guy in the world. There's lots of things we may think about, but we would never dare do. The Marx Brothers dared do it."

The Marx Brothers were born between the late 1880s and early 1890s—but that's only a historical fact, and mere facts could never contain the Marx Brothers. Perhaps it's more appropriate to say the Marx Brothers were born in the early 1900s, when they were pushed onto the vaudeville stage as the singing Nightingales by their domineering mother, Minnie.

Or perhaps the Marx Brothers were born in 1909 in Nacogdoches, Texas, when the audience ran out during the middle of their performance to watch a runaway mule. When they returned, an angry Julius (later Groucho) ad-libbed insults like "Nacogdoches is full of roaches" and

"I'd horse-whip you if I had a horse," generating huge laughs, while Leonard (later Chico) began playing piano and Arthur (later Harpo) began performing physical stunts on stage. The Marx Brothers' madcap mayhem had begun.

Of course, there's speculation that that famous story is just a myth pushed by the brothers—several Marx Brothers historians, including the esteemed Paul Wesolowski, believe they never even really played in Nacogdoches—so maybe the real birth came in 1914, when Minnie promised vaudeville houses new material and the brothers' uncle, comedy star Al Shean, wrote a script that had only three lines for Arthur. When Arthur got panned for his delivery of those few lines, but raves and big laughs with his physical performance, he decided never to speak on stage again. "Though they never knew it, they had stumbled on a formula that had been created in the fourteenth or fifteenth century called commedia dell'arte," says Marx historian Bill Marx, Harpo's son. "It was rooted in a triumvirate of the authoritarian figure, which became Groucho, the idiot who was Chico, and the mime, whom my dad became. And it was amazing how they stumbled upon it, just by accident."

But the story of Harpo's "last lines" may also be apocryphal; it may have been a more gradual realization. So maybe the Marx Brothers really began a year or two later, when according to legend a monologist named Art Fisher

And since the Marx Brothers were still being billed as Leonard, Arthur, Julius, and Herbert when they finally made it to Broadway stardom with their musical revue *I'll Say She Is* in 1924, maybe the Marx Brothers were finally born when the critic Alexander Woollcott came backstage and heard the brothers bandying their nicknames back and forth in private. He persuaded them to publicly transform themselves into Chico, Harpo, Groucho, and Zeppo. Woollcott then brought the Marx Brothers together with writers George Kaufman and Morrie Ryskind, who created *The Cocoanuts* and *Animal Crackers*, the plays that made the brothers into theatrical superstars and that were adapted into the first Marx Brothers movies. That was perhaps the true moment of their "birth," the moment when they brought to raucous life the full potential of talkies and created their first lasting performances.

Unraveling all the myths behind the Marx Brothers' origins are impossible, partly because their evolution as an act was gradual and a long time in coming—they were in their thirties and forties when they attained movie stardom—and partly because the brothers themselves had a habit of making up stories, just as they famously ad-libbed their way

was playing cards with them backstage: Fisher dealt a card to Leonard, who had a reputation for chasing the chicks, and called him "Chicko," then dealt a card to the harp-playing Arthur (born Adolph but changed his name to Arthur) and called him "Harpo," then dealt a card to Julius and called him "Groucho," either because of his dour temperament or because of his "grouch-bag," which people used to wear around their neck to store money and candy, and then Milton became "Gummo" because he wore gum-soled shoes. (Herbert became "Zeppo" later, after Gummo dropped out of the act.) Once again, though, that may be nothing more than a good story—Wesolowski and biographer Simon Louvish were unable to find any traces of an Art Fisher outside the brothers' imagination.

through every performance. ("Shhh, I think I hear a line from my original script," Kaufman once said during a stage performance.)

Regardless of how they came to be the iconic Marx Brothers, they were a perfect comic foil for the Depression era, which hit right when their movie careers began, and yet they were rediscovered and embraced by the Sixties generation in large part because of the Brothers' affinity for anarchy and mocking authority.

"Larger and more lunatic than life, the Marx Brothers have become a metaphor for the improbable," wrote Paul D. Zimmerman and Burt Goldblatt in their book *The Marx Brothers at the Movies*. "Their wildness stirs something deep within even the meekest citizen. They act on our forbidden desires. . . . The answer to their survival is simple—they are very, very funny, so funny that they transcend their time."

The Marx Brothers succeeded because they were a very modern, quintessentially American, and totally unique creation. They were embraced by Salvador Dali as the ultimate surrealists, yet they were always focused mainly on getting the next laugh.

"They never laughed during a story conference," perennial co-star Margaret Dumont once said. "Like most expert comedians, they involved themselves so seriously in the study of how jokes could be converted to their own style that they didn't even titter while appraising their material."

And as Bill Marx says, they adapted the material to themselves naturally because their public personas were really just an "extension of their real beings." Groucho, the intellect, loved books and language from an early age; Chico was the chick-chasing gambler who always had an angle but was always in over his head; and Harpo was the quietest but also joyful and relentlessly impulsive, and he just couldn't resist taunting authority figures. (Harpo's famous "Gookie" face, in which he inflates his cheeks while crossing his eyes, was born when he was a kid and would watch through a window as a New York tobacconist unknowingly made that face while rolling cigars.

The mischievous lad would then bang on the store window and make that same face at the enraged cigar-roller.)

They brought their own twist to a tradition tracing back through Mark Twain and H. L. Mencken, using their humor to attack phonies and the high and mighty. Bill Marx envisions "all the pompous people in the world" on a rug and the Marx Brothers' having "the guts" to "pull that rug out from under those people—and just say, 'Sorry.' Boom."

The Marx Brothers made thirteen films, but their lasting reputation is built on the first seven, all chock full of classic comic scenes—slapstick physical chases, verbal battles between Groucho and Chico, the pranks of ne'er-do-wells Harpo and Chico, and of course Groucho's word-fire, rat-a-tat-tatting down every target in his path, especially Margaret Dumont, who perpetually played a society lady Groucho would woo for her money but insult for her lifestyle.

Groucho's most famous lambasting came in *Duck Soup* when he snaps at her moments after arriving: "Well, that covers a lot of ground. Say! You cover a lot of ground yourself. You'd better beat it. I hear they're gonna tear you down and put up an office building where you're standing. You can leave in a taxi. If you can't get a taxi, you can leave in a huff. If that's too soon, you can leave in a minute *and* a huff. You know, you haven't stopped talking since I came

here. You must have been vaccinated with a phonograph needle." (Groucho later claimed that much of Dumont's charm was that she never understood the movie's jokes.)

The brothers debuted with a film version of *The Cocoanuts* in 1929 (made during the day while they performed *Animal Crackers* on Broadway at night). Despite the unbearably primitive moviemaking and the inane plot—in most Marx Brothers movies, plots existed merely to set up their vaudevillian antics—the movie holds up well, featuring all the quintessential Marx elements. (The brothers were so funny that co-director Robert Florey continually cracked up during shooting, forcing extra retakes.)

The movie's highlight—one of filmdom's all-time great bits of absurd wordplay—comes when Groucho tries to explain to Chico about the property he's auctioning off and points out the "viaduct." Chico interprets it as "Why a duck?"

GROUCHO: *I say, here is a little peninsula, and here's a viaduct leading over to the mainland—*
CHICO: *All right. Why a duck? Why a—Why a duck? Why-a-no-chicken?*
GROUCHO: *I don't know why-a-no-chicken. I'm a stranger here myself. All I know is that it's a viaduct. You try to cross over there a chicken, and you'll find out why a duck. It's deep water, that's viaduct.*

This smash was followed by an adaptation of *Animal Crackers*, an even more direct attack on faux sophistication and high society. Groucho plays an African explorer, Captain Spalding, and gives a memorable off-the-wall recitation of his time in the jungle featuring one of his most famous lines:

"One morning, I shot an elephant in my pajamas. How he got in my pajamas I don't know. Then we tried to remove the tusks, but they were embedded in so firmly that we couldn't budge them. Of course, in Alabama, the Tusk-a-loosa. But, uh, that's entirely *irrelephant* to what I was talking about."

And of course Harpo runs rampant until the classic ending, when a suspicious detective, finally convinced that "the professor" (Harpo) was not involved in any crime, shakes Harpo's hand, only to have some stolen knives fall from his coat of tricks. Then more knives come out, then dozens and dozens more, until Groucho, knowing the bit from Broadway, ad-libbed, "I can't understand what's delaying the coffeepot," and then a coffeepot dropped to the floor.

After adapting these two Kaufman classics, the brothers went to Hollywood and teamed up with the legendary

S. J. Perelman for *Monkey Business* and *Horse Feathers*. But whether it was written by Kaufman or Perelman didn't matter—the madmen of mayhem made every script their own. "They improvised four to one over whatever was written," Bill Marx says. "They would forget their lines and it didn't matter, or they went in another direction."

The Marx Brothers were peaking now, with critical and popular acclaim, and their next two films may have been their zenith. *Horse Feathers* mocked the pomposity of elite colleges and the hypocrisy of mixing sports and education.

Their approach to filmmaking was also more ambitious. At one point, while Chico is playing the piano, Groucho approaches the camera and snickers directly to the moviegoers, "I've got to stay here, but there's no reason why you folks shouldn't go out into the lobby until this thing blows over."

Then came the antifascist, antiwar satire *Duck Soup*. The Depression was bottoming out, and America was not ready to focus on Europe and Hitler, or deal with seemingly unpatriotic snipes at the government and our soldiers. As a result, the film was the Marx Brothers' biggest critical and commercial disappointment, and it was responsible for Paramount's not renewing their contract. Today, however, it is considered their true classic, the ultimate statement of their beliefs.

Rufus T. Firefly (Groucho), president of Freedonia, is asked if he finds a cabinet report clear. "Clear? Huh! Why a four-year-old child could understand this report! Run out and find me a four-year-old child. I can't make head or tail out of it."

Later he asks Chicolini (Chico), an enemy spy he has foolishly made secretary of war, what kind of an army Freedonia should have. Chicolini endorses the idea of "a standing army," explaining, when Firefly asks why, "Because then we save money on chairs."

Perhaps the biggest difference, beyond the topic, is that instead of great writers they actually had a great director, Leo McCarey, who later directed such comedy classics as *The Awful Truth* and *An Affair to Remember*. McCarey stripped away any romantic subplots and musical interludes for Harpo or Chico, maintaining a frantic pace in their quickest film.

Beyond the big thematic satires were the unparalleled small set-pieces, each becoming a classic Marx moment: Harpo and Chico as Pinky and Chicolini are posing as peanut sellers when they torment a rival vendor (played

by Edgar Kennedy, master of the slow-burn comedic style) with the classic three-headed hat-switching maneuver. Later Harpo, disguised as Groucho in nightclothes, accidentally shatters a mirror, and then when Groucho arrives Harpo pretends to be Groucho's image, matching Groucho's every increasingly silly wiggle and shake. Only when Chico, also disguised as Groucho, shows up his jig is up.

But being ahead of their time could have meant being behind on their bills if the Marx Brothers hadn't bounced back from Paramount's rejection by signing with MGM producer Irving Thalberg, who guided them to their biggest commercial success in *A Night at the Opera*. Thalberg brought back George Kaufman and Morrie Ryskind to write the script, then sent the brothers out on the road to perform the scenes live. "As funny as they were on film, they

were a thousand times funnier on stage," Chico's daughter Maxine once said. "They were unpredictable."

In fact, the movie's most famous scene in the crowded stateroom was on the verge of being dumped before the brothers added their own brand of chaos to it. The scene begins on a boat with Otis Driftwood (Groucho) and stowaways Fiorello (Chico), Tomasso (Harpo), and the opera singer they hope to ride to a fortune, Ricardo (Allan Jones), jammed into Otis's tiny room. Driftwood goes out and orders food from the steward, egged on by Chico's shouts and Harpo's honks—everything he orders they punctuate with an additional "and two hard-boiled eggs—*Honk!*"

While they're waiting for their food, and Otis is waiting for his assignation with wealthy Mrs. Claypool (Dumont, again), two chambermaids, an engineer, a manicurist, an engineer's assistant, a random young woman, a wash-woman all pile into the room. Then four egg-bearing stewards jam themselves in—just before Mrs. Claypool arrives and opens the door, only to have everyone and everything spill out on top of her.

The other equally celebrated scene comes when Driftwood and Fiorello forge a deal to manage Ricardo. They literally dismantle the absurd legalese of "The party of the first part shall be known in this contract as the party of the first part" by tearing up every phrase they don't like—and Fiorello "donn-a-like-a most-a dem."

When Fiorello says he "no like-a the second party, either," Driftwood quips, "Well, you shoulda come to the first party. We didn't get home till around four in the morning—I was blind for three days!" Finally, they've discarded everything except one last clause, about everyone being in their right mind, a "sanity clause." But Fiorello just laughs. "You can't fool me. There ain't no Sanity Clause!" (Bill Marx says it's the line people most often cite as their favorite Marx movie line.)

The Marx Brothers were at the top of the film world, but the hill down would be steep. Thalberg died of pneumonia at just thirty-seven years old while they were making *A Day the Races*. The movie was another hit featuring memorable scenes, but in structure it was still somewhat derivative of *A Night at the Opera*.

Worse still, Thalberg was gone, and studio head Louis B. Mayer didn't like the Marx Brothers, leaving them largely on their own. For the rest of their career they floundered through productions like *Room Service, At the Circus*, and *The Big Store*. After World War II, they briefly reunited for *A Night in Casablanca* and *Love Happy*, reportedly to help Chico out of gambling debts. By that time, Groucho was on his way to another career as host of the television game show *You Bet Your Life*.

But their best movies have stood the test of time, and the influence of these anarchic comic free-spirits can be seen in everyone from George Carlin (antiauthority) to Woody Allen (intellectual absurdism) to David Letterman (irony and the puncturing of the pompous) to *The Simpsons* (the insults, the wildly unpredictable plot turns).

Perhaps the ultimate tribute to the Marx Brothers' staying power comes in Woody Allen's classic film *Hannah and Her Sisters* when the character Mickey (Allen) is feeling suicidal and aimlessly wanders into a movie theater where a revival of *Duck Soup* is playing. Forget all the political satire—the hilarity that comes from the Marx Brothers' unbridled lunacy and outsized love of life inspires Mickey, giving him a reason to go on living.

In a way, the Marx Brothers do that for us all. Hooray, hooray, hooray!

CREDITS

Authored, produced, and directed by Joe Garner

Editorial/text assistance provided by Stephan Michaels, Stuart Miller, Todd Schindler, and Bill Stroum

Narration written by Mark Rowland

Footage, music, and talent clearances managed by Stephan Michaels and Garner Creative Concepts, Inc.

Original musical score composed and orchestrated by Richard Kosinski

Studio production facilities provided by the Production Group Studio, Hollywood, California

Director of photography and associate director: Chris Monte

Production coordinator and assistant to Joe Garner: Abigail Ray

DVD supervising editor: Chris Monte, Magic Hair Inc.

Additional editing services provided by Jeannie Gilgenberg, Mark Needham, and Davo Weiss

Audio production engineering by Mike Forslund

Main title, animation, and menu design by Castle Digital Design

Creative director: James Castle

Senior animator: Robert Dixon

DVD authoring provided by Los Angeles Duplication and Broadcast, Burbank, California

Television, motion picture, and performance clips provided by:

"Who's on First" provided by, used with permission, and copyright of TCA Television Corp., Hi Neighbor, and Diana K. Abbott-Colton

NBC Studios Inc. and the Estate of Milton Berle

Hope Enterprises Inc.

The Flip Wilson Show—Research Video

Rodney Dangerfield: Paper Clip Productions Inc.

Bill Maher: Home Box Office

Robert Klein: HBO Independent Productions

Laugh-In: Schlatter, Friendly, Romart

Garry Shandling

Jerry Lewis

The Daily Show with Jon Stewart courtesy of Comedy Central © 2004

CBS Entertainment Inc.

Columbia TriStar Domestic Television

WHACKO Inc.

Knave Productions

Python Pictures Limited

Worldwide Pants Inc.

Home Box Office

HBO Independent Productions

Broadway Video Enterprises and NBC Studios

Calvada Productions

Carsey-Werner-Mandabach

20th Century Fox Television

Castle Rock Entertainment

Warner Bros. Television

Warner Bros.

Peter Rodgers Organization

The Television Distribution Company Inc.

Hackett Entertainment Inc.

John Magnuson Associates

Cablestuff Productions, Inc.

Burt Sugarman Productions

Schwartz and Company Inc.

Historic Films Archive

Joan Rivers Worldwide Enterprises/Bill Sammeth Organization

Joe Siegman Productions

Will Rogers Heritage Trust

Chris Rock Enterprises, Inc.

Creative Light Worldwide

Carpe Iuris Consultos Inc.

Bubble Pictures Inc.

MK2 SA

Buster Keaton / *Sherlock Jr.* courtesy of The Douris Corporation

Crown Media Distribution LLC

Harold Lloyd Entertainment Inc.

C3 Entertainment Inc.

MGM CLIP+STILL

Universal Studios Licensing LLLP

Columbia Pictures

Paramount Pictures

StudioCanal Image

New Line Productions Inc.

Universal Media Incorporated

We would like express our heartfelt gratitude to all of the actors and comedians who have graciously permitted the inclusion of their performances.

GCC would like to extend a special thank-you to the following people: Chris Costello, www.abbottandcostellocollectibles.com; ® © 2004 Lynne Unger Children's Trust by www.CMGWorldwide.com;

www.Petersellers.com; ™ © 2004 Estate of Marty Feldman by www.CMBWorldwide.com; Pat Lowe at the Will Rogers Memorial, www.willrogers.com; and Sperdvac (Society to Preserve and Encourage Radio Drama, Variety and Comedy), sperdvac@aol.com, (877) 251-5771, P.O. Box 7177, Van Nuys, California 91409–7177.

I would like to extend a very special thank-you to the following people for their generous contributions of their time and insight: Irving Brecher, David Brenner, Tim Conway, Chris Costello, David Crane, Phyllis Diller, Budd Friedman, Darrell Hammond, Alexa Junge, Bill Kinison, Robert Klein, Carol Leifer, Jerry Lewis, Leonard Maltin, William Marx, Joan Rivers, Phil Rosenthal, Bob Schiller, George Schlatter, Tom Shadyac, George Shapiro, Joel Siegel, Dick Smothers and Tom Smothers.